Sir Stephen Powle
of Court and Country

Sir Stephen Powle
of Court and Country

Memorabilia of a Government Agent
for Queen Elizabeth I, Chancery Official,
and English Country Gentleman

Virginia F. Stern

SUP

Selinsgrove: Susquehanna University Press
London and Toronto: Associated University Presses

© 1992 by Associated University Presses, Inc.

All rights reserved. Authorization to photocopy items for internal or personal use, or the internal or personal use of specific clients, is granted by the copyright owner, provided that a base fee of $10.00, plus eight cents per page, per copy is paid directly to the Copyright Clearance Center, 27 Congress Street, Salem, Massachusetts 01970. [0-945636-22-9/92 $10.00+8¢ pp, pc.]

Associated University Presses
440 Forsgate Drive
Cranbury, NJ 08512

Associated University Presses
25 Sicilian Avenue
London WC1A 2QH, England

Associated University Presses
P.O. Box 39, Clarkson Pstl. Stn.
Mississauga, Ontario
L5J 3X9 Canada

The paper used in this publication meets the requirements of the American National Standard for Permanence of Paper for Printed Library Materials Z39.48-1984.

Library of Congress Cataloging-in-Publication Data

Stern, Virginia F.
  Sir Stephen Powle of court and country : memorabilia of a government agent for Queen Elizabeth I, chancery official, and English country gentleman / Virginia F. Stern.
    p.   cm.
  Includes bibliographical references (p.   ) and index.
  ISBN 0-945636-22-9 (alk. paper)
  1. Powle, Stephen, Sir, 1553?–1630. 2. Great Britain—History—Elizabeth, 1558–1603—Biography. 3. England and Wales. Court of Chancery—Officials and employees—Biography. 4. Administration of estates—England—Essex—History—17th century. 5. Landowners—England—Essex—Biography. I. Title.
DA358.P68S74   1992
942.05′5′092—dc20
  [B]   90-50632
                                                                                            CIP

PRINTED IN THE UNITED STATES OF AMERICA

Your true knowledge of the Honour of the Court, and the Pleasure of the Countrey: your judiciall Observation in your Travels abroad, and your sweet retyred Life at home.

—From Nicholas Breton's dedication
of *The Court and Country,* 1618
to Sir Stephen Powle

Contents

List of Illustrations	9
Preface	11
Introduction: The Significance of Powle's Manuscripts	15
1. Education in the Liberal Arts and the Law	19
2. Travel: A Modified "Grand Tour"	32
3. England and Scotland	53
4. Agent for Queen Elizabeth at Casimir's Court	58
5. Agent for Queen Elizabeth in Italy	69
6. Home	95
7. Interlude: Recovery from Tragedy	100
8. Early Years in Chancery	104
9. Family Life	108
10. Recording the Essex Rebellion	113
11. Suits, Paradoxes, and Slanders	122
12. Lord of the Manor of Smyths-hall	126
13. Country Squire at Mylend	132
14. Sir Stephen Powle as "Adventurer" in the Virginia Company of London	137
15. Later Years at Smyths-hall and Mylend	157
16. "Indian Summer"—A Third Marriage	175
Appendix A: Catalogue of Manuscripts and Their Provenance	181
Appendix B: Printed References to Stephen Powle	185
Appendix C: Funerary Monument of Powle's Parents	187
Appendix D: Books Dedicated to Thomas Powle, Clerk of the Crown	188
Appendix E: Transcripts of Typical Letters from and to Powle and Other Representative Pages from His Notebooks	190
Notes	222
Index	237

List of Illustrations

Walter Ralegh on first coming to Court	25
Unidentified English gentlemen of Stephen Powle's age	28
Robert Sidney c. 1588	50
Holograph page from Powle's Commonplace Book (Tanner MS. 169, fol. 17v)	56
William Cecil, Lord Burghley	61
Duke John Casimir's letter to Lord Burghley praising the services of Stephen Powle	64
Map showing routes of Powle's travels	70
Sir Francis Walsingham	92
Stephen Powle's escutcheon	96
Robert Devereux, second earl of Essex	114
1609 Virginia Company broadside	140
Lottery broadside, February 1614/15	146
Title page and dedication to Powle of Breton's *The Court and Country*	168
Two views of seventeenth-century Westminster by Hollar	177
Powle genealogy	180

Preface

I became curious about Stephen Powle when I learned some years ago of his voluminous travel diaries, letters, legal reports, and miscellaneous memoranda among the Tanner manuscripts at the Bodleian Library. Soon afterward, when visiting the British Library, I came across other manuscripts relating to him. At the Public Record Office while looking through the State Papers of the late Elizabethan period, I noticed many letters from Powle to Principal Secretary Sir Francis Walsingham, and later among the Burghley papers I found some letters from Powle to William Cecil, the lord treasurer. These further whetted my curiosity so that I resolved to find out something of the life of this Renaissance Englishman who has left us so many records of his times yet is almost unknown today.[1]

Born to a family of landed gentry, Stephen Powle (pronounced "Pole"[2]) was in his youth a government agent in the Rhenish Palatinate and in Italy; on his return to England he became deputy clerk of the crown in Chancery during the dramatic last years of Elizabeth's reign. There followed other service in Chancery as one of the six clerks and in Essex as a justice of the peace. He was among the first knights created by King James I, and by 1609 he had become an enthusiastic investor and administrator, for he was one of the original thirteen members of the Council of the Virginia Company of London. Yet later in life he retired quietly to the country to administer his wife's large estates and to correspond with family, learned friends, and eminent acquaintances of a lifetime. In 1618 Nicholas Breton aptly dedicated the dialogue *The Court and Country* to him.

Powle himself has much to tell us, since he kept copies of most of the letters he wrote throughout his long and interesting life. Several hundred of these letters are extant as well as diaries of his travels and varied memoranda contained in his Commonplace Books. The foregoing, together with copies of some of the letters he received and other related manuscripts, have made it possible to construct a biographical study of his life.

In order to facilitate the reading of those manuscript sources quoted in the ensuing text, I have expanded contractions and modernized spelling and punctuation except in a very few instances where there is a specific reason to quote precisely as written.

There were certain differences from modern times in the calendars then in use, and they require some explanation. In the England of Powle's time the year was considered to begin on 25 March (Lady Day), and this is the dating that Powle himself customarily used when in England. On dates falling between 1 January and 25 March I have therefore given the modern date along with his as, for example, February 1578/9 (where 1578 is Powle's dating and 1579 is the modern one). This does not, however, apply to Italy, where the year customarily began on 1 January. There is also another factor that comes into play at the time that Powle visited Italy. The Italians had realized that the Old Style or Julian Calendar was becoming increasingly divergent from the solar system. A correction was therefore effected in the year 1582, whereby ten days were removed from the calendar by making 15 October follow immediately after 4 October 1582. Thus a date in Italy (and in most other Catholic lands) would be ten days later in the Gregorian or New Style *(stilo novo)* than the date in England, which continued to use the Old Style or Julian Calendar.[3] To clarify this difference when discussing letters to and from Italy and France, I have usually given both the Old Style and New Style date, as, for example $\frac{10}{20}$ January, where 10 January is the English date and 20 January the Italian. In those letters where Powle did not indicate the type of calendar, he was apparently using the local dating.

Unless otherwise specified, manuscript references in parentheses are to Tanner manuscripts. They form the largest single group of references to Powle and consist of copies of his letters, legal notes, and miscellaneous memoranda. They were purchased from book dealers or at auction in the early eighteenth century by the antiquarian Thomas Tanner (1674–1735), bishop of Saint Asaph in Wales. On Tanner manuscript 169, folios 229r&v, are two pages of brief scrawled notes in Tanner's hand stating the basic facts of Stephen Powle's life and career. It is likely that Tanner made these notes at a time when he was considering the purchase of a batch of Powle manuscripts. An ardent collector who ultimately bequeathed his manuscripts to the Bodleian Library in Oxford, he is credited with having bound the Powle material into volumes. However, Tanner was quite careless about the chronological order of the volumes' contents, with the result that the documents need considerable rearranging to form a proper temporal sequence. Fortunately, Powle himself dated nearly all his entries.

As for the manuscript volumes themselves: Tanner manuscript 309, which I shall refer to as Powle's Letter Book, starts about 1578/9 and contains for the most part the earliest material; manuscript 168 is composed largely of legal records kept in the 1590s and 1600s at the time that Powle was an official in the high court of Chancery; it is followed by manuscript 169, which together with 168 is considered his Commonplace Book and was originally foliated consecutively with it, manuscript 169 beginning with folio 208. Modern librarians have simplified the foliation by numbering each volume separately. Other Powle material is found in Tanner manuscripts 76, 78, 130, 231, 283, 284, and 314.

Among other original sources on which this biographical study is based are the Elizabethan State Papers, Lansdowne, Cotton, Harleian, Additional, Rawlinson, Salisbury (Cecil), and Middle Temple manuscripts, parish records, and documents at the Essex Record Office and at the Public Record Office in London.

Although Powle's early manuscripts are in his own hand, many of the later ones are copies, made by his then-current clerk, of letters written or received by him. It is not known what happened to the originals of the letters he received. Presumably they were lost or destroyed, except in a couple of instances: for example, one from John Chamberlain is found bound into Tanner manuscript 309 (folios 300r–301v),[4] and two letters from Thomas Lodge are inserted in Tanner manuscript 169 (folios 190r–92r).

Sir Stephen Powle was surely of far more importance in his day than one would expect from the dearth of information about him in print, but one cannot claim that he was a major figure. Nevertheless, a survey of his life and manuscripts should prove of value because he has left such extensive and detailed records that an intimate contact can be established with him and his times, thus providing further insight into an important historical era and some of its leading personages. His carefully recorded official communiqués during the end of Elizabeth's reign and his habit of keeping drafts or making copies of all his letters have endowed today's historians with a rich collection of late sixteenth- and early seventeenth-century notes in somewhat the same way that Arthur, Lord Lisle, and Samuel Pepys have done for their periods.

I am more than grateful to the staffs of the Bodleian, British, and Folger Libraries, the Middle Temple Library, Westminster Archives, Public Record Office, and Essex Record Office for their courtesy and assistance, which enabled me to inspect the original records on which this study is based. I am also beholden to Elizabeth Story Donno, who at a very early stage read my manuscript with a discerning eye and made invaluable comments; Paul Oskar Kristeller generously gave me assistance with some of the more puzzling Latin and Italian passages; S. F. Johnson saw an early section of my project and provided helpful suggestions and encouragement.

I am especially indebted to Jane C. Apple, who first acquainted me with Powle's Bodleian manuscripts, supplied a number of genealogical notes and other tidbits that proved useful, and steadily evinced her supportive interest in this study. I wish also to mention Irene Cassidy, a veteran researcher in Britain who helped educate me in the mores of sixteenth- and seventeenth-century England and was ever on the alert for material that might be pertinent to the life of Sir Stephen Powle.

Introduction: The Significance of Powle's Manuscripts

Stephen Powle has certainly left a substantial legacy in his extensive and detailed manuscripts. They portray many aspects of life in his day in England, Scotland, France, Germany, the Rhenish Palatinate, and Italy. He reports his liberal arts education at Oxford and his intellectually stultifying study of the law at the Middle Temple, which nevertheless proved valuable in later years. His notes reveal the yearning of a young man for religious training in Geneva, wellspring of Protestantism. He also communicates the wide-eyed enthusiasm of a youth traveling outside his native land for the first time, absorbing many kinds of impressions. His interest in all that he saw led him to record details that he felt might later be useful to him and others: geographical features, historical points of interest, local customs, types of government, defense measures, pageants and magnificent spectacles, as well as an extensive listing of various currencies. He made a practice of continuing his education whenever opportunity arose in other lands and so sheds light on the universities of Geneva, Basel, Heidelberg, and Saint Andrews during the sixteenth century.

One reads his carefully framed letters seeking employment in civil or legal service; one learns of the problems of aspiring Elizabethans and how they wrote letters and sent gifts to ingratiate themselves with officials who might be helpful. Powle's letters to Lord Burghley and to Sir Francis Walsingham from abroad portray his experience as a foreign agent for Elizabeth in the Palatinate and in Italy, giving his perceptive appraisals of the political situation, alignments, and threatening dangers in the four years preceding the Armada expedition and providing some understanding of Walsingham's vast spy network. Powle also has left us his legal records of the court of Chancery, supplemented by correspondence and information about the government's handling of the Essex Rebellion. Later memoranda and letters refer to Powle's involvement in the Virginia Company of

London, tell of family life in England, dealings in land, financial loans, manor administration, and give insights into English country life. The account is punctuated by frequent religious and philosophical reflections as well as by occasional intimate details of his better known contemporaries: Walter Ralegh, George Carew, John Chamberlain, Robert Sidney, Andrew Melville, John Casimir, William Cecil, Nicholas Breton, and Thomas Lodge. From Powle's early adulthood in 1576 until his final years in the late 1620s he kept records—a span of fifty years. Most of the records have survived.

Sir Stephen Powle
of Court and Country

1
Education in the Liberal Arts and the Law

Stephen was the youngest of the three surviving sons of Thomas Powle, clerk of the Crown in England from 1549 to 1596. Thomas also held the important Chancery offices of senior six clerk and controller of the hanaper and served as high steward to Queen Elizabeth, clerk of Her Majesty's Forest of Waltham, and justice of the peace in Essex. That Stephen was not the oldest son and heir of this prominent government official had much to do with the shaping of his early life.

His letters to his father show the young man trying to win paternal favor or to impress his father with his filial obedience and conscientiousness in the hope of receiving much needed financial aid or being allowed to pursue a desired career. Despite Stephen's eloquent appeals, his father usually remained unresponsive. Although well-to-do, Thomas Powle was a stern and not overly generous parent and could be coldly unforgiving when he was in any way disobeyed. The one exception was his relationship to his oldest son, Thomas, upon whom he bestowed whatever favors he chose to give.

The result was that young Thomas, aware that he was the favored child, grew up with a devil-may-care attitude and no sense of obligation to his family or others. However, he evidently developed considerable charm and an attractiveness to women.

Young Stephen, on the other hand, had to make his own way in the world with minimal help from his family. But his difficulties with his father may have made him resourceful and taught him how best to handle the unyielding men in positions of political influence whose favor he later sought.

Stephen was born about 1553 in Essex, probably in Cranbrook, Great Ilford (Becontree Hundred)[1] of a prosperous gentry family. His mother, née Jane Tate of Waxham Norfolk, was, according to the epitaph on her London tomb in Saint Dunstan's the West, "descended from a line of honorable ancestors." She had one daughter and five sons, of whom two died in childhood. Apparently she was a rather meek woman completely dominated by her husband. Unlike his father, she is rarely mentioned in Stephen's letters or memoirs.

Stephen's childhood seems to have been a relatively happy one under the tutelage of Master Hopkins, a beloved schoolmaster who took the boy in charge at the age of seven. Hopkins was a monk devoted to scholarship who found a position with the Powle family after the dissolution of the monasteries. Stephen corresponded with him well into adult years and at times sought his sympathy and advice when overwhelmed with filial problems (169:48r, 55r).

As a youth Stephen was studious and of a quiet sort. He entered Broadgates Hall (later to become Pembroke College), Oxford, in about 1564 and had as fellow students such later luminaries as William Camden and George and Richard Carew. Broadgates, one of the more important halls at Oxford, was customarily the undergraduate preparation for would-be law students. Stephen mentioned his instructor in logic there as [Richard?] Stanihurst, "a sophistical Catholic." The "learned Papist" Richard Bristowe was another of Powle's instructors (309:80r). Bristowe left Oxford in 1569 and eventually became director of studies at the English College of Douai and died in 1581. Stephen later wrote that while at Oxford he had studied the Scriptures seriously and frequented Friday disputations of divinity in Christ Church. Little is known about his other studies except that they were in the liberal arts (309:3v). In March 1568/9 he received his Oxford bachelor of arts, and on 9 December 1572 (seven terms having elapsed since he received his bachelor's degree) he was licensed from Corpus Christi, Oxford, for his master of arts. Apparently he had migrated at some point from Broadgates to Corpus.

On 2 July 1571, at the age of sixteen, while waiting for his Oxford Master's degree, he was incorporated at Cambridge (under the name of "Pole") to study with Lucas Gilpyn, an ardent Calvinist who was lecturing there in theology in 1570 and 1571. Stephen, who came from an Anglican family, was evidently not influenced by the Catholicism of his early instructors, but his subsequent studies with Gilpyn seem to have moved him profoundly and opened the way for a deep preoccupation with Calvinism. Stephen revealed that it was at this time that he had "the taste and feeling in his heart of election by God" and thus felt assured of eternal life (309:80r). There is no record of "Pole" having attended any further lectures at Cambridge or of proceeding master of arts there.[2]

On 26 November 1574 the elder Thomas Powle (together with one Thomas Fanshawe[3]) was granted the manor of Aldersbrooke, Essex, by alienation of John Bullock, Esq. In anticipation of the conclusion of this transaction, when a fortnight earlier Stephen entered the Inns of Court, he registered as from Aldersbrooke, Essex.[4]

Since his father desired that he follow in parental footsteps and choose a legal career, on 9 November 1574 Stephen enrolled at the Middle Temple. The particulars of his admission (the original of which is in Latin) are according to *Middle Temple Records*[5]: "Stephen, third son of Thomas Powle of Aldersbrooke, Essex, esq., specially; fine—. Bound with Messers Thomas Powle, his father, and Thomas Powle. his brother. Stephen Powle to a chamber to be newly built in the Old Hall; fine—." The "fine," or fee of special admission, would usually have been four pounds, which was considerably more than that for general admission, since the former exempted the student from the ordinary duties and charges of membership. He was not obliged to attend all the designated periods of study or to pay commons fees when not in attendance, nor was he obligated to execute offices that might otherwise fall his lot for the celebration of "Public Christmas." In consideration of these exemptions, the additional admission charge was made. Special admissions were occasionally granted *honoris causa* without a fee and this may have been the case with Stephen, as his father then held the important office of clerk of the Crown as well as several other government posts. Annual rent for chambers was 5 percent of the value of the chamber. As long as the rental was paid, and provided commons was attended at least six times a year and the rules of the Middle Temple were observed, the chamber could be held for life. Otherwise it was forfeited to the house. The attire worn was customarily a student's gown and cap. Boots, spurs, swords, and cloaks were forbidden.[6]

Charles Worsley, writing in the late seventeenth century, described the four Inns of Court (that is, the Inner Temple, Middle Temple, Lincoln's Inn, and Gray's Inn) as "the highest order of collegiate institution in the land, to which sons of nobility and best gentry resorted as a matter of course to complete their studies." Some prepared for the bar, others for judicial positions, and some for government posts. In the 1570s there resided at the

Middle Temple during term time about two hundred Inner Barristers (seventeen years old or more), some having come directly from grammar schools but most from the universities. During reading time this number dwindled to about one hundred. These Inner Barristers, or beginning students (although a step above the entering neophytes who were called merely Gentlemen or Students), were ruled and counseled by a lesser number of Utter Barristers, who were graduates in the law. Of the latter after an extremely lengthy period the most distinguished rose to a further step of preferment as Benchers (or Readers), who comprised the governing parliament of the Middle Temple.[7]

Since Stephen was an earnest and conscientious young man, upon entry into this prestigious institution he must have involved himself in the traditional scholarly exercises: attending conferences and the disputations that were known as "moots." From lectures and readings he would have learned about pleadings and putting cases and would have immersed himself in the Laws and Statutes of England. Twice a year, during Lent and August, especially important lectures would be held with great display and magnificence. In term time, as he learned more, he would frequently have gone to Westminster Hall to hear actual pleadings, arguments, and judgments by eminent professors and judges of the law.

Serious students were involved in long and diligent studies, but at the end there was the prospect of attaining important legal offices or government positions. Whether they were to become worthy magistrates or founders of great and noble families, their knowledge of the law would in many circumstances stand these candidates in good stead.

But all the students were not studious, nor were all the activities at the Inns of Court serious ones; there was an abundance of gaiety, reveling, carousing, and involvement in pageantry, the high point being the special revels known as Grand Christmas, at which time the Lord of Misrule, or Christmas Prince, presided over a topsy-turvy model of the Royal Household. At other times there were poetry readings, singing, all varieties of music and dancing such as was usually practiced at court.[8] Occasionally there were performances of plays in the new Middle Temple Hall built in 1572. The handsome hall (still extant today) is over one hundred feet long and sixty feet in height, with a magnificent hammer-beam roof and a screen with rich carvings supporting the gallery. Windows are of stained glass and depict the arms of some of the prominent early members of the Society of the

Middle Temple. One bears the escutcheon of Stephen's father, Thomas Powle the elder, clerk of the Crown in Chancery for over thirty years.[9]

Before the time of Henry VIII, a simple library chiefly of law books had existed, but it had gradually been robbed of all its contents. By 1574 it is unlikely that a library still remained, for those who wished to study had to buy their own books. Stephen wrote to his father that during his first two years he spent ten pounds on law books (309:9v).

The atmosphere at the Middle Temple was at this time mainly one of noisy and raucous disorder that, as one gathers from Powle's letters, would not have been to his taste. Since he was not required to be present at all times and would have had little inclination to join his confreres in carousing, he probably left the Temple at the height of the reveling.

On 30 January 1578/9 he wrote his father the welcome news that he had become a "professor of law" (309:6r), which meant that by then his diligent studies had achieved for him the rank of Utter Barrister, which qualified him to practice law.[10] Even some years before this he must have been considered a promising student, for as early as 10 February 1576/7 he had been admitted to the Lord Chief Baron's chamber, located in an area reserved chiefly for Benchers and "ancient Utter Barristers."[11] Ordinarily one was not allowed to become an Utter Barrister unless one had performed nine exercises, kept eight terms of commons and one vacation commons, and was of at least six years' standing at the Middle Temple. In Powle's case, his Oxford degree and his conscientiousness may have been taken into account to shorten the length of his necessary Middle Temple sojourn, for in January 1578/9 he would have been at the Inn only about four years.

Despite Stephen's serious-mindedness, there evidently were times when he would have liked some diversion or recreation that was unavailable to him because of lack of spending money (309:8v). On 25 May 1579 he wrote home, begging for further funds, explaining that during his first two years at the Middle Temple his father had allowed him only twenty marks[12] above the ten pounds he needed for books and ten pounds for furnishing his chamber. Although in the past two years his allowance had been increased by four marks, it was far from sufficient, for he had been "charged by" his "mother's commandment" with the finding of a serving man. Stephen explained to his father that because of his financial embarrassment he was "barred from the company of learned men" (309:9v). Despite this, he seems to have made a number of friends at the Inns of Court whom he kept throughout life, among them Walter Ralegh and John Chamberlain, the renowned letter writer.

On 27 February 1574/5 "walter Rawley" of Budleigh, Devon, had been admitted "generally" for a fee of twenty shillings to the Middle Temple from Lyons Inn (one of the Inns of Chancery) and, according to Stephen's notes (309:91r), they roomed together. Ralegh apparently did not study law, but he remained at the Temple until at least 1576,[13] probably using it as a stepping-stone to the court. The two young men were opposites in temperament and tenets, although they adjusted and admired each other in many ways, remaining on terms of friendship until the end of Ralegh's life. Stephen mentions him many times throughout Tanner manuscripts 309, 169, and 168: receiving medical and other "scientific" advice from him, quoting from some of his Parliament speeches, investing in his Guiana expedition and in the Virginia Company, serving on the council of the latter, and probably writing him an anonymous letter of spiritual counsel several days before his execution (169:205r). Ralegh, who was about a year older than Powle, seems to have been a rather boisterous young man, while Powle was shy and perhaps a bit straitlaced, for in 1590, looking back at this period and thanking God for saving him from many possible adverse influences, Powle included among these "my bedfellow at the Inns of Court and many years' companion riotous, lascivious, and incontinent Rawlegh" (309:81r). Nevertheless, Powle referred gratefully to Ralegh's introducing him to Sir Edward Stafford and Jean de Simier. He was to meet both gentlemen again aboard ship when he left England late in 1579.*

At the Middle Temple Stephen also became friendly with a delightful but less ostentatious young man, John Chamberlain, who was precisely Powle's age. As with Ralegh, it was a friendship that continued into future years.

Stephen remained at the Middle Temple until at least August 1579 (169:59v), which would have been five years. Although during this period he applied himself assiduously to his legal studies, he disliked almost every minute of it and soon became convinced that it was utterly wasted time. Stephen succinctly and forcibly summed up his feelings about the law when on 17 June 1578 he wrote to his old schoolmaster, Hopkins: "I have

---

*See p. 32.

Walter Ralegh (1552?–1618) on first coming to Court in 1582. Kunsthistorisches Museum, Vienna.

small liking for this study which I account for the knowledge rude, for the order confused, and for language barbarous" (169:48r).[14]

During this period Stephen had begun keeping an album of musings, memoranda, copies of letters he had written, and sometimes of those he had received. The opening paragraph of this interesting volume (now in the Bodleian Library, classified as Tanner manuscript 309) reflects his personal thoughts and annoyances. It opens with a paragraph expressing his determination to seek permission from his father to leave the study of law and head for Geneva for further theological studies. He reveals that even if his father refused to give him further maintenance, he was determined to satisfy himself in spiritual matters. Furthermore, he was convinced that by travel on the Continent he could gain proficiency in foreign languages, and this would aid him in securing a niche at court when he returned home. Stephen put into letters those matters that he was unable to discuss face-to-face with his father, for in the latter's awesome presence the son became tongue-tied, or as he graphically phrased it, *"magis mutus quam piscis"* (more mute than a fish) (309:9v). Very gradually he would learn how to maintain his own individuality despite adamant paternal directives.

Following the opening paragraph of this album, one finds a long and persuasive letter to his father written in January 1578/9, in which Stephen expressed his desire to "return to the University," this time in Geneva in order to immerse himself in spiritual studies and closer reading of the Scriptures. He supported his arguments to his father by innumerable biblical quotations. He emphasized "the contrarieties of his natural disposition to the study of the law: his bashfulness instead of boldness and his taciturnity in place of garrulity." In addition, he pointed out that unpleasant effects had been wrought on the health of his body and spirits, such as sickness and dullness because of this long and unwilling labor from which he has gained little profit. He argued further that he was certain that the disorderly method of legal study would deny him progress in as short a period as his father looked for or preferment so soon as he expected. When despite all these arguments Stephen received no answer from his father, on 25 May he wrote again—a still more urgent and insistent letter.

One wonders whether Stephen's intense preoccupation with religion at this time may have been partially due to a desperate search for a benevolent father in heaven to compensate for the harshness of his earthly parent. Although from the age of about seven to seventeen it was quite usual for a Tudor father to exercise rigid control over his offspring, by the time young men reached their late teens, they were customarily released from parental jurisdiction and allowed to be on their own. Thomas Powle's practice was far different: he continued to rule with an iron hand and not always justly.

Signor Angelo, a religious counselor at the Middle Temple, evidently sensed Stephen's religious yearnings and advised him to visit Geneva, the fountainhead of Calvinism, to hear Theodor Beza and other leaders of the Calvinist church. The young man's desire to attend the university at Geneva and study divinity there began to grow steadily in insistence (309:4r), but he temporarily acquiesced to his father by staying a bit longer at the Inns of Court.

Meanwhile, he sought financial help from various friends (although unsuccessfully); then in late November 1580, when he would have been about twenty-four or -five, he resolutely left for the Continent. By means of pleading letters to Thomas Powle from various close or otherwise influential friends such as Lord Chancellor Sir Thomas Bromley,* the father became somewhat reconciled and was ultimately persuaded to continue at least a portion of the stipend he had paid annually for Stephen's tuition at Oxford and at the Middle Temple. After all, travel was considered to be an important part of a courtier's education. In addition, he gave Stephen ten pounds spending money toward his journey (Rawlinson MS. D 913:82r).

Stephen's mother, Jane, had died on 24 November 1577 at the age of fifty-seven, and within the next two years his father, then about sixty-six, had married Winifred Mordaunt Cheyney, widow of John Cheyney and mother of three sons, Sir Francis, John, Esq., and Thomas (Rawlinson MS. D 913:80; Tanner MS. 309:9v). Stephen seems to have tried to establish a pleasant relationship with his highborn stepmother, to whom he now referred as his "mother." When he left on his journey, she gave him a token gift of forty shillings (Rawlinson MS. D 913:82).

Curious as one might be to know what this young man looked like as he set off for his European travels, there is, unfortunately, no portrait of Stephen Powle known to exist, and there are no allusions to his physical appearance other than to his heavy

---

*See p. 190.

Three portraits of unidentified English gentlemen.

Unknown man inscribed 1598, aetatis suae 39. Courtauld Institute of Art, London.

An unknown man c. 1610, attributed to
William Larkin. Yale Center for British
Art (Paul Mellon Collection).

An unknown man ca. 1610, attributed to William Larkin. Yale Center for British Art (Paul Mellon Collection).

eyelids (Lansdowne MS. 88:43r) and an inference that he was tall.[15] His notes indicate that he was extremely conscious of and quick to mention his defects. Since he mentioned none in connection with his appearance, it seems likely that he may have been quite nice looking.

On pages 28–30 are late sixteenth- and early seventeenth-century portraits of several unidentified English gentlemen of about the same age Powle would have been at that time. One longs to speculate whether one of them might be he.

2
Travel: A Modified "Grand Tour"

After waiting two days for favorable winds, Stephen sailed from Dover in the queen's ship at the end of November 1579. He commented that as the weather was temperate, he was "not very sick." On board were Sir Edward Stafford, envoy from Queen Elizabeth to "Monsieur" (duc d'Alençon), and Jean de Simier, Alençon's proxy in wooing Elizabeth. Both gentlemen had previously been introduced to Powle by his friend Walter Ralegh. When they disembarked at Calais, Stafford was helpful to the young traveler in advising him as to lodging and diet while in France. Through the diplomat's hospitality, Powle dined daily with him and Simier during the three days they were together, and he thus saved considerable expense. From Calais Powle traveled sometimes on horseback, sometimes by coach through Abbéville, Amiens, and Saint Denis to Paris, being especially delighted by the "fair buildings and churches" at Amiens.

Arriving in Paris on 7 December, he was grateful for Resident Ambassador Henry Cobham's assistance in placing him in good lodging near the University (in Saint Jean de Beauvais Street at the sign of the Bellerophon) and for his generosity in daily inviting him to his table (Rawlinson MS. D 913:79v). He favored Powle even further by giving him a ride around Paris in the ambassadorial coach with Lady Cobham and himself. Despite these many favors, Powle found living in Paris very expensive. A simple chamber and slender meals for himself and his man cost him fifteen French crowns a month, that is, twenty-seven English shillings. Because of the high prices of essential French goods, even old shoes and boots from England were shipped to Paris, which boasted a street where they sold nothing else. The only inexpensive item of good quality that Powle had thus far found in Paris was velvet (Rawlinson MS. D 913:80r, 19 December 1579), but he could not take advantage of its value, as his slender funds were already so near depletion that he needed to conserve to the utmost if he were to be able to remain in Paris any longer.

Stephen had deposited with Master Bodley[1] (or Bodligh), a London merchant who lived on Maiden Lane, a sum of money consisting of the yearly allowance from his father, a small sum that he himself had saved, and possibly a few loans from friends, and with this he had arranged for a bill of exchange so that he could from time to time draw against this sum during his travels. At the outset, Bodley was to have sent his son in Lyons[1] a letter of credit for Powle, but this was either lost or agonizingly delayed, and Stephen grew more and more worried until mid-December, when, with Bodley's help, he was able to procure fifty-five crowns from a Master Gaudy in Paris. There were other problems for Powle. He had discovered that a "license to travel" would probably be necessary when he left France, so he had written to his eldest brother, Thomas, begging him to obtain such a permit for him. Stephen wrote six such letters to him before the end of December but to no avail. He also urged Thomas to try to persuade their father to send some additional money for his travel expenses. No response was received from his brother or from any of the other members of his family to whom he had written (Rawlinson MS. D 913:82r). He wondered, probably in desperation, whether Robin, the Devonshire boy to whom he had entrusted a packet with some of these letters, had failed to deliver them. It is more likely that neither his father nor his eldest brother felt inclined to help him.

He also wrote to Signor Angelo, asking him to collect, if possible, money owed Stephen by "the little black man," James "Buttes," whom he had befriended while at the Middle Temple. Powle had written a series of love letters for James to a very young lady named "Audrey" who was living (and likely serving) in the household of Lady Will Buttes at Thornage, Norfolk. James had probably worked there previously. The suit was successful, for he eventually married Audrey,[2] but he apparently had not yet paid Powle the agreed-upon fee for his letters.

While in Paris, Powle attended the university there and became proficient in French, with which he already had had some experience, however distorted, in his legal usage of the barbaric "Law French." He may also have been studying Italian, for not too much later he had become fluent in this tongue, also.

It is not clear when (or even if) he received his license to travel, but in early February he was able to find company with whom to set forth toward Lyons; it would have been far too dangerous to travel alone, since bandits and highwaymen were a frequent threat to those traveling alone or in small groups. Geneva was, of course, his real goal, but while in France Stephen pretended to be heading for the University of Padua, as this would have been more acceptable to the Catholic French than Geneva, with its detested religion (Rawlinson MS. D 913:80v).

Leaving Paris with a group of dyers, Powle proceeded to Lyons by a cheaper route than he had originally planned. The party went via Dijon and Chalon and along the river Saône to Lyons (Rawlinson MS. D 913, 79v, 80r). The dyers, who were experienced travelers, advised Powle that the thriftiest plan was to buy horses in Paris and sell them in Lyons or at the end of the journey, as otherwise the charge for horse hire would be well over forty crowns. Apparently Powle took their advice and accompanied them to Lyons. From there it was only a short distance to Geneva. He does not say whether he covered the final lap of his journey on horseback or by coach.

In his Letter Book (Tanner MS. 309), starting on folio 116r, one finds a detailed diary of his memorable sojourn in Geneva during the spring and early summer of 1580. There he heard Beza and Danneus and "the other holy prophets," and on 3 April 1580 he received Communion from the great Beza himself. Powle seems to have been deeply influenced by Beza's version of Calvinism: one can be assured Christ has designated him one of the elect (to be saved) if one can find instances in one's life when God was especially good to him. This doctrine probably accounts for Powle's frequent citing of events that seem to exemplify God's benevolence to him. A particularly apt example of this type of reminiscence is the long "Meditation" that Powle wrote at Clayhall Manor in 1590/1 (309:79v). At this time, he reviewed the whole course of his life as "a thanksgiving to the Almighty" for all his spiritual and temporal blessings—this despite the harrowing tragedy he had suffered earlier that year in the deaths of his beloved first wife, Elizabeth, and their twin sons. Powle concluded that there are times when God's ways are too inscrutable for man fully to understand.

Powle's religious feelings were strong ones, but they seem sometimes to have been intermingled with a tinge of pragmatism. Among his manuscripts are frequent prayers to achieve a specific goal: seeking God's help in procuring a desired office for which he had already written the necessary petition letters or, another time, eloquently praying that his services at Duke Casimir's court would prove successful (309:83v, 78).

Powle provides a vivid picture of Geneva in 1580, perched as it was very high on a small hill in the county of Savoy. It was a free state governed by four magistrates elected annually and known as the Sindex. The precinct of Geneva was less than half a mile in circumference—somewhat smaller than Canterbury and with its ministers all of equal authority. Modeled as nearly as possible on the primitive Church of the Apostles, its religion was based on the word of God and was "free from all ceremonial superstition." Powle describes their rites of Communion, marriage, and baptism, all of which aimed for simplicity. Crime was punished with severity.

In addition to absorbing religion and satisfying some of his spiritual longings, Powle increased his experience in more mundane ways: he took an interest in the political structure of the Swiss cantons, the customs and cultural differences to be found in Geneva, its laws, religious practices, architecture, and antiquities. He also learned certain oddities: how to make water look like wine in color and taste pleasant and how to make powder of molten lead, salt, and ashes, with which he could shoot birds without leaving any marks on their bodies (309:124r).

Because of the advent of the plague, Powle found it wise to leave Geneva earlier than planned, and on 2 September he set off for Basel. This town on the Rhine, to which he traveled on horseback through Lausanne and Berne, was five days' journey (309:41r, 125). There he stayed about six months and attended its university.

Upon arriving in Basel, Powle became acquainted with a young Polish knight, Adam de Goraisky, to whom he had a letter of introduction (309:129r). Adam and his brother, Peter de Goraisky, residents of Basel, became close friends of Powle. He kept up a correspondence with them for many years and in August of 1585 while in Heidelberg he received from Adam a folio of notes in Italian describing salient points about Portugal, France, Persia, Milan, Venice, Muscovy, Malta, and Germany, listings of the various dukes, counts palatine, and the like, together with a tract on the office of ambassador and some historical notes on England (231:1r–100v). Perhaps Adam had envisaged Stephen as a future ambassador.

In Powle's spare time he saw the sights of Basel. His most moving experience was his visit to the study and tomb of Desiderius Erasmus, who had been a resident of Basel before his death in July 1536. Powle felt a rapport with this man of common sense who had struggled against abuses of the church and the dogmatic pendantries of schoolmen and had been a major force in establishing humanist education in the liberal arts.

On the south side of the Great Minster there still stood a huge linden tree with widely spread branches that afforded shade to those who sat under it. Here Erasmus was said to have been utterly delighted with the pleasantness of this place from which he could scan all of Basel from east to west, viewing the mountains and towers round about and the river Rhine directly beneath. Near the river stone seats were to be seen, one carved with Latin verses as a memorial to the great scholar. Erasmus himself was buried near the chancel in the Great Minster.

On 6 December there came to Basel four Englishmen whom Powle had seen in Geneva: the young nobleman Henry Hastings and his tutor Master Church, Master Farmer, and a Master Cooper. These last two stayed only a few days and then continued on to Strasbourg by boat up the Rhine, while Hastings and Church remained in Basel and attended the university with Powle.

On 20 February the theologian Danneus arrived from Geneva and that night supped with Powle. Present also were Ottoman Jacobus Grynaeus, professor of historiography at the University of Basel,[3] and a certain Baron Kulish. There probably were spirited discussions of religion, for years later Powle recalled Kulish's attempt to dissuade him from Calvinism (309:81r). Basel was known as a congenial meeting place for scholars from various countries; there they could enjoy discussions and a free interchange of ideas. In 1571, when the French philosopher Pierre de la Ramée wrote his eloquent Latin panegyric to Basel, he referred to its great men and its sense of freedom and humanity.[4]

Before he left Basel in March 1580/1, Powle heard disturbing reports of the death in Ireland of George Carew and Walter Ralegh, but, as was frequently the case, the news proved false. On 8 March Powle, Hastings, and Church departed by boat for Strasbourg. It was only a day's journey costing two batts[5] per person.

Having visited the two great Protestant cities of Geneva and Basel, they arrived at a third, Strasbourg, to find it in an uproar because of attacks by intolerant Lutherans against the Calvinist humanist Johann Sturm, who had shown sympathy for the French Huguenots. Lutheranism was conservative, emphasizing ceremonies, altars, and vestments, as opposed to Calvinism, the so-called Reformed Religion, with its simpler and more personal forms of religious observance. Its most distinguishing feature, however, was its well-known doctrine of predestination.

In a book titled *Formalis Concordia*, the German Lutheran theologian Jacob Andreae (1528–90) of Wuerttemburg and a few coauthors had awkwardly tried to reconcile the teachings of the Lutherans and the Calvinists. The book had evolved from six sermons delivered by Andreae about 1572. These became the basis of the Swabian *Concordia*, which developed into the *Formalis Concordia*, or Formula of Concord. The work had taken final shape at a 1577 conference at Bergen Abbey, near Magdeburg, and was therefore sometimes referred to as the "Bergen Book" when it was published in 1580.

In reaction to this publication, some Latin verses had made their appearance that, according to Powle, were reciprocal ones that could be read either as a commendation or dispraise of Andreae, and they were believed to have been written by Sturm (309:138v). Powle revealed this interesting information in his notes and quoted the verses, although with at least one minor error:

Encomium libri Bergensis et Authoris

Eximii liber est fructus nec publica pacis
formula durabit tempus in exiguum,
unamini[6] liber hic coniungit pectora sensu
Dissona, nec gliscet plus grave dissidium
perpetuo tua laus vivat, nec Suevice Doctor
Gloria decrescens te tua destituat.
Arbitrium ad pacis toxit te gloria Christi
unica, non turpis quaestus et ambitio.

Whether the poem was in fact reciprocal is difficult to say. If it was intended only as commendation, however, it is unlikely to have been written by Sturm, who at this time had no love for Jacob Andreae. Charles Schmidt, in *La Vie et les Travaux de Jean Sturm*,[7] refers to a 1581 work of Sturm's, *Epistola apologetica contra Jacobum Andreae alteram flagrum Aegyptium, suae theologiae doctorem Tubingensem*.[8] To have called Andreae "another Egyptian plague" was using strong words.

"Toxit" in line 7 of the poem is, of course, not a true Latin word. Did Powle mean to write "traxit" (drew) or "toxicat" (poisons) or was the poem itself ambiguously combining the two words? If the word was intended to be "traxit" (drew), the verses could be commendatory, according to Professor Paul Oskar Kristeller for whose translation I am extremely grateful:

A praise of the Bergen book and of the Author

The book is of extraordinary fruitfulness, nor will its public formula of peace endure for a short time. This book joins discordant hearts in a unanimous sense and great dissent will not slide further. May thy praise live forever and, O Swabian Doctor, may thy glory not decline nor abandon thee. To the arbitration of peace the glory of Christ alone drew (traxit) thee, not ugly gain nor ambition.

However, if the rather ambiguous second line is interpreted differently and if the next to last line contains the notion of poisoning (toxicat), then the poem was in fact reciprocal, as Powle stated, and could be read as derogatory of Andreae and the *Concordia*.

Johann Sturm (1507–89) in his youth had been invited by Strasbourg to reorganize its educational system, and through his efforts the city had developed an important educational center. In 1538 he had established a humanist "gymnasium" and by 1564, an academy. The aim was to inculcate "piety, knowledge, and eloquence" with a ten-year course of studies graded according to the difficulty of the subject matter. Sturm's academy gradually evolved into the great university of which he became rector.[9] And he also played an important part in Strasbourg's politics and religion, siding with Zwingli (precursor of Calvin) against Luther. Now, in 1581, as Powle reported, libels were being published against Sturm because of his criticism of the Lutheran Church of Strasbourg, and on 30 July 1581 he had voluntarily exiled himself about six miles away in Neustadt within Casimir's Palatinate, which was sympathetic to Sturm's religious doctrines. Soon Sturm was forced to relinquish the rectorship of the university.[10] In 1589 he died, embittered, at the age of eighty-two.[11]

By the time that Powle arrived in Strasbourg, many students had departed. On 6 April he, Hastings, and Church registered at the university and, after paying a fee of ten batts, went before the dean and were incorporated as noblemen.

The following day Powle spent visiting the Tower of Strasbourg, which was, according to his notes, "accounted amongst the wonders of the world for height and workmanship." He measured the height with his astrolabe and found it to be about five hundred feet tall. The astronomical clock that had been installed in the tower in 1574 seemed especially miraculous, and Powle sent two letters to England describing it in detail.[12] Among the other sights that interested him in the city were the three sawmills and an arsenal, whose extensive weaponry Powle listed in his diary. On another day he and Hastings enjoyed a few musical hours across the river listening to the sweet-voiced nuns sing early morning prayers in the nunnery. Also included in Powle's memoranda of this period are notes on how to keep roses fresh until Christmas (309:142v), how to prevent injury from the shot of a harquebus or gun, and a medicine "for the stone in the reins and bladder." It was expected that such miscellaneous information would prove serviceable later in life.

During Stephen's long absence from England, his father's customary harshness toward him seems to have somewhat moderated, for Thomas Powle had apparently been sending Stephen funds from time to time during his travels. On 20 June 1581 Stephen wrote a long letter to his father to thank him and to assure him of the value he had derived from his eighteen months of travel. After expressing gratitude for his maintenance, Stephen explained that through observation and inquiry he had endeavored to understand certain aspects of each country he had visited: the government, the strength and power of its princes and magistrates, its league of alliance with neighboring nations, the size of its dominion, its outstanding personages with their affinities, its type of religion, the number of its chief cities, the nature of its people, and the fertility of the soil.

After briefly describing the countries seen, he proceeded with a lengthy, historically based discourse touching on the beginnings, development, and government of most of the important commonwealths throughout the ages (169:149r–173r). One of his conclusions, based on observation and supplementary reading in works by such authors as Aristotle, Justin, Bede, Guicciardini, Bodin, Machiavelli, and Regiomontanus, was that laws should be made according to the natures of the people and that magistrates should govern with reason, for people differ markedly according to the areas and climates in which they live. As Stephen analyzed it:

> By dividing the world into three parts, cold, temperate, and fervently hot, philosophers have noted that as air is affected with divers qualities so the minds of inhabitants be disposed by divers affections. The Northern people be strong of body, and apt to be cruel, yet very faithful and secret, of wit dull and lumpish, therefore they must be governed by force. Temperate persons be apt to speak and therefore by laws and pleadings polished. The Meridianal persons be melancholic, *propter adustam choleram*, therefore to be governed by religion and ceremonies. And it hath been observed that the Northern people have prevailed in conquest over the Southern, that the Meridian people have filled the world with arts, sciences, and ceremonies, that Temperate climates first invented laws and pleadings.

Going back to ancient times, he referred to the Assyrian and Chaldean monarchies, which were overcome by the Medes; the Grecian sovereignty, which succumbed to the Romans, "people in respect of them Northern." He pointed out that at present the Turks ruled Greece, held Judea tributary, and bore sway in Egypt, "south regions far off," and yet were not able to prevail against the Muscovians, Scythians, and "Polonians," northern neighbors. "The Venetians being but one city have extended their dominion on the islands of the Mediterranean" but "have not one parcel in Germany northward or nigh them. . . . The Spaniard always warreth on the Moors and never essayeth his force with the French nation. And how many times hath our little island been Lord over most of the continent of France," he noted, adding that it was never found that "the French King hath by force of arms worn the English crown." He continued his rather simplistic analysis by discussing the development of arts and sciences (astronomy, philosophy, oratory, languages, physics) by the Egyptians, then the Greeks, and later the Romans. Superstitions, he wrote, were to be found mostly in Africa, Spain, and Italy, although not so often in Germany, Poland, England, or Scotland (169:159r).

He noted that in hot countries the people are inconstant and variable, while in cold countries they are constant and immutable; the Florentines, for example, had changed their manner of government eight times in 300 years, whereas the Swiss had remained an immutable aristocracy for three hundred fifty years.

He further observed that those who, because of long peace or because of abundance as a result of the fertility of the soil, incline toward effeminacy and "daintiness" can be swayed by courtesy rather than broken by force; in contrast, those who dwell on the frontiers of different regions are daily exercised in war and acquainted with scarcity and inclined to rob, and they can be kept within civil limits only with difficulty. Such men must be controlled by constraint and harsh punishments. As examples he cited the inhabitants of the Pyrenees, those of Hircinia Silva (the western part of Bohemia), those of the Alps in Valetia who are within Italy, Savoy, Switzerland, and Geneva, and those on the borders of England and Scotland.

Stephen inferred from the foregoing, based as it was on limited geographical knowledge, that whosoever aimed to rule successfully in the north would need other means besides law, but in France or other temperate countries, he would need mainly courts of justice. In hot countries the ruler could use the inhabitants' superstitions to augment his power. Powle here gave

Christopher Columbus as an example. Being "desirous to keep in subjection the Indians who superstitiously reverenced the moon as a goddess," Columbus informed them that he would shortly deprive this goddess of her light, for he knew from astronomy that there was about to be an eclipse. After this did in fact occur, the Indians submitted themselves completely to his authority and "honored him as their chief sovereign, so well did he use the ignorant natures of the people to be a mean to effect his enterprise" (169:160r). Powle allowed that all the above theories could, of course, be modified by the power of almighty God when it seemed good to his omnipotent will.

Powle concluded that laws should be enacted and magistrates should govern reasonably, and superiors should eschew tyrannical humiliation, for it proves to be a perilous form of government.

Powle then turned to a brief consideration of astrology and of numbers (no doubt influenced by his reading of Cardanus and Regiomontanus), noting all the critical happenings of various Septembers.

He next discussed at some length the subject of musical harmony as described by Plato (169:169r&v). Harmony in music, the dance, and in life[13] was a subject much written of in Powle's milieu, for it was felt to be applicable to the concord of well-governed commonwealths as well as to life in general.

Powle concluded the long letter to his father by observing that since the most flourishing states eventually come to an end, partly through influence of the heavens, partly by disruption of musical harmony, partly by "consent of numbers," but chiefly by the "will of almighty God," men labor in vain if they rely solely on political laws to establish tranquility at home or if they depend solely on arming themselves and on fortifying their cities to prevent overthrow by foreign powers.

Therefore we must not build assurances of our safety on any sandy foundation or strive to follow the vain, ambitious pomp of magistracy or government, he noted, for "high places of estate have commonly dangerous downfalls." Powle urges that we find our freedom in that only city where is eternal rest and never-ending happiness—the heavenly Jerusalem, high throne of the only triumphant King, our glorious God (169:172v).

Stephen apologized for this long, wordy discourse in which he had tried to condense and evaluate all that he had seen and learned in his eighteen months of travel. His musings show him to be a meditative and thoughtful young man with deep religious feelings who was trying to avoid false values and ambitions while speculating and seeking deeper understanding of the world around him. Signing his long letter "Your loving and obedient son, Stephen Powle," he noted that it was "begun and ended in sixteen mornings, 1581 May 22 . . . penned in a water bath at Strasbourg being an extremely hot summer . . . but perused and enlarged at sundry times sithence." It was sent to his father 20 June 1581.

On the same 20 June Stephen made a notation in his diary that he had seen that day the canopy of state, which was of yellow damask and gilded thereon, carried by four of Strasbourg's leading citizens who were transporting the Emperor Rudolph II from the entrance of the city to his lodgings (309:151v). Stephen seems not to have been impressed by the man with all his trappings who was the center of this pomp and show. Stephen felt similarly about many of those persons he was later to meet at Elizabeth's court.

About a month later (22 July) Powle received from a certain Doctor Beuter, whom he had sought out in Nuremburg, listings of the genealogies of most of the princes of Germany, the genealogy of Charles V, and the seats of ecclesiastical princes, as well as a list of civil and imperial cities with the dates of their congresses and assemblies of consultation. Accompanying this data were four sheets of paper containing "the whole description of Germanie." Powle was surprised to learn that sometimes the title "count palatine" was bestowed by the emperor's favor on persons otherwise mean of estate and poor of living and that such persons were granted the privilege of making bachelors and masters of art and of conferring legal and medical degrees at the university (309:152r).

Powle left Strasbourg on 12 August and traveled by coach via Speyer, arriving at Heidelberg 14 August. There he learned that the seat of Duke John Casimir, count palatine of the Rhine,[14] was only three miles away. Four days later the duke arrived from a hunting trip attended by forty horsemen, and the following day Powle was granted permission to visit the count palatine's fabulous garden. There Powle saw a great variety of devices, exotic plants, strange fruits, and infinite numbers of unusual herbs "sufficient to furnish an herbalist with unknown knowledge and to delight any other beholder" (309:169v). He described the spectacular garden in detail. In the midst was a fountain at the corners of which stood exquisite statuary of Diana and her nymphs. The garden also contained aqueducts, waterfalls, groves of unusual trees, banqueting houses, a tiltyard and other areas for sport and pleasure, as well as a section filled with various kinds of beasts and birds, arbors, labyrinths, paintings, and statues. After his visit, Powle was given as a keepsake a branch with pomegranate buds and a varicolored herb.

The Palatinate property was extensive. In the suburbs of Heidelberg in the Church of the Holy Ghost (Heiligen Geist), Powle visited Casimir's extensive library, which contained four to five thousand volumes in the sciences (309:176r). Three hours from Heidelberg was Scheinam Abbey, situated in a valley surrounded on three sides by hills of great height, while on the fourth side flowed the river Neckar. There Powle saw the handsome abbey with its stately buildings and rich revenues, which also was within the domain of the wealthy count palatine.

On Sunday, 10 September, when Powle finally left Heidelberg and proceeded toward Frankfurt by coach (paying eighteen batts for its hire), even at some distance from Heidelberg he again passed several castles belonging to the Palatinate.

On 11 September Powle and his man finally reached the river Main and Frankfurt. Powle explained that the city was in Vederavia, a free state governed by two burgomasters and a senate. The city, Powle wrote, although as big as Strasbourg, was not comparable to it either in strength or beauty, Frankfurt's houses being of wood.

He further commented that the Jews were confined to one section and were permitted no occupation except usury so that the younger ones were brought up in idleness and sat in the streets talking and "recreating themselves." Although they dressed in costly silks and gold, they were dirty and untidy in their houses and food. They were distinguished by a round circle of yellow cloth worn on the left shoulder of their robes. Although they were extremely oppressed, their numbers steadily increased. They charged only eight coins for each hundred borrowed and received an item in pawn that, if not claimed by repayment of the loan in one year and six weeks, they retained as belonging rightfully to them (309:189r). Probably these were the first Jews that Powle had ever seen.

On Sunday, 17 September, he departed from Frankfurt toward Strasbourg by coach, paying three florins for himself and the same for his man. It was twenty-four "German miles"[15] and took four days. En route he bought a whistle with which he was able to mimic the songs of all birds. At a village called Linkenau he saw a wedding in progress; then, passing over the Rhine by the long bridge, he and his man once again entered Strasbourg.

His return to Strasbourg was for the purpose of joining ranks with a fellow traveler to continue on to France. Powle remained in Strasbourg until Tuesday, 26 September 1581, at which time he left for Paris via Lorraine in the congenial company of Master Robert Sidney, who was then nineteen and about eight years Powle's junior.

Robert's eminent older brother Philip Sidney had been an Oxford college mate of Stephen's: first at Broadgates Hall and subsequently at Christ Church (the latter while Stephen was at adjacent Corpus Christi). If Robert visited his brother at Oxford, he likely would have met Powle previously in England. Robert, who seems to have been more vivacious although perhaps a bit less studious than Philip, had (under Hubert Languet's direction) after some continental travel spent a season in the Strasbourg area living with the famous Johann Sturm.[16] This must have been an inspiring experience, as the great scholar was a strong proponent of humanist education.[17] Now, before returning to England, Robert decided to set off with Powle on an excursion to Paris so as to become better acquainted with France and French ways.

Powle portrays their journey together in detail (309:189v). Shortly after leaving Strasbourg, they passed by Sturmianum, Sturm's home in Dortheim, and proceeded from there to Kocherberge, a castle seated high on a hill and belonging to the bishop of Strasbourg. They stayed overnight in the walled city of Taverne, which also belonged to the bishop. There the young travelers were interested to see an eagle "thayned"[18] and fed. Stephen's notes describe the surrounding countryside as "champion,"[19] with plentiful corn and wine. Veering northward through various towns in Lorraine as far as Saarbruck, where the inhabitants spoke a mixture of French and Dutch, the travelers then headed south and west, toward Paris. Continuing by coach through the towns of Luneville, Saint Nicholas, Nancy, Surcy, Ligny, Steinville, and Anserville, they eventually crossed the border into France.

The first French town they came to was Saint Disier, which was small but strongly fortified. They stopped next at Vitry, where Powle and Sidney played tennis; they enjoyed the game, but Powle does not report who won. From Vitry they proceeded to Poire de Champania, a little village where they unfortunately had only "slender entertainment" because a fortnight before soldiers had lain waste the countryside so that there was now a shortage of water and of wood. A little farther on they came to the walled town of Porroy, which six weeks before had been utterly sacked (309:191r). After passing Bois de Vincennes, the king's house where Henry V of England died, Powle and Sidney traveled one more league to reach Paris and lodged that night at the Croi de

Fer. The next day they were glad to enter pension in the house of Madame Aunray at the sign of the Bellerophon, where Powle had lodged on his previous visit to Paris. The journey from Strasbourg had taken them eleven days.

Meanwhile, at the Parisian court magnificent entertainments were being given by King Henry III of Valois[20] in honor of the marriage of his favorite, the duc de Joyeuse, to the queen's half-sister Marie de Lorraine. The wedding itself had been held on 18 September, but an elaborate celebration had been continuing from 14 September through early October accompanied by a different gorgeous presentation—visual, musical, poetic, or chivalric—nearly every day. Some took place in the courtyard of the Louvre and others proceeded through the city on floats or on the river Seine. Antoine Caron, as major artist, and Claude le Jeune, as composer and musical director, created the presentation.

Beyond the very considerable artistic importance of this festival was its political and religious purpose to draw together in amity the rival factions of the Guise party, to whom the bride was related, and the emerging Catholic League in praise of the French Valois King Henry. He was endeavoring to bolster his tenuously held throne through his own and his favorite's marriage into the Guise family and through his display of splendor throughout his kingdom. According to Powle, there had been "much triumphing, jollity, and gathering of the states of France and foreign princes."

An interesting work by Frances Yates[21] describes the earlier part of this fabulous program of entertainments during the Joyeuse wedding festival. Although Powle and Sidney arrived in Paris too late to see the main portion of the celebration, what they did view was staggering to them in its intricacy and magnificence. They were delighted to find that part of the program was considerably behind its originally scheduled time: certain events that were supposed to have concluded by 19 September actually were given in early October, after the young men had reached Paris. One of these took place on Tuesday, 9 October: the cardinal de Bourbon feasted King Henry III in Paris at the Abbey Saint Germain, of which the cardinal was abbot. At twilight, before supper, a marvelous show was presented. Powle conveys his open-eyed amazement at the scene on the waters of the Seine (309:192r&v).

He describes the twenty-two boats made in the shape of various sea creatures: porpoises, sea calves, whales, dolphins, sirens, and mermaids. Chained together, they were towing a great castle, at the rear of which stood a gigantic Neptune, god of the sea, holding in his hand an imperial crown below which was a throne for the king of France and seats for the rest of his princely assemblage. As lord over the seas, Henry III and his entourage were being drawn by these monstrous creatures. From within their bodies issued forth musical harmonies of various sorts. The pageant seemed a miraculous one, for the boats made their way a full mile upstream against the current from the Bonhomme Abbey to the Louvre although they were not self-propelled. The manner of operation was a hidden device with cords tied under the isle above the Louvre so that the boats were being pulled by the turning of submerged wheels. The effect was described as delightful to the senses of both hearing and sight.

This wonderful show continued for three or four days during the daytime, and at night there were maskings on horseback, in which King Henry and Queen Louise[22] danced on horseback. The horses, which had been imported from Naples, kept time so artfully that it was, Powle reports, an utterly amazing sight.

On the Tuesday following, the king, the duc de Mercoeur, the duc de Guise, and the duc de Lorraine became challengers at tourney and at barriers. Their entrance on "Mount Parnassus" was a spectacular one, with the nine Muses playing several kinds of wind instruments. The float was propelled by "inward motion," as was another mountain on which could be seen dryads, nymphs, and other minor divinities with their consort of string instruments. Then followed the flying horse, Pegasus, "whose hooves had created the fountain of Helicon which the Muses frequent." Behind, mounted upon a high throne glistening with spangles and adorned with gold cloth eight yards in length and at least ten in height, followed Duke Mercury (Mercoeur) in complete gilt harness "to signify that as God of Eloquence he was an attendant on the Muses and as messenger a precursor of Jupiter who was represented by the King himself following in a great ship to show that he was so omnipotent that he could make mighty vessels by nature designed to move on watery seas now proceed forward and sail on immovable earth. This ship was sumptuously rigged as a fit palace for such a mighty monarch with its mast covered in cloth of gold, its sails with cloth of silver and all the tackling fashioned of silken cords" (309:193r).

The duke of Guise rode on the left, mounted on a black horse with bases and caparisons of green and white in front of the king's ship; on the right side of the ship rode the duke of Lorraine, attired in silver armor with bases and caparisons of white and yellow. After the four challengers had marched once around the court, the king and duke of Lorraine proceeded to their pavilions on the right side, and the duke of Mercury to his pavilion on the left, ready to defend their challenge at the barriers, while the duke of Guise kept himself on his horse "to adventure his strength and fortune by Tourney."

> At the other end of the court came the defendants mounted on gallant steeds caparisoned with cloth of gold ready to deliver their swords as by force they should be broken and those incontinently betook themselves to tourney with the Duke of Guise who, afterwards being dismounted, fought at barriers with the King. (309:193r&v)

There followed six or seven companies, some on horseback, some on foot, among whom were the twenty-two-year-old duc d'Aumale (brother of the duke of Guise) and the eighteen-year-old duke of Genoa. Then came the duke of Joyeuse and Monsieur la Valetta (the former had married the queen's sister and the latter was to marry the other sister shortly after), sitting on the side of a model of burning Aetna supported by a Cyclops whose face was in the fore part of the mountain and whose feet were at the rear, so that he seemed to bear the mountain on his belly. Preceding the mountain were ugly dwarfs carrying the armor and ensigns of these two princes. On either side, smiths pounded on anvils with their hammers as they followed their master, Vulcan. After descending from the mountain, the two knights marched around the great court and betook themselves to tourney and to barriers. Immediately after them came a whole pageant of golden-haired nymphs whom Powle identifies as Venus's darlings, since she was associated with Vulcan and his forge and also favored the affairs of Mars and therefore would be present to behold the forthcoming feat of arms and chivalry. In her chariot was "all manner of melodious harmony and consorts of music with wire strings as well as the best voices to be found in Paris."

Next came a great whale on whose back rode ancient Neptune, "desirous of seeing these solemn triumphs and willing to make trial of his champions." As the whale opened its mouth, it yielded forth four drums, six pages, and six knights who were to perform at tourney and barriers both for their honor and for the delight of the spectators. The king himself, "in keeping with his dignity and place, confirmed his superiority by winning the highest degree."

> Thus the heavens by the presence of *Jupiter, Mercury,* and *Venus;* the seas by *Neptune* and the great whale; the infernal parts by *Vulcan* on the burning mountain; the woods and groves by the *Muses;* and the

Earth itself by so many knights having presented signs of joy at the solemnizing of this marriage, it behoveth that the air also should yield forth her tokens of this triumph . . . sometimes there fell (as it were) stars . . . sometimes thunders by astonishing noise and clap to be heard, sometimes in the air *Candelae accensae* were to be seen. (309:194r&v)

The foregoing description, hardly a brief one, indicates that Powle was a thrilled and intelligent spectator well versed in mythology. For him and for Sidney, this Renaissance court fete was a source of breathtaking amazement. However, there is no indication to what extent he was aware of the underlying shakiness of the political situation. As Roy Strong has so aptly commented, "Nothing could have been more optimistic and, at the same time, further from political reality than the Joyeuse 'magnificences' that were the final glorious swan song of Valois festival art."[23]

On Thursday, 18 October, there was in solemn manner a tourney by fourteen contestants against fourteen, among them the king himself with Monsieur d'Alençon, the duke of Joyeuse, and La Valetta, the younger brother of the queen, on one side, and on the other side the dukes of Guise, Aumale, and Genoa.

Powle wrote next about a visit on 25 October with Don Antonio, pretender to the throne of Portugal,[24] when he came to Paris. Powle reported that the following day (Friday) he and Robert Sidney "took their footcloths" (their formal regalia) and went to pay their respects. The Portuguese "King" gave them "great caress," and when he embraced Powle used these words: "Toto quanto son vostro" ("I am completely yours"). Don Antonio had visited England previously and now "Monsieur" (d'Alençon), Henry III's brother, had just gone to England "to further the 'King' of Portugal's affairs" (as some thought), but others imagined it was "to celebrate an English marriage" with Queen Elizabeth.[25] Powle's notes continue: "About this time the King of Spain proclaimed 'Monsieur' to be his enemy, and all his partakers: as well for the taking on him the government of the Low Countries . . . as also for that he feared he would take part with the King of Portugal and help to restore him to his kingdom" (309:194v).

The foregoing refers to the fact that the States General of the United Provinces and the prince of Orange had offered to make the duke of Anjou ("Monsieur") commander-in-chief of their forces, for they believed that French support would give them added strength against Spanish aggression. By June 1581 Anjou had assembled fourteen thousand soldiers, and in July, Holland and Zeeland declared their independence from Spain. But he lacked the backing of his brother Henry III of France and therefore had insufficient funds to pay his troops. Since at this time "Monsieur" was the foremost candidate for Queen Elizabeth's hand, he sought financial aid in England. Elizabeth, on her part, eager to make a show of Anglo-French solidarity in order to deter Spain, gave her suitor ten thousand pounds (with a promise of more to follow) to pay his troops and urged him to proceed quickly to the Netherlands. Anjou thereupon crossed the Dutch frontier and siezed Cambrai, which the Spanish had been attacking, then entered Ghent and Antwerp and was crowned duke of Brabant and count of Flanders. However, in his haste to become ruler of the Netherlands, he overstepped and met calamitous defeat from Antwerp's citizens. After many of his troops were killed and the balance driven out, he was forced to retreat to France. Meanwhile, Catherine de Medici, his politically minded mother, had sent an expedition to take Don Antonio to the Azores in hope of keeping the Portuguese throne from the Spanish. However, it was to no avail. Philip soon ousted them.[26]

A Turkish ambassador arrived in Paris on 11 November, attended by his son and two servants, who were all attired according to Turkish custom in gowns and turbans of white wreathed cloth. Powle reports that he visited his chamber and watched the entertainment that the ambassador provided for his guests, although he did not describe it (309:195r).

On 24 November Powle was present at an audience with the Turkish ambassador, first in the king's chamber and then in that of the Queen Mother Catherine de Medici. About the twentieth of the month another Turkish ambassador arrived with further privy instructions. Perhaps this was an occasion when Turkey and France were joining together in one of their frequent struggles against the Empire.

On 29 November a report, later to be proved false, reached Paris that "Monsieur" was betrothed to Queen Elizabeth. At this time, the duke of Joyeuse's brother was espoused to Monsieur la Valetta's sister and was to be married two days later. In the meanwhile, Monsieur la Valetta was made duke of Épernon and thus a peer of France.

The same page of Powle's manuscript bears notation of another sort: on 12 November he had learned from Master William Gent to swallow a knife without any harm and to divide any circumference by means of a compass. On 11 December Powle learned from Master Robert Sidney the way to pierce any harness and to

Robert Sidney, Viscount de L'Isle c. 1588 (1563–1626). National Portrait Gallery, London.

shoot farther with the like quantity of powder, same bullet, and same piece than anyone could who did not know this secret. Sidney had learned this process of heating and cooling and specially treating the ammunition in the Low Countries (309:195v). Like other Renaissance gentlemen, Sidney was a young man of varied developing talents in the military field, in statesmanship, and in poetry[27] as well.

On 12 January Powle sent his man back to England, probably to prepare for his own return in March. A couple of days later Robert Sidney went with Powle to visit Saint Denis, burial site of French kings. Although Powle had been there once before, this time he saw far more than he had two years earlier. Because of their mutual avid interest in history, Sidney had persuaded him to make a return trip to the site before leaving France, and it proved to be a rewarding excursion for both young men. They viewed with fascination the precious relics and riches of France, including a gorgeous robe of blue velvet embroidered with pearls that the king had worn when consecrated at Rheims, the Imperial Crown, the sword carried by Joan of Arc and by Saint Louis. In addition to these authentic historical mementos, Saint Denis boasted a number of suppositious relics: a piece of wood from the Cross, bones of Elias the prophet, a piece of linen cloth in which Christ was buried,[28] and one of the cups from Solomon's Temple. Powle does not indicate that he and Sidney were at all skeptical of these.

He next reports that on 18 January thirteen Swiss ambassadors came to Paris to demand payment of a three hundred thousand crown debt owed their country by the king of France. The ambassadors had been instructed to dissolve the league with France unless the sum was paid, for the king of Spain had offered the Swiss discharge of this debt if they would enter into league with him.

On 23 February, the Thursday before Shrovetide, Powle saw coming from the Tuileries gardens the "zany," together with a servant on horseback, who "fished" for boys along the way as he went with toothsome "comfitts" dangling.[29] Powle also saw many masqueraders in the streets, some on horseback and some on foot. It seemed that all the inhabitants of the city were crowded onto Notre Dame bridge to watch them (309:198r).

Powle's next diary entry, made a number of months later, recounts that on a Saturday in June he learned from Erneste, a "Purnegian" nobleman, how to make rachetti fly in the air and how to make "caylys," a fiery ball, burn in the water and boil above it. Presumably these were varieties of fireworks. Powle and Erneste tested and "proved" them that night.

The remainder of this diary page has been torn away. What is left indicates that it was devoted to methods of secret writing that would have been of especial interest to a government agent. Powle probably found these notes useful later in his career. Brackets denote those parts of the manuscript that are illegible or were lost because of the torn page. The following is the gist of what remains (309:199):

> Sometimes in the inward parts of the [   ][30] that covers the wax of seals, which Sergeants commonly have, there are written letters which can be seen by removing the wax.
>
> Pigeons have been used as messengers of letters as when the Consul Hircius sent messages to Decius Brutus [   ].
>
> The Egyptians covertly expressed their meanings by Hieroglyphics as for instance, *Crocodilus infortunium significabat, accipiter celeritatem, manus dextera*[31] *expensa liberalitatem.* [The crocodile signifies misfortune, the hawk speed, the right hand generosity.]
>
> If you use a sheet of paper similar to one that your recipient has, you can write the letters of your secret message through the holes of the paper onto another sheet of paper. Now take this sheet and fill up the rest of it with any other letters so as to confuse anyone (not possessing the grid) who tries to decipher it.
>
> Bede invented a system whereby one could express his meaning by figures. This system is called Dactilogia and Artologia.
>
> There are three main kinds of invisible writing:
> *Dormaticum* which is writing with a kind of herb called "lactaria" or "lactuca-caprina" out of which, when crushed, there issues a milk-like kind of juice. When it is dry, it must be read by casting ashes thereon.
> *Highasmaticum* which is by writing on linen cloth with alum water. *Aleoticum*, a juice which is variable and diverse both in form and matter and is used to write in the spaces between the lines of a letter [   ].

Powle gave page references for the above notes on secret writing but there is no indication, on the portion of the page that is extant, from what source book or books they are derived.

3
England and Scotland

Powle's last dated entry from France is 12 March 1582, from Paris. Shortly after this he returned to England. He was now twenty-nine and had been away from home over three years, of which the last six months had been spent in France. This period of foreign travel had effected certain modifying changes in the rather staid, intense young man who left England in 1579. A new self-assurance had resulted from his challenging and maturing experiences: opening his eyes to new cultures, studying in the universities of various countries, being cordially received by a number of eminent personages, and, above all, being removed from the dominating influence of his father. As anticipated, Stephen acquired skill in languages: considerable facility in French and Italian and, to some degree, in German. Well aware of the value of his experiences, he had managed to keep voluminous records of what he had seen and had noted miscellaneous bits of information that he believed would some day be useful. He was still far more introspective than most of his contemporaries, but he had acquired a new ease of manner and a confidence in himself.

When he returned home he was to feel the force of his father's domination once again, but now he was better able to cope with it. His health improved; he no longer became ill with frustration and emotional turmoil. His deepening religious faith had provided him with a cushion against adversity; his earlier tense seriousness had moderated to more reasonable limits, allowing his latent sense of humor to put in an occasional appearance in response to some of life's absurdities.

On 14 September, in one of his lighter moments, he wrote a teasing letter to his second brother, William, purportedly from his father (169:34r). The story behind it is that William Poole (as his brother called himself) by allowing his horse to stray onto his father's property had angered him, and as punishment the irate elder Powle had asserted his "legal" right to take possession of the horse as waived or forsaken goods. In June William had written his father apologizing for the trespass, explaining how badly he needed his horse and how much he would appreciate having it returned. His father, however, did not relent.

When Stephen returned home from France, he heard of the incident and, much amused by its inanity, wrote a fictional letter to William from their father. The letter has his father taking literally the phrases in William's letter of apology, "I crave pardon for my boldness," and his subscription, "Yours to command." Stephen has his father saying:

> because you have made such a liberal offer of dutiful obedience, I mean to make proof of the performance of your promise by this one simple charge: from henceforth forever I will you to be silent, and by that means peradventure you may purchase me to be your friend hereafter in some other matter of less moment than the delivery of a gelding.
>
>   Clay-hall
>   Essex, 1582   14 Sept
>   Tho. Powle

The address "Clay-hall" at this time was probably, like the letter, fictional, or at least teasingly premature. Thomas Powle and various business partners were from time to time involved in the buying, selling, and renting of land and various important properties. By 1588 he did formally lease Clay-hall Manor, with its extensive meadows, pastures, woods, gardens, and outlying buildings, for thirty-four years at an annual rental of only forty pounds.[1] Probably he anticipated making a tidy sum by turning it over in due course to an affluent client. It is conceivable that as early as 1582 Thomas Powle may have been considering acquiring this prestigious estate.

Whether or not William Poole ever retrieved his horse is not known, but Stephen's Letter Book contains the notation that his chaffing letter to his brother was never sent.

After returning to England Stephen entered Lord Treasurer William Burghley's service. Presumably this had been arranged by Powle senior, then clerk of the Crown and in a position to have considerable influence with Burghley. However, Stephen did not at this time continue in government service (169:17v), for we learn from his letters that by April 1583 he was at Saint Andrews University, Scotland at New College (later known as Saint Mary's), and there he became friendly with its master, Andrew Melvyn (more commonly known as Melville).

When visiting Edinburgh during this period, Powle had the honor of being invited to dinner at the residence of Ambassador Robert Bowes. In a letter of 30 April to Lady Bowes from Saint Andrews, written because she had expressed an interest in learning more about a sermon that Powle had attended at Edinburgh, he reported that unfortunately he had nothing further to tell her of the sermon by Master Lawson other than what Powle had already related to her when he had dined (apparently at a large dinner) at her home, for he had arrived late at the sermon and was further hampered by not being familiar with the Scottish tongue. In lieu of this, he sent her other "wine" from "the Lord's holy vineyard," a sermon by Master (Tobie?) Matthews. Powle had written down the contents of the sermon together with the discourses of sundry other preachers and had bound them together in a gift booklet for Lady Bowes. In closing his letter he asked to be remembered "unto my Lord Ambassador" and as a postscript asked Lady Bowes to deliver his "most dutiful service" to the following "honorable ladies" (whom he had possibly met at the dinner): the countess of Argyle, the countess of Orkney, and "my good Mistress the lady Marie Stewart the hands of which honorable personages I kiss with all duty, humility, and reverence" (309:96r).

Powle was well received and made many friends in Scotland, but while there he had an accident. On 8 May while in the garden of New College he stumbled and fell headlong in the orchard and, as a result, was unconscious for four hours. In September, after his recovery, he received from Melvyn some Latin verses of sympathy about the fall (168:205r). Powle replied appreciatively in Latin prose. He seems to have been much liked by those he met at Saint Andrews and in Edinburgh, for in 1590, when reminiscing about this period, he wrote that when he departed from Scotland (at the end of October), he was "escorted by a greater convoy than either Master Secretary Walsingham or any other Ambassador since that time" (309:82r).

Upon Stephen's return home matters were far less pleasant. He found Thomas Powle indignant that his son had "visited the King of Scots," an act that, as a loyal servant of the queen, his father considered almost treasonable. He was also angry that Stephen had not continued in Lord Burghley's service. At this time Stephen wrote despairingly to his old schoolfellow and long-time friend George Carew:[2]

> I have laboured long by many means for a reconcilement: I find my father's displeasure to be a labyrinth that hath many intricate pas-

Holograph page from Stephen Powle's Commonplace Book, Tanner Manuscript 169, folio 17v. Draft of Powle's letter to Lord Chancellor Bromley. Bodleian Library, Oxford.

sages but no outgoing: a main deep sea that hath many stormy tempests but no calm quiet, nor secure shore or haven. And my bolid³ is too short to sound the bottom, for which cause, I must of force follow the course that I resolved to undertake in your chamber: that is to *Polonia* where I will hope to find some secure shore for this seabeaten bark of mine, and some happier haven for my harbor. (169:18r)

It took well over a year with the earnest efforts of Lord Chancellor Bromley* and other prominent friends to whom Stephen had written for help to effect even a partial reconciliation with his father. Meanwhile, Stephen considered going to Poland, perhaps because of his friendship with the Polish knights Adam and Peter de Goraisky, whom he had met in Basel.

Later he modified his plans and chose instead to go to Bohemia. Stephen needed funds to finance such a journey, so he asked Carew to lend him money temporarily, and in return he offered his pistol and copies of his notes on France or Scotland. Stephen next wrote to his godfather Lidcote (169:18v), to a close friend, Anthony Cooke (169:34v),[4] and to other special friends begging for a loan of five pounds from each. According to later annotations on copies of these letters, Powle received no favorable response from any of them.

On 1 January 1584/5 he sent his father as a New Year's gift Robert Parson's *Book of Resolutions*,[5] which had recently been published in Rouen. With it, Stephen wrote a long letter to his father describing the book's virtues despite the author's Catholicism (309:93v). No answer seems to have been forthcoming from Thomas Powle.

---

*See appendix E, p. 190, for transcription of Powle's letter to Bromley.

4
Agent for Queen Elizabeth at Casimir's Court

Stephen now proceeded to ask Secretary Walsingham for a passport to travel "toward the Emperor's Court in Bohemia," and in February of 1584/5 wrote to Treasurer Burghley begging to be "feet, eyes, or ears to his Lordship" (309:95r) and requesting letters of introduction to the Calvinist Duke Casimir, who was now elector of the Empire, because, wrote Powle, he deemed Casimir's court "in respect of his power, religion and league with her Majesty the fittest place wherein I may do either my Country or your Honor service." Walsingham and Burghley complied with Powle's requests, and he shortly set off as an agent of Queen Elizabeth to the court of Johann Casimir at Heidelberg, arriving there 2 April 1585 (309:79r).

Johann (or John) Casimir, born in 1543, was third, and supposedly favorite, son of Friedrich III, the elector palatine. Friedrich had been Lutheran in his youth but soon swung enthusiastically to the religion of the Swiss reformers and developed a deep hatred of the papacy and its ceremonials. He was sympathetic to the Huguenots, many of whom had sought refuge in Heidelberg, and he endeavored to halt their persecution in France and the Netherlands by sending Casimir to their aid with a considerable force under his command. The expedition was successful, and a peace was achieved that granted the Huguenots liberty of worship. But soon after Casimir's return home, the truce was broken by the horrible massacre in Paris on Saint Bartholomew's Day in August 1572. Friedrich also tried to secure tolerance for the Calvinists of Germany, and this was effected until his death in October 1576, when he was succeeded by his eldest son, Ludwig VI, who, having been bred in his father's earlier views, remained a strict Lutheran; on the crown prince's accession, the state religion was changed from Calvinism back to Lutheranism, with emphasis on the altar and the sacred symbols.

However, Ludwig's rule was mild, and he did not survive long enough to reverse his father's policies completely, for he succumbed to tuberculosis at the age of forty-four. At his death in October 1583 he left his eight-year-old son and nine-year-old daughter in the guardianship of Casimir, whom he had previously appointed administrator in Heidelberg. Casimir now assumed regency of the Palatinate for his nephew and took careful charge of the boy's upbringing, changing his and his sister's former harsh and rigorous schooling to a more liberal type of education. The boy became strongly attached to his uncle, who, conscious of the fact that he was nurturing a future ruler, spent considerable time with him.

Casimir proceeded to reorganize the state according to his strong Calvinist beliefs and transformed the church, the university, and schools. Lutheran councillors were dismissed and were replaced by those of the "reformed religion." Distinguished professors and preachers Ludwig had dismissed were reinstated wherever possible. Festivals of the saints and other holy days were not observed; Christmas and Easter were observed quietly in private homes or were ignored. Once again, as in Friedrich's time, "the pulpit was all, the altar nothing." Life and morals were strict: drinking, dancing, dicing, and fortune-telling were forbidden. Casimir assumed government leadership with *Constanter et sincere* as his motto, and the people endorsed his changes.[1]

He seems to have been a high-minded, well-intentioned man, but he was unable to see both sides of a question and he angered easily. Throughout his life he remained dedicated to the Calvinist cause and retained a strong antipathy to anything Roman Catholic. As champion of Calvinism, he tried to form a Protestant League to counterbalance the Holy League in which Spain, the pope, and the emperor had united. But, unfortunately, because of factionalism the ideal of a league of Protestant states was not achieved at this time.

Johann Casimir valued friendship with England and had always been on excellent terms with Queen Elizabeth, who seems to have liked him and admired his strong leadership. In fact, she had awarded him the Order of the Garter.

Despite his usual amity with the English, Casimir chose to ignore the warm letter of introduction which Burghley had written for Powle, because Casimir had shortly before been irked by what he considered Burghley's adverse influence on the queen at a time when the elector was seeking English aid to reinstate the archbishop of Cologne in his seat.[2] When Powle tried to present

Burghley's letter to Casimir on his arrival in Heidelberg, he was denied an audience with him and was not given any sort of proper assignment at the Palatine court. In other ways also he was treated in an insulting or belittling fashion, being "placed among the pages," who were young boys "rude in behaviour and ignorant in all knowledge whatsoever" (78:95r). After considerable time had passed, he was given a bit of translating to do from Latin or Italian into French, the official language of the court, since Casimir had received his boyhood training in France. Because of Powle's skill in languages, he was occasionally asked to interpret for foreign ambassadors but was never employed in any work he considered significant.

When Burghley was informed of the insults to Powle, he wrote to him in his own hand apologizing for this unjust treatment and reassuring him that the cold reception was evidently intended as a slight to Burghley rather than to Powle (309:46v). Burghley's attitude toward Powle seems here, as elsewhere, almost a paternal one.*

To occupy himself constructively, Powle attended the University of Heidelberg (78:95r-99r) and spent his spare time putting together the family tree of Casimir's ancestors, which had been requested by Burghley, who was himself an ardent genealogist. To carry out this undertaking, Powle made two trips to Nuremberg and assembled much information. Periodically, Powle sent to the lord treasurer long newsletters telling of any important "occurrants," political alignments, or diplomatic intrigues that could be of English interest (78:95r–99r). These intelligence letters, which are now among the Burghley papers, range widely, seem perspicacious and informative, and probably proved of value to Burghley.

In March of 1585/6, after almost a year had elapsed since Powle's arrival at the elector's court, Powle wrote him (78:106v) in French of his intention to return to England and of his willingness to carry any letters that His Excellency needed to have delivered to the queen or her councillors.

Casimir then entrusted Powle with certain important letters: to Master Ségur (the king of Navarre's ambassador, who was residing at Frankfurt on Main), to the earl of Leicester in the Netherlands, to the bishop of Cologne (then resident at Vianen in the Netherlands), and one to Casimir's mother (also in Vianen).

---

*See pp. 66, 213–15.

William Cecil, First Baron Burghley (1520–98) Lord Treasurer, attributed to M. Gheeraerts after 1585. National Portrait Gallery, London.

Powle was departing not only because his time and energies were being put to inadequate use at the court but primarily because the funds he had brought from England were now running low, and Casimir had provided no living expenses for him. However, in order to make his departure a courteous one, Powle presented to His Excellency a beautifully illustrated copy of the genealogy of his ancestors and a pair of gloves; to Casimir's nephew, the young prince, Powle sent a portrait of the queen of England together with a handkerchief of fine English workmanship (78:106r).

Powle stopped briefly in Frankfurt on Main, from where on 2 April 1586 he wrote Burghley a newsletter. Among other items is the following disturbing notice:

> There be sundry libels written and printed in Dutch and French sounding greatly to my Lord of Leicester's dishonor. Master Ségur did first inform me thereof and wished that some English gentleman would be a suitor to the Burgomaster to inhibit the sale of them. He himself did buy as many as he could burn. (Cotton MS. Nero B IX, 136v)

Apparently the scandal-filled quarto, later known as *Leicester's Commonwealth*,[3] was just then appearing on foreign shores. It accused the earl of various heinous crimes, including the murder of his first wife, Amy Robsart.

In the late summer of 1584 English authorities had first learned of the publication of this slanderous diatribe and took prompt measures to suppress it, for they assumed it to be of limited circulation. Queen Elizabeth denounced its "abominable lies" and ordered all copies surrendered immediately. Despite attempts to confiscate as many copies as possible, little was achieved, and further insult was added when it became known in the spring of 1585 that a French translation had just been issued. How widely this vicious attack on the earl of Leicester had been disseminated was acutely brought home to Lord Burghley by Stephen Powle's letter of June 1585, which made clear that not only was there a recent French translation but now a Dutch version that had made its appearance in the Netherlands.

When Burghley and Walsingham read the text of the libel, they realized that it had undoubtedly been brought out by supporters of Mary, queen of Scots, who was then an English prisoner, and they unsuccessfully endeavored to track down the author. In their efforts to retrieve copies of the tract, various punitive measures were proposed by the Privy Council, but it was soon apparent that the situation was out of control. Although Sir Philip Sidney, Leicester's nephew, had written a brief essay defending his uncle, it was deemed wiser to forego publishing it lest it open up further discussion of the earl's morals. Burghley and Walsingham eventually concluded that the wisest course was to allow the furor to subside of itself as readers became aware of the scurrilous falseness and excessiveness of the libel. Perhaps Powle's letter had made Burghley recall the judicious advice given to him by Archbishop Matthew Parker on an earlier occasion[4] that "some things are better put up with in silence than much stirred in."[5]

Stephen Powle left Frankfurt for Holland to deliver Casimir's letter to Leicester, who was then in command of English forces in the Netherlands. Queen Elizabeth had at last decided to intervene so as to prevent Spain from appropriating Dutch ports, which could prove all too convenient for an invasion of England. Elizabeth also feared the growing influence of France in the Low Countries. After the assassination of the prince of Orange and the fall of Antwerp to the Spanish in August 1585, a treaty had been signed by which England agreed to furnish troops to the Netherlands with the proviso that the towns of Flushing and Brill and the fort of Rammekens be held by the English as pledges for sums advanced. Thereafter, the queen had sent six thousand foot soldiers and one thousand horse soldiers under the leadership of Robert Dudley, earl of Leicester. They arrived late in 1585.*

Powle wrote to Burghley of his visit to Leicester's headquarters.[6] The letter related that the earl had bestowed "whole showers of speeches" on Powle while discussing the proposed Protestant league to be made among four princes: Duke Casimir, the duke of Saxony, the marquis of Brandenburg, and the landgrave of Hesse. Powle summarized Leicester's various comments to be passed on to Burghley with the recommendation that in his view Lord Buckhurst (Thomas Sackville) would be most fit to handle negotiations.

After stopping in Holland, Powle was delayed in getting a passport and making connections for England. Furthermore, his purse was near depletion, as Casimir had given him no funds to cover the extra traveling necessitated by delivery of his letters.[7] But, surprisingly, despite the neglect and almost insulting treat-

---

*See p. 202.

Nº 5.

Joannes Casimirus Dei gratia Comes Palatinus Rheni,
Tutor et Electoralis Palatinatus Administrator Dux
Bauariæ etc.

S.

Literæ vestræ quibus Stephanum Polum nobilem Anglum
diligenter nobis et accurate commendastis tantum
apud nos ponderis habuere vt eum in numerum nobilium
aulæ nostræ libentissime recepermus cuius quidem
facti nos non pænituit. Nam is quandiu nobiscum
vixit, morum probitate et elegantia, vitæ innocentia
obsequijsq; suis non solum abunde (nobis) satisfecit, sed et om-
nium sibi beneuolentiam conciliauit. Et sane nobis
gratum fuisset si rebus ipsius ita ferentibus tantisper
hic perstitisset, donec occasionem probandi eius operam
et industriam in negotijs nostris tandem nacti essemus.
Verum reditum adornanti nobisq; summisse ualedicenti
moram injiciendam non putauimus quem omnino di-
gnum iudicauimus qui Serenissimæ Regiæ Angliæ etc.
dominæ et consanguineæ nostræ charissimæ a uobis
commendetur idque ut faciatis, et Ser.ti eius nostris
uerbis officiosissime salutem nuncietis, rogamus. Valete.
Data Heidelbergæ Idibus Martij. Anno a partu Vir-
ginis cIↄ Iↄ xxcvi.

Casimir

Duke John Casimir's letter (1586) to Lord Burghley praising the services of
Stephen Powle. Lansdowne Manuscript 50, folio 11, British Library.

ment of Powle while he was at Heidelberg, Casimir evidently valued his services, for in a letter dated the ides of March 1586, the duke wrote to Lord Burghley that his high commendation of the "noble Englishman Stephen Powle" had proven well warranted, for Powle had lived at Casimir's court "in probity of manners and refinement." In the "blamelessness of Powle's life and in his compliance he not only exceedingly satisfied us but also brought together the benevolence of all to himself and was wholly pleasing to us." The letter is written in Latin in a formal Italic hand and has Johann Casimir's flourishing signature (Lansdowne MS. 50, fol. 11).

Powle's letter to Burghley after his arrival in London is dated 17 May 1586, from his father's house in Maiden Lane. Presumably, by this time, there had been a reconciliation with his father, possibly due to the fact that Thomas Powle had recently suffered financial reverses and was perhaps less arrogant.

Upon his return to London, Stephen sent to Lord Burghley the long genealogy of Casimir's ancestors with replicas of their escutcheons in color (78:105r). The accompanying letter is dated 3 June 1586. About the same time, Stephen presented gifts purchased abroad to several members of Lord Burghley's staff: to Henry Maynard (chief secretary) "a castle of bone curiously wrought at Nuremburg"; to Richard Spencer (a secretary) "three Dutch toys"; and to Walter Cope (gentleman usher) "a German's handiwork" (78:105v).

According to Powle, Lord Burghley welcomed him home and wanted him advanced to clerk of the (Privy?) Council but found to his dismay that the queen had already promised the office to another. Powle's appointment was deferred; he was now about thirty-one years old.

On 12 December 1586 he wrote to Burghley from Maiden Lane telling of the unfortunate decline of his father's estate and of his own need to procure such employment as would provide him a living either in England or elsewhere. He requested a passport so that at the time of the approaching Frankfurt Mart he could travel eastward in the company of others to seek relief in some foreign place, for, as he explained, he could not bear to suffer penury before the eyes of his friends. Perhaps, Powle offered, he could carry Her Majesty's packets to Casimir if there were any occasion of sending to His Excellency. As a postscript, Powle suggested that it might be helpful for English intelligence to order the monthly Venetian "occurrences" from Padua, Venice, or Augsburg, since they were based on weekly intelligence letters from most parts of Europe (309:66r).

Burghley sent his letter to the principal secretary, Sir Francis Walsingham, to peruse, and thereupon order was given for Powle's departure to Venice with fifty pounds annual pension plus thirty pounds for travel to Venice (309:65v). He was well prepared for such an assignment since in 1583 he had made extensive notes on Italy with regard to its chief cities and their governments, important families, history, outstanding monuments, hospitals, ports, and so forth (309:97r).

In late March 1587 Powle set off from England by boat (309:67r) and, on board, met a former ward of Burghley, Edward Lord Zouche, who was then about thirty-one. In Zouche's party were Hawkins, late proctor of Cambridge, Holliband, the French schoolmaster, and Zouche's servant, Warde. Zouche and Powle traveled together via Hamburg to Frankfurt on Main, the commercial and banking center of Germany. There Powle delivered to Horatio Palavicino, Queen Elizabeth's financial ambassador, a packet from Walsingham.[8]

On 8 April Powle wrote to Burghley from Frankfurt. The letter suggests the warm relationship that existed between Powle and his "Master":

> Touching your commandment [to go to Venice] I hear that the Inquisition is more strictly observed there than ever heretofore for of late one Donzellino a learned Physician was drowned there only for that he had a book of the Religion sent him enclosed in a letter; yet I mean by the favor of God to remain there till some extraordinary occasion drive me from thence, be it never so dangerous: and am to depart hence Wednesday in Easter week (which is the end of the Mart) with the merchants of this town. I would it stood with your Lordship's pleasure to command me any particular service by message of word of mouth, or by other men's letters: and not by your own writing: for the times being so dangerous your Honor's letters would be construed in the worst sense if they should be intercepted. Without any commission from your Lordship I will presume to send your Honor such things as I shall value at any worth for rareness being hard to be recovered, or newness being of any singular invention. Thus my gracious good Lord, I rely wholly on your Honor as on my own father, making your Lordship's favor mine only inheritance to procure any increase whereof I will hazard my life, in such a case to any danger whatsoever. (309:66v)

On the same day Powle sent a newsletter to Walsingham by his man, Daniel Simpson. In it he told of the mixed reactions to the queen of Scots' death: that at Hamburg, Luneborg, and Brunswick it was "very heinously taken," but that it was highly commended in Protestant areas such as at Cassells in the Landgrave William of Hesse's country and at Frankfurt by "all those of wisdom who were of the religion or wish well to lawful proceeding." Those of the meaner sort and common soldiers were discontented with England because the previous summer many Rutters were commandeered by Grave Meurs using her majesty's name. The Rutters were German cavalry soldiers who were engaged to fight in various sixteenth-century wars. They were frequently swaggering bullies who showed no respect for the lands they traversed. Most departed home without payment of any charges; others wandered through the countryside complaining and showing their wounds. Powle observed to Walsingham, "Your Honor at home may apply at your pleasure medicines thereunto."

Powle traveled with Lord Zouche and his party toward Heidelberg and en route stopped at Cassells, where they were invited to the landgrave's. However, they did not dine with the duke but with his counselors because he himself was then "in his diet to reform fatness." Powle was shown a pamphlet, written by Dr. John Dee, the famous English mathematician and occultist, which had that day been presented to the landgrave. Its title was *Liber de Secretis et Magnalibus Dei qui in Apocalipsi vocatur Alpha et Omega (A book about God's secrets and Mighty Works called in the Apocalypse "Alpha and Omega")*. The book opened with these words from the twenty-seventh chapter of Genesis: "De rore et pinguitudine terrae det tibi Deus" ("May God give thee the dew and richness of the earth"). Underneath was written "Deus Londinensis" ("$\frac{Dee}{God}$ of London"), profanely alluding to Dee's own name. The August before, Dee had been at Cassells for a season with his train of four coaches, affirming openly that he lived at her majesty's charges. People considered him "a proud and fanatical spirit, disliking all religions and delivering this doctrine to the world: that there must be forthwith a restorer of the house of Israel to its wonted terrestrial glory which message he said he had from the Angel Gabriel" (309:67v).

On 13 April Powle and Lord Zouche reached Heidelberg, where Zouche and his party remained. This was Powle's second visit to Casimir's court, and he stayed only briefly, as he needed to proceed to Augsburg, where he was to meet merchants from Frankfurt who were traveling toward Venice. On 15 April he left Augsburg for Venice with them (309:68r). He had already informed Walsingham that following Sir Francis's direction, he would proceed from Augsburg to his appointed place, but he apparently had considerable trepidation about staying in Venice, because his letter contains the following lines:

> Hoping that your Honor will leave this free to myself that if I find it dangerous in respect either of the Inquisition, passage, or other troubles, to stay elsewhere near there. . . . But wheresoever I remain your Honor shall be informed by me every three weeks of the occurrents: and though I adventure never so many dangers, I will by the favor of God go to Venice to take order that the weekly advices be sent me; and if any other intelligences may be procured by my industry, I will acquaint your Honor therewith likewise. But herein if I do not perform so much as your Honor looks for, then if it please you to command Master Doctor White of St. Dunstan in London to put down my error herein by letter, he will convey the same to me by the way of Nuremberg and Augsburg. And if it is impossible for an Englishman to enter Venice, then if it please your Honor to apply me to some Dutch service I will discharge that duty faithfully. (309:68v)

5
Agent for Queen Elizabeth in Italy

The Englishman William Thomas visiting Venice in the mid–sixteenth century described it as

> The most magnificent, beautiful, and wealthy city . . . queen of the sea . . . inhabited by a very great number of people of many nations, who have flocked hither from almost the whole world in the pursuit of trade. And there all tongues are spoken, and there are the most disparate of human costumes.

Thomas also wrote that "this city abounds in all the comforts of living" and enjoys "a climate which is most temperate and serene." He continued:

> I think no place of all Europe able at this day to compare with that city for number of sumptuous houses, specially for their fronts. For he that will row through the Canale Grande and mark well the fronts of the houses on both sides shall see them more like the doings of princes than private men. And I have been with good reason persuaded that in Venice be above 200 palaces able to lodge any king.

The Venetians, he tells us, "rather practice with money to buy and sell countries, peace, and war than to exercise deeds of arms," although they did have a fine arsenal and nearly two hundred galleys. "Most Venetians are at these days become better merchants than men of war."[1]

Venice had long been an international emporium, and during the late sixteenth century her activity as a port was considerable. Her government was relatively stable and had managed to stay clear of foreign control. Citizens of Venice enjoyed much independence, being allowed to criticize provided they took no action against the state. Venice was well known for its anticlericalism and freedom of religion but recently the Papal Inquisition had been stretching out its tentacles so that by the late 1580s non-Catholics were becoming increasingly wary.

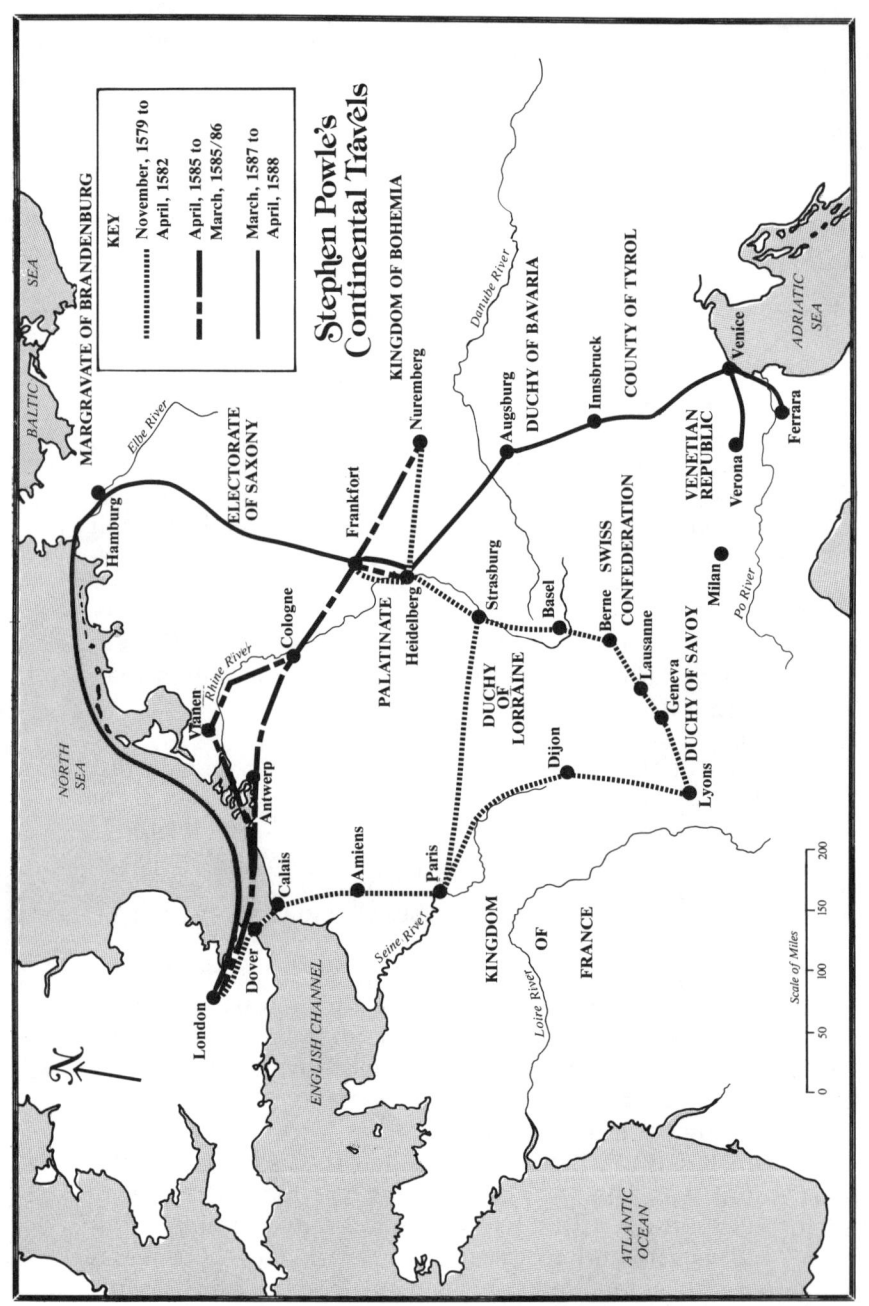

Map of Stephen Powle's continental travels 1579–88. Drafted by Nicky Gelfer.

For Stephen Powle as an agent of Principal Secretary Sir Francis Walsingham, Venice served as a center for news, since it was at the hub of many trade routes. Powle was able to operate here with more freedom than would have been possible in most other areas of the Italian peninsula. He arrived in Venice on 27 April 1587, having been delayed because of having to obtain *Gleide* (safe conduct) through each province of Germany; without this, no one was permitted to pass during mart time. On 16 May Powle sent Walsingham the first of a series of biweekly newsletters from Venice (309:63r). In it he mentioned that his previous letter was written 8 April from Frankfurt, and that on 22 April he had reached Innsbruck in Tyrol where Archduke Ferdinand held his court. There he heard an amusing tale:

Four days previously, the rector of the College of Jesuits and the rector of Aall had been requested by Maximilian, duke of Bavaria, to loan thirty thousand ducats in support of the Catholic cause. They agreed to this and were conveying the money by mule to Munich (the duke of Bavaria's court) when they were intercepted and the money was captured by men sent from the Archduke Ferdinand, who, having had secret intelligence of this, ordered the money seized while the mules were passing through his lands. In the meanwhile, Ferdinand commanded both the rectors to appear before him, and he made known to them his need of money and craved them to lend him some. The rectors replied that they had no funds at all because they lived wholly on the alms of the church and the charitable contributions of well-disposed Catholics; so, with regrets, they departed from his presence. Within an hour after this, the mules with their treasure were brought to Ferdinand in Innsbruck. Since the rectors dared not acknowledge their wealth, which would have been contrary to their former protestation to the archduke, they could not complain of any harm or injury and, therefore, lost the thirty thousand ducats.

Powle continued his letter to Walsingham with news from Italy:

> The chief princes that wish good success to her Majesty's proceedings be the Dukes of Mantua, Ferrara, Florence, and the Signoria of Venice. All are moved therunto by the general dislike of the Spaniard's tyrannizing greatness, her Majesty's known enemy. . . . The Duke of Florence . . . hath at this time a private difference with the Pope (whom I account a principal member of Spain) about a claim the Pope maketh to Borgo Santo Sepolchro, that many years since did

belong to the See of Rome but became the Duke's because it was not redeemed after it had been pawned for money. The money this Pope Sixtus Quintus offereth to pay, the Duke refuseth it. Moreover, he would have him at the least pluck down the Castle thereof because it standeth too nigh Forli, a frontier fort of Romagna, and sundry banditi from Rome be harboured in Tuscany to increase the heartburning betwixt them.

The Venetian in particular honoreth her Majesty in regard of her gracious, calm, and peacable government in these stormy times; and now all her neighbors' countries be afire, her highness only keepeth her realm in a moderate temper. He is also well affected to our country in respect of his sale of his chiefest commodities in those parts to his exceeding gain. Moreover, sundry principal men of this state have remained long in England and do daily increase their wealth by trading thither, as Giacomo Foscarini, Ragazzoni, and sundry others of less account. (309:63v–64r)

The rest of the letter covers the following news items:

The Spanish King had tried through his Ambassador Jerrari to effect a peace with the Turks for three years, but Master Harborne, the English ambassador, had managed to prevent it and Jerrari had returned to Milan 9 May empty-handed. There was as yet no mention of the removal of Spaniards from Milan, although the report was that about 25 April four well-appointed galleasses[2] departed for Spain from Naples and two from Sicily.

It was reported that the Franche Comté[3] had joined with Lorraine to aid each other with two thousand foot and six hundred horse soldiers to prevent the passage of the Rutters through their countries. These disgruntled and destructive bands of swaggering bullies returning from the wars were inclined to pillage the countryside as they passed through. Powle realized that Walsingham had closer sources to inform him which way these Rutters would pass into France.

German Protestant princes were to meet the king of Denmark at Lüneburg on 23 June about confirming an offensive and defensive league against the enemies of their religion, by that means offsetting the Holy League made by the Catholics the previous year.

Maximilian (the Catholic prince) was hoping to be king of Polonia and was using three means: (1) the support of the queen widow (of Stephen Battori, who had died in 1586) and all her partisans, (2) marriage to the young princess of Sweden, and (3) the favor of Samoisky, chief strongman in Polonia, who was wholly devoted to the house of Austria. But it was suspected that

Samoisky might be secretly trying to promote one of the Battori family. The election was to be held the end of June in the fields outside Cracow. The king of Spain feared, and had so written to the emperor, that the rivalry among Ernestus, Matthias, and Maximilian would work to their detriment, and he therefore advised that only one should stand for election in order to make a united party more assured.[4]

Powle wrote from Venice that no prince of Germany had either an ambassador or agent there; even the king of Spain had merely an agent, secretary to the last ambassador.

Recently a little pamphlet about the queen of Scots had been printed, touching the proceedings of her cause and her execution. It was a simple narration of all of the relevant circumstances. Because the decision to execute her was an action approved of by sundry chief princes in Italy in their secret discussion, the only thing disliked was the open manner of justice to a person who was a queen.

Powle closed the letter by expressing some of his fears:

> I deliver unto your Honor at this present diffusedly such occurrents as my small continuance and acquaintance have afforded me means to attain. If I had a direction from your Honor by writing to send them, I might both adventure to deal with the Secretaries here of Ferrara, Mantua, and Florence, as being warranted thereby; and also it would be a good shield of defense against any of my promoting countrymen which lurk here to put such into the Inquisition as they find to hinder their endeavours by any labour or letter. I write thus much because sundry have been drowned here for religion since Donsellinus' execution, both of French and Dutch by means of the Inquisition; and Wolfgangus a secret Intelligencer here for the Duke of Saxony (and not an Agent for his Honor to the state of Venice) had a commission from his prince to the same end, which he was constrained to show to the Signoria of late being accused by the French King's Ambassadour to lie here as a spy.
>
> Thus with humble remembrance of my duty I beseech Almighty God to bless you in this world with increase of honor, and after this life, to bestow on you everlasting happiness.
> From Venice 16 May 1587.
> Your Honor's for ever most bounden.
> S.P.   (309:65r)

Powle's second letter to Walsingham from Venice is dated 30 May 1587, and in it he mentions that his previous letter of 16 May was sent by means of Jieronimo di Bonna and was enclosed in a letter to Niccolo di Gozzi. Powle was apparently being as cautious as possible. He wrote that the king of Persia was said to have turned over both the civil and military administration to his son Emirdas. The wars there were continuing without hope of reconciliation until the Turks recovered Tauris.

Election of the king of Poland was to take place about midsummer. At least sixty thousand horse would be assembled in the open fields of Posnania, and orders had been given that no man bring with him any dagger or harquebus. Those who were candidates were the three archdukes of Austria, the young prince of Sweden, and one of the Polish noblemen[5] (but not of the Battori family, as they had been commanded to leave the country). Maximilian was considered the most likely to be chosen. Powle continued with some local Italian news, but the end of this letter (following 309:69v) is missing, as are the pages beginning the next letter, which is dated 18 June 1587.[6]

In a 20 June 1587 letter (309:17r) to Thomas Powle the younger, Stephen's elder brother, Stephen described, as if by hearsay, the present state of the country of Italy, the nature of the people, and various other particulars, but he referred to these things as "*audita*" not "*visae*," as he dared not reveal that he was then in Italy. He stated that he expected to return to England the following spring. Writing of Italy's wonderful climate and its fertile soil, in which in some places as many as five crops were grown a year, he commented that if the goodness of the governors were equal to the fertility of the soil, Italy would in all likelihood recover its lost monarchy for the second time. Many held their authority from no other sovereign than God and the sword. Those "more accounted of" for richness of wealth and greatness of estates were: (1) the king of Spain, who held the two kingdoms of Naples and Sicily and the duchy of Milan, (2) the pope, who had temporal jurisdiction in Romagna and ecclesiastical authority all over Italy, (3) the great duke of Tuscany, who held the commonwealths of Florence, Siena, and Pisa and possessed infinite treasure, (4) the signoria of Venice, which extended its bounds farther than any and was mightier on the sea than all (Powle gave them only fourth place because they were but an aristocracy, which was subject to many alterations), (5) the duke of Ferrara, who was greatly accounted of for his wealth and feared for his power, especially by those that stood in awe of the French faction, for the recovery of the duchy of Milan, and (6) the duke of Savoy, who was also prince of Piedmont and was honored by the pope with the title of "the shield of faith" because of keeping

Geneva in awe and of being a bulwark against the Protestants in France should they attempt to conquer Italy. He was of the Spanish faction, although his father married the aunt of the present French king. Powle ennumerated sundry other commonwealths and princes, such as Genoa and Luca, the duke of Mantua, the duke of Parma and Piacenza, the duke of Urbino, the prince of Massa, and other little principalities (309:18v).

In closing he said (feigningly) that he was then in Strasbourg and expected to be at the Frankfurt Mart in September. He advised Thomas that he could write to him in care of English merchants who would be there the next September, and he added that he would much like to hear particulars about his home and his old friends. He sent his regards to Thomas and his wife but made no mention of other members of their family, possibly for safety's sake. Their father and stepmother were then presumably living at their home in Maiden Lane; their married sister, Dutton, had probably been widowed by this time and was living with her daughter, Jane, in Buckinghamshire (309:21v; 130:135v).

The fifth letter to Walsingham from Venice is dated 12 July 1587 (309:70r) and is an unusually long one written in both English and Italian. Powle stated that he had been writing regularly every fourteen days and would like to know whether his letters were being received with safety and speed. He noted that the reports arriving in Venice at the signory were often quite different one from the other as they came daily from sundry places, for example, those from Naples were quite different from those from Milan and Rome, even when they concerned the same subject, and sometimes one week's occurrences were contrary to those received the week before. He tried to reconcile such discords as best he could. Powle's reports seem to have been of particular value to Walsingham and Burghley* in giving an overall view of foreign happenings.

Powle now switched to writing the next paragraphs in Italian, as he did for several pages later in the letter and from time to time in other letters to Walsingham. The rationale for this may have been that those who waylaid and inspected letters read Italian far more easily than English, and if they found that the Italian passages contained nothing to alert them, they usually did not bother to translate the English. The Italian sections would have

---

*See, for example, Burghley's letter to Powle in appendix E on pp. 213–15.

seemed fairly innocuous to those trying to gather evidence for the Inquisition and might reassure them to the point that they would not inspect the letter further. It is the English sections that contain matter that Powle probably would have preferred not to be disclosed en route.

In Italian, in which Powle by this time was fluent,[7] he wrote of the daily pillages and incursions made by the Galleotts of Algiers around Sicily and Otranto and of the harm done by the Turkish Rovers. He related that letters received from Rome revealed that certain scholars of the English College at Rome and other Englishmen and Scotsmen believed that the king of Scotland (since the death of his mother) was no longer pretending friendship with the queen of England, had resolved to return Catholicism to the Scottish throne, and had recalled three bishops who had previously been expelled from Scotland for wanting to restore their church.

Powle now turned to English and wrote:

These be R.H. [Right Honorable] their devises and the boasts of ill disposed persons who attempt to defame her Majesty's just proceedings and farther their own wicked attempts. The wagers among merchants about the Pope's choice of Cardinals next Christmas has already come forth privately; and among them Dr. Allen, Dr. Lewes, Mr. Hayes an Irishman, and my Lord Prior are named. My Lord Prior [Signor Richard Shelley] is sick of the stone and in great want and has requested me to ask you and my Lord Treasurer whether his annuities and rents for his houses (one in Trinity Lane and two in Westminster) might be sent to him for relief. He says that your Honor knows that though in religion he be a Catholic, yet in his heart he is a most dutiful subject, preferring the good of his country before his private advancement, in regard whereof he has refused a pension from the King of Spain "because he would serve only her to whom his whole obedience belongs."

In Italian he then summarized various reports he had received from Venice, Milan, Rome, and Genoa and then turned to English to relate that on 4 June he had received a report dated 15 May from Lisbon about Sir Francis Drake's foray near Cape Saint Vincent. Powle observed, "your Honor will have learned of this long before my letters can arrive in England."

Returning to Italian again, Powle wrote about His Catholic Majesty, Peru, Brazil, and the Portuguese Indies, and added that Signor Guglielmo Santo Clemente would be in Polonia as ambassador of the king of Spain.

Now reverting to English, Powle wrote that the Englishmen who went to Naples on a "bon Aventure" came back this way about the fourth of July. Powle did not see them because they arrived very late and stayed in Venice only one night, but he suggested that if they returned to England, they could report what preparations they had seen in their journey, since they were *occulati testes* (eye witnesses). It was thought in Venice that all things both in Spain and Italy would be in readiness about the middle of September for some "Impresse" of importance (elsewhere he referred to this as the "enterprise of England"). Powle closed the letter with the request that if Walsingham wished to command him any specific service, he could send Powle letters either by means of Master Loe, the merchant dwelling in Milk Street, London, or to the trading Venetian merchants, in case Master Gozzi himself did not write so often as these traders. Powle added that Master Loe wrote regularly to Nuremberg and that his factors sent letters from there to Venice weekly.

Powle's sixth letter (309:76r) from Venice to Secretary Walsingham is dated 24 July 1587, and more than half is in Italian. In the English portions he wrote of the two Altanni brothers, who were appointed by the king of Spain to convey from Venice to his ambassador at Constantinople letters of some moment concerning King Philip's intent for the "enterprise of England." However, the brothers disappeared for five months and the letters were undelivered. For this reason, King Philip gave orders to the Venetian signory to apprehend the Altannis, accusing them of being disloyal to Spain in conveying (as the king supposed) these letters to Her Majesty in England by means whereof (as he imagined) Her Highness made preparations for Sir Francis Drake to prevent his enterprise. The brothers were at first prosecuted by the Spanish secretary, but after his death two months before, they were heard, freed, and now enjoyed their usual liberty without punishment or penalty.

Signor Richard Shelley, Lord Prior, having had some conflict in arguments with certain Jesuits sympathetic to the English traitors executed in England last summer, grew ill from these discussions and died about 12 July. He gave his servant John, who had attended him for twenty-eight years, most of the arrearages of the pension due him and the rents of his three houses in London. John planned to travel to London to seek Walsingham's help in obtaining the same. Lord Prior had large debts among certain merchants resident in Rome. The Knights of Malta buried him the day after his death and seized his goods as their rightful property, but John lived in hope that by means of the pope and cardinals at Rome he might recover these goods for himself.

It was given out as a matter of great secrecy that, because the "enterprise of England" was delayed, men levied in Naples, Romagna, Tuscany, Genoa, and Urbino would be used in the kingdom of Algiers, and the Turks would be unable to prevent this surprise because they were busied with the wars in Persia and were keeping an eye on the election of the king of Polonia, besides having men in the field under the Bolliherbey in Greece. In every state of Italy soldiers were now being levied, ostensibly for the purpose of annoying a common enemy with their united forces. Powle reported that since writing this, information had been received from Naples that those soldiers departed 17 July because of an urgent message three days earlier from Spain.

In closing, Powle entreated Walsingham for a note confirming receipt of his letters, for he was anxious to know how long it took them to reach England. He observed that a man with an open full purse and a commission from Her Majesty to warrant his writing could, if he remained in Venice, obtain firsthand knowledge of the basis of these reports. As it was now, Powle could acquaint Walsingham with only secondhand information. Thus levies of men and enterprises of princes were known publicly before Powle heard of them and therefore, he assumed, could be of minimal use by the time this news arrived in England.

On 1 August 1587, in the seventh letter to Walsingham (306:76r), Powle wrote that his previous letter was dated 24 July and for purposes of security had been sent by Bonna within a superscription to Niccolo di Gozzi in London. Again Powle mentioned his uncertainty as to whether his letters were being received, since he had no confirmation. Unknown to him, Walsingham was ill at this time with a recurrent kidney infection that had caused him temporarily to withdraw from official tasks. Since Powle was concerned that his recent letters might not have arrived, he repeated some of the information already sent, such as the names of captains employed in Italy and levies of men for Spain, France, Lorraine, and the Low Countries.

The prince of Butera[8] came from Naples to Sicily about 23 May for the purpose of receiving the Order of the Golden Fleece and to see their musters, for at that time there was a secret proposal that men be levied from Spain. In the dukedom of Urbino there were one thousand foot soldiers under the conduct of Signor Guerra Andrione, viceduke of Senogallia. But letters received that morning said that they were unwilling to serve the Spaniard since they had heard from others of the Spanish tyranny over Italian soldiers. Since the duke was for a time pensioner to the king of Spain, he was bound to furnish him that number. Among the families of the *paesani*, a sum of money was therefore imposed on those unwilling to serve, and by this means the required number of soldiers had been obtained. In the states of Parma, Piacenza, and Castro, and places thereabout, they levied so many men that they recruited a total of five thousand. These were to be conducted to Milan by Captain Biaggio Capezucchi, and he was then to dispose of them as directed by the king, either for Flanders or Spain. Powle reported the levying of troops in other parts of Italy, citing numbers levied and their commanders.

The money to enable these captains to make levies came from the king of Spain's credit in Italy; from his creatures the Fuchers;[9] from one million six hundred thousand scudi given by the prince of Salerno; and from the same amount raised by Baldezar Lomelino, to be paid by thirds through Milan, Genoa, and Flanders, with the allotment of 14 percent. Powle also wrote that the "welcome news" was received 30 July of my lord of Leicester's arrival in Holland and passing by Sluys.

The next relevant letter extant is a 12 September 1587 communication from Walsingham to Burghley (Harleian MS. 6994, fol. 96r), which contains the following section:

> My very good Lord . . . How greatly it importeth her Majesty to have the King of Navarre upheld is shown by the enclosed which I received this morning from your servant Master Powle. It would be advisable to have his letter read to her Majesty by Master Wooley or at least so much thereof as concerneth herself. There would be some expedition used in taking order for the sending of some present supply unto the King of Navarre. Mr. Horatio [Palavicino] will attend on your Lordship this afternoon to be ready to be employed in case her Majesty shall like to use his service. If the Duke of Montpensier[10] shall find her Majesty resolved to back the King of Navarre there is no doubt but that he may be drawn to make himself a party. There is no way so apt to stop the Spanish preparation against this realm as the upholding of the King of Navarre and the keeping under of the house of Guise, whom Spain seeketh to advance. If her Majesty shall lose the opportunity either by long delay in resolving or by not sending such a portion of treasure as may do good, she shall have cause, I fear, to say farewell my days of peace.

Powle's "enclosed" letter no longer accompanies this. He apparently foresaw, as did Walsingham, that Henry of Navarre, then a young man of the same age as Powle, was the French leader the English should support. Henry, king of Navarre, had been raised as a Calvinist and since 1569 had been head of the Huguenot party and, since the death of the duke of Anjou, was presumptive heir to the throne of France; after the death of Henry III, he was to become Henry IV, one of the great kings of France.[11] Navarre was a man of good character and a fine military leader at a time when France was torn into factions between the three Henrys: Navarre, the duke of Guise as head of the insidious Catholic League trying to assume power at whatever cost, and the weak King Henry III, who was afraid to oppose the duke.

In August 1587 Navarre was hoping to levy troops in Germany to help suppress the aggression of Guise and the Catholic League. Desperately in need of monetary support, he had sought funds in England for this purpose. In July, after he had won an important victory at Coutras over Henry III's anti-Huguenot army under the command of Anne, duke of Joyeuse, Navarre's remaining funds were dangerously low.

Walsingham had long felt that the wisest policy was to give vigorous support to Henry of Navarre, but Elizabeth had been reluctant to loosen her purse strings. In January 1586/7 she had given Casimir one hundred thousand crowns to aid his army's pro-Huguenot invasion of France, but his badly organized troops had been unsuccessful. Elizabeth was now resistant to further financing of a foreign army. With receipt of Powle's letter, Walsingham strongly urged the queen to back Navarre's more promising effort. She seems to have acquiesced at first but later weakened. She did not want to repeat her useless support of Casimir. Her sympathetic rapport with Navarre was therefore not at this time translated into financial aid, despite Powle's letter and Walsingham's urging. Later, however, she grudgingly did give Navarre support.

About six months later in Venice Powle received from Lord Burghley in his own hand a heartwarming letter of thanks and commendation for the helpful services Powle had rendered to him and to Secretary Walsingham (309:46v–47r).* The letter was written 15 February 1587/8 and tells of Burghley's delight at seeing Powle's "capacity and judgment" and his industry and conscientiousness as shown in his careful reports. Burghley was also grateful for Powle's long letter to him at the end of November (309:12r–17r), which "did at length and in good method anatomize the whole body of Italy, describing the conditions, the sympa-

---

*See appendix E, p. 213, for a copy of Burghley's letter.

thies, and jointures of all the states and potentates, in such plain and probable manner, as any discourser or inward counsellor of their countries were able to do." Burghley remarked that he had taken much profit from this report and esteemed Powle's "labor bestowed . . . to be of more value than any service at any time since I have had servants." In closing, he cautioned Powle in a somewhat Polonius-like manner "to be circumspect in the place where you are, to avoid the craftiness of false brethren, and the malice of such as may be your enemies for your country's sake," and he thanked him for the "delicate and costly token" of the mother-of-pearl spoons Powle had sent him. The letter is signed "Your assured loving friend, W. Burghley."[12]

On 27 September a light-hearted, chatty, and, in part, risqué letter was written by Powle to his good friend John Chamberlain in England (309:53v). Since neither this letter nor the one that Chamberlain wrote, with its amusing reply and lurid anecdote, are mentioned by Norman Egbert McClure in *The Letters of John Chamberlain*,* they are here quoted in full. Powle's letter follows, and Chamberlain's reply is found in appendix E, pages 202–5.

To Mr. John Chamberlaine.   27th Septem. 1587

Master Chamberlaine: if you esteem no more of our occurrants than men commonly do of wares that have lain long in shops for signs, nor be pleased with letters better than our Italians be with their wives who upon the first night's trial they find overyeared or not maidens, then I have small hope you will value this token of my good will at any worth nor delight yourself in reading of this present letter; for by remaining many months (I fear me) in the Post's chamber it carrieth an ancient date and having been touched with many unchaste hands and peradventure been forced by sundry dishonest persons before they be presented to your good self (unto whose service they were wholly dedicated). For that cause whether you shall find them unspotted vestals with their holy girdles unbroken or not when they be presented to you I greatly doubt. Therefore, unless you mean to receive them with all their faults, give them no entertainment, but cast them away before you read them any farther.

If I should make a chronology of all adventures I have passed or a journal of every day's progress since I left England and begin *ab ovo* (because I am well acquainted how much particular circumstances do delight you), I should report (I am sure) my Ambassador Daniell's[13] message, who hath imparted all this unto you (for so was his charge) at his first arrival. But to supply his wants may it please

---

*American Philosophical Society, Philadelphia, 1939.

you to be advertized (because we will have our beginnings formal after the Dutch manner) that at Cassells we supped with William, the Landsgrave of Hesse, being ceremoniously invited with a long Latin oration according to their troublesome custom. The charge was mine (for so it was my Lord Zouche's pleasure who travelled in most private manner to Francfort) to make some short answer thereunto. *Postquam incaluere maero*,[14] we had many discourses, and of Dr. Dee's being the summer before there was made up the last act of our comedy, who came hither with a train of 4. coaches, and therein all his family, as discontented with the Emperour for his too slender entertainment of him, and therefore he desired leave (to show his greatness, for otherwise he needed not to have made any such suit) to remain there for a time, where bestowing one month, he returned back to Prague (as he gave it forth) being sent for by the Emperour. But before his departure he presented a book to the Landgrave, the title whereof was *De virtutibus et magnalibus Dei qui in Apocalipsi vocatur Alpha et Omega*. Underneath was written *Monas Hierogliphica* and at the lower end of that page a sentence out of the 27th of Genesis: *De rore et pinguidine terrae det tibi Deus* and at the end of that page his own name (unto which he had profanely alluded in those before) *Deus Londinensis*.

At Francfort I met Master Palavicino who was returning back and Master Evars in his company who had lived in the university of Heidelberg a whole year. From thence I wrote to all my friends and forgot my good Master Chamberlaine (to put in my faults also) for which I crave pardon. But in truth Sir it is my manner to be most bold with them to whom I think myself most beholden. Master Rodwey meeting me here, we travelled together to Nuremberg where I met Master Luther and delivered your token to him. At Augsburg I had Moyses the proccaccio[15] for my guide to Innsbruch, to Trent, and from thence to Venice. I leave not out this circumstance because, although I came not out of the land of Egypt, yet you know I departed out of the house of bondage.[16] By Master Luther's direction I was provided of a very good lodging where I grew acquainted with the Gentleman the bearer hereof, Master Egerton, a knight's son and here my especial friend with whom I desire you to be acquainted for my sake. The seat of Venice when I beheld it in my gondola as I came from Margera, methought resembled some Flemish painted table of landscape or some mathematical demonstration in perspective: the towers and monasteries in the sea and especially of Murano divided from Venice resembled it so well. But how this place contented me when I came in, I must tell you my opinion. At the first I was rather amazed than delighted therewith because being the day of the Duke's marriage in the Bucentaure to the Sea as Leo, the streets were stuffed up with a world of people. But since that by continuance I have been acquainted with the infinite number of delights here, I think it be the

Paradise of all pleasures that may be possibly devised or imagined the pattern of all well governed commonwealths for policy, and for territory and jurisdiction the greatest state in all Italy.

Since my coming hither, I have seen the Arsenal, the Sala di Dieci, the Patriarch of Aquileya's antiquities; St. Mark's treasure, and all other places worth the beholding. I have been at Treviso, Padua, Vincenza, Verone, Brescia, and Bergamo; I have seen Mantua, and was at the coronation of the young Duke the 22 of September; I have seen Ferrara, Ravenna, Rimini, Urbino, Pesaro, Ancona, Loretto, Angubio, Perugia, Borgo Santo Sepolchro, Concordia, Goro, and Chiozza. If I go any farther I am afeard I shall make you a map of Italy in this letter. Though it be of a later edition than that which you do daily behold within your own memory, yet it cannot be so perfect because I did see these places *tanquam Canis Nilum: bibit et abit* [just as the dog the Nile: he drinks and he departs]. And now that I am returned hither, I am but where I was at the first, which I make the centre where I do *quiescere* this winter. This rest have been but my circumferences.

Our Comediantis many years since banished Venice be renewed at Murano where I wish you to hear Madonna Francischina, Horatio, and the old Pantalon with his Zane.

If to be well neighboured be no small part of happiness, I may repute myself highly fortunate, for I am lodged amongst a great number of Signoras. Isabella Bellochia in the next house on my right hand and Virginia Padoana, that honoreth all our nation for my Lord of Oxford's sake, is my neighbour on the left side. Over my head hath Lodovica Gonzaga, the French King's mistress, her house. You think it peradventure preposterous in Architecture to have her lie over me? I am sorry for it but I cannot remedy it now. Pesarmia with her sweet entertainment and brave discourse is not two canals off. Ancilla (Master Hatton's handmaid) is in the next Campo; Paulina Gonzaga is not far off; Prudencia Romana with her courtly train of French gentlemen every night goeth *a spasso* [unemployed] by my pergola. As for Imperia Romana, her date is out which flourished in your time. I must of force be well hallowed amongst so many Saints. But in truth, I am afraid they do condemn me of heresy for setting up so few tapers on their high altars.

I do observe Guicciardini's method, that in every city's description forgetteth not the person that flourisheth therein. And you, having heard the names of the chief ladies of account, I must put down likewise the names of the famous mountebanks: Antonio Milanese for a cunning Ciarlatano, Lucasino for a good voice, but of all Tabarino passeth for a Zane, and Frittado for a mask ball and short comedies in the Piazza of St. Mark.

Do you not marvel Sir to see me write in this kind. I am bold to make myself merry in your company hoping no man shall see these follies of mine but your own self in your private Chamber. And I do use this kind of music as an *Antidotum* against melancholy wherewith I am sometimes overcharged when I turn my thoughts to behold that daily decaying house and almost ruinated to the foundation, for I hear the land is mortgaged.[17] Moreover, I have been writing these two days to my Lord Treasurer of matters of more gravity and therefore I delight in this vein for change. This humor of voluntary is almost spent, now to set songs!

The occurrents followed of that week as in Signor Georgio's hand appeareth and I wrote unto him besides many other particularities of Persia, Polonia, Turkey, and of sundry discontentments between the Princes in Italy, and of a proffered marriage to Parma's son Prince Raniccio by the Pope for Madonna Flavia, his niece, by Florence of his daughter, of the death of Admiral Occialli in Turkey, and of his successor, Ebiam Basha, the Turk's son-in-law.

I mean to put you Master Chamberlain to your ciphering because I scribble this letter in haste. I perform in measure that which I want in weight and I make you a miser's feast because having long time starved you, I glut you with a volume of lines.[18]

If you write to me every fourteen days, I will requite it after the manner of the old world: ware for ware, when *commutatio mercium* was used.

Send by Farrington, not by Parvis' brother, to me because I like him not; not for injuring me but because I hear many complain that he hath a commission to open men's letters.

Of Master Gent's not writing to me from Nuremberg, being in my debt for a token and a letter from Bremen, I take Parvis to have been the cause of all this unkindness, whom etc. *sed motos praestat componere fluctus* [but it is better to calm the aroused waves][19] Commendations to Master Cope, Master Bodleigh, Master Litton, Master Evers, Master Dr. Gilbert.

P.

Chamberlain's colorful and very long, newsy reply to Powle's September 1587 letter is dated from London, 25 December "1588," but must have been written in December 1587. It is found in Powle's Letter Book (Tanner MS. 309) in two different places: the complete letter in Chamberlain's hand is inserted on folios 300r–301v, and a copy of the end by Powle's clerk is on 56r. The full text of this letter can be found in appendix E, pages 202–5. An apt retort to part of Powle's letter and a few lines relevant to Powle's older brother Tom are excerpted below:

You are marvelously beset with Signoras if you be so round besieged. I see not how you can escape without passing the Pikes. If you live still among such saints you are very obstinate if you be not edified.

Ywis your brother [Thomas] would not make it so dainty, for of all things he loves plenty. It was told me that this last summer at Bergen op Zoom [in Brabant in the Netherlands] he kept almost a whole regiment of wenches. He carried two from hence of my acquaintance, for the rest he furnished himself there and kept four or five in one house. Oh he would have made a goodly Basha![20] But I must seal up your mouth that this come out no more. You write nothing how your diet there contents you, nor what taste you find in those sugared melons and other delicate fruits. Belike you were loath to set my teeth on water, or else you thought me not so licorous of that part as of the other thing.

On 7 November 1587 Powle wrote to Walsingham (Harleian MS. 296, fol. 48) warning him of impending danger to Queen Elizabeth. Powle had recently sent Stephen Rodwey to Rome to procure information for him. Powle had made Rodwey's acquaintance three years previously in Bohemia and had found him to be a man "of great secrecy" who spoke French and Dutch so fluently that he could pass for a native of either France or the Netherlands. On Rodwey's return journey from Rome he met four strangers near Verona who were traveling with him in the same coach. Rodwey became quite friendly with one of them, Giuseppe Giraldo, an Italian merchant from Bergamo, who told him of his forty-five-year-old cousin Michael Giraldo, a Bergamo merchant for the eastern countries who had recently returned from Constantinople and upon his arrival in Venice had made a hurried and secret trip to Rome, after which he returned to Venice and almost immediately afterward embarked for England purportedly as a merchant. When Giuseppe asked him the reason for such a long and dangerous voyage by sea, Michael answered that he carried "una pasta nella scatula per la regina d'Inghilterra" (a pastry in a box for the Queen of England), which Giuseppe believed contains some exquisite poison and that the service was undertaken on order from the pope. Moreover, Michael urged Giuseppe to pray for his prosperous success in the enterprise he had in hand. In Powle's previous letter he had explained why he believed this surmise to be true. Powle's earlier letter had apparently not been received by Walsingham, so Powle was here reiterating the major facts. After investigation, Powle had ascertained that only two boats had left for England this last summer. The one that left in August seemed more likely to be carrying Michael Giraldo. It was called the *Gallion Tizzon* and carried a shipment of Malmsey. The other, which had left a bit earlier, was *La Stella Evidale*. In point of fact it was *La Stella*

Evidale that had had Michael Giraldo on board but, according to a later letter of Powle's to Walsingham $\frac{\text{Feb.28}}{\text{Mar.10}}$ 1587/8 in the State Papers), Giraldo was "cast away" (shipwrecked) on the coast of Wight about Michaelmas last. Whether by providential accident or by stratagem of Walsingham's, the poisoning was aborted.

Powle's earlier letter continues with many news items for Sir Francis, some in English and some in Italian. A new excommunication order by the pope was soon to be published against Her Majesty, as there already had been against the king of Navarre. Recently, the pope had imposed excessive taxation of wine, corn, oil, meal, and on the trees growing in the Via Regia. By means of these taxes, he had infinitely enriched his treasury, supposedly for the wars against the Huguenots in France, Flanders, and England and for preparations very shortly for "an imprese of importance."

On 26 December (309:57r) Powle wrote from Venice to his young friend and protégé Edward Egerton, who had recently left Venice to return to his home in London. Powle had received three letters from Egerton since his departure from Italy and was hoping to hear of the safe arrival in England of this promising young man he had referred to in his letter to John Chamberlain. Powle also expressed his hope that Egerton soon would be "luckily matched to some honorable gentlewoman." Powle continued: "I have performed the most part of my journey" (apparently an assignment from Walsingham, and a risky one) that

> was both less dangerous and more comfortable to me by the good company of Master Geratt. For whose courtesy I thank you as the author, and I repute myself greatly bound unto him for being an actor with me in so dangerous a tragedy as this voyage might have brought us unto. What was the cause we performed not every point of our former determination I suppose Master Geratt hath himself acquainted you by letter. Nevertheless I account that travail both to have satisfied me, as no other like unto it that ever I made. Not that I gained any thing more thereby than variety of solaces, which was the only fruit I gathered. And in truth, Sir I have learned this one thing since I came into Italy that *Chi va et ritorno fa bon viaggio* [he who goes and returns makes a good journey].

This caused Powle to dwell on his intense desire to return to England, for he had had his fill of all the pleasures that travelers commonly relish; now the waters of his own country would content him "far more than any wine from Greece, Germany, or Montefiascone." He continues:

> The smoke of mine own chimneys in Ithaca[21] will please better my sight than foreign fires were I never so cold, and the shadow of an English oak would give a more perfect refreshing to my whole body than the stately Pines of Ravenna, to me smothered with heat, or the sunshine of some hotter climate would give comfort to me if my limbs were frozen with chilling cold. I write this much to welcome you home . . . lest any discontentment might enforce your mind to a second travail. By this means presenting unto you a remembrance only of what you have felt hitherto and we poor pilgrims do daily endure.
> I look for some restraint of this unpleasant liberty I enjoy,[22] by some good means shortly of calling me home by commandment of her Majesty. . . .
>
> Your most assured friend to command,
> S.P.
> (309:57r&v)

Since November 1579 Powle had been away from England a total of almost six years, and his homesickness was now becoming persistent. In his Letter Book (309:205r) are found a few sardonic lines about travel:

> A traveller ought to have
> The back of an ass,
> The belly of a sow,
> The cares stopped,
> The eyes shut up
> His purse open,
> The ears of a merchant.

In his letter of 16 January 1588 (N.S.), now in the State Papers (101/81), Powle voices his alarm at the deteriorating situation for foreigners in Venice. There had been new laws against giving intelligence about the political situation, and strangers with no acceptable cause for staying in Venice were daily urged to depart. Powle had been unable to renew his permit *(bolletino)* for more than fifteen days. He was now the only one of all "our English gentlemen" here. He begged Walsingham to procure for him a warrant for his security or else transfer his service to some other place, for he needed commandment from the queen or Privy Council to show the officials who periodically examine such causes. Powle's servant, Daniel Simpson, would transmit Walsingham's command.

He continued with his usual bulletins of intelligence. Although the Spaniards there spread word that the Armada was ready, 21 December letters from Lisbon indicate that it would not be in order for another six months because of the sea-beaten condition of their ships and the exhaustion of their mariners. The scarcity of food in Lisbon, where so many thousands more needed to be fed, had produced much misery "by reason of the Fleet putting to sea for the enterprise of England about the beginning of December last, when by the unseasonable time and wonderful storms, they were driven back to the coast of Portugal." However, this excuse for the long delay of the Spanish enterprise is believed to be fictitious.

Among other letters from Powle to Walsingham in the Elizabethan State papers, Foreign (101/81), is one dated $\frac{\text{Feb.28}}{\text{March 10}}$ 1588, in which Powle wrote that this was his thirty-first letter to His Honor since 6 May last. Although most were only of the ordinary occurrences, two were of especial importance: one of 7 November (N.S.) concerning the discovery "of a most heinous intent of Giraldi, a Bergamasco, who departing hence in the ship called 'La Stella Evidale,' was cast away on the Isle of Wight about Michaelmas last"; the other, of 2 January 1588 N.S. (State Papers 101/81), contained an answer to His Honor's of 15 October in which Powle replied to the three questions posed to him: (1) whether the peace offered by the duke of Parma was a true intent of performance by the king of Spain and why this peace was offered when nothing was less meant; (2) reasons why some enterprise was in hand and why at that particular time, when it had been so long deferred and when the pretended wrongs were of so many years' continuance; and (3) what intelligence France and Scotland had of these matters. Powle included a copy of his detailed answers to these questions, for there was always the possibility that Walsingham had not received his previous letter. Powle's answers, in brief, were that the so-called peace was a snare to lull their enemies to sleep and to lessen the likelihood of aid from their friends. Philip, who now had the eager support of the pope, was aged and wanted to ensure his son's reign over Portugal, the Low Countries, and the Indies, which were at risk as long as the queen had forces in Holland, Don Antonio was in England, and English ships were threatening the Spanish fleet in the Indies. Powle felt that the positions of France and Scotland were uncertain and dependent on many factors, but he did not believe that the Scottish king, having received so many favors from Her Majesty, would aid a foreign plot against her. After giving his reasons for the above in detail, Powle added that his arguments were no more than opinions of his friends and himself and not to be weighed "in comparison with your Honour's experienced judgment."

Walsingham seems to have valued Powle's judgment and written reports, as so much of them rang true. It was becoming evident that the "peace negotiations" in the Netherlands were simply a delaying tactic and maneuver to throw England off its guard until such time as the Spanish Armada would be ready to make its onslaught against her.

Like Powle, Walsingham had long been worrying about the possibility of Scotland being used as a point of attack against England from the north at such time as the Armada should arrive from the south. He had been continually pressing Elizabeth to increase her pension to James so that he would feel a stronger allegiance to her, but the queen could not be persuaded to deplete her treasury further. Fortunately, Powle's guess was right that the Scottish King would not at the last minute aid a foreign plot against Elizabeth.

Among Powle's newsletters to Walsingham (in State Papers 101/81) is an "Abstract of the principal pointes of the letters from Mr Powle" covering those of late December and early January 1587/8. It was a summary probably made by one of Walsingham's staff at a time when he was ill.

Returning to Powle's original letter of 10 March, one finds he now continued in a worried but more personal vein:

> By that time this letter can be presented your Honor, my first year will be expired which having been employed wholly in her Majesty's service in this place, without any remove and for that I have bestowed herein not only her Majesty's allowance, but as much more of my own (by reason of the dearth and manner of living here, besides the ordinary charge [   ] in paying for the carriage of my letters weekly, with the purchasing of intelligence by money) my hope and humble desire is that your Honor will send the allowance augmented according to my first petition being in England, by procuring me one French crown the day, for otherwise I must be enforced to give over that service to my great grief which I entered into with a most earnest desire. And to conceal nothing from you, the maintenance I have received this last year from my father is much diminished, partly because his estate beginneth to decline more than is meet I should

impart unto any, where my chiefest support was; partly also for that [my family] presume her Majesty's allowance is so large that it serveth to defray all my charges without their further help, whereof Master Doctor White, the preacher, can give your Honor more particular notice. I most humbly crave pardon for my importuning your Honor with my private suits in these general troubles whereabout your Honor is greatly busied. Let my present wants (which before your Honor can send supply thereuto will be increased) excuse this fault, for necessity doth carry always his privilege.

The last paragraph of Powle's nine-page letter is in Italian and described the feeling in Italy that war was imminent. There had been much literature circulated praising the Scottish queen and exhorting all princes to avenge her unjustified execution. Powle had bought as many as he could and had taken measures to try to prevent their further distribution. He added that in his letter of the previous week he had sent Walsingham the names of the cardinals recently created and a note about the Spanish king's treasure brought from the Indies by his last fleet. The letter is signed "N.N.," as are other of Powle's more secret communications of this period.[23] It is in Powle's handwriting with his seal.

In Powle's Commonplace Book 169:40r is a copy of a portion of his thirty-second letter to Walsingham[24] "concerning the warlike provisions made by the king of Spain for the invasion of England wherein was set down all the particulars of ships, men, money, and victuals." Powle expressed his amazement at how such a large number of men were mobilized. He wrote "all here wish that Sir Francis Drake were abroad upon the coast of Portugal to abate the pride of the monarchical Spaniards." This letter was dated 19 March 1588 (N.S.).

On the same 19 March (a Saturday, habitually Powle's day for correspondence) he wrote to Master Kyrton at Ferrara (309:58r). He was a wealthy and rather careless young Englishman who had written asking to hear from Powle but had neglected to give him a specific address. The few Englishmen left in the area seem to have made a practice of corresponding regularly with one another as a safety measure lest they meet with foul play. Since Powle's answering letter to Kyrton was of necessity addressed only "Ferrara," he was careful not to write anything incriminating lest it get to other hands than Kyrton's. Powle did, however, comment on the fact that he had not heard from Master Rodwey that week, which made Powle fear "either his sickness or some false measure." He wished Kyrton good success with his suit that, as Powle later noted in the margin of his copy, was to be the duke of Ferrara's gentleman. On Wednesday 23 March, having received an exact address from Kyrton, Powle wrote to him again scolding him gently and advising him next time to be more economical with writing space: not to use so much paper for so few words, for the last time Powle had had to pay a large carriage charge. His own extant letters from Venice are very closely written.

Powle reported to Kyrton that he was leaving on Monday for Verona on foot (about sixty-five miles) if his feet would carry him, as he was "almost choked" for want of exercise in Venice. If his legs did not hold out all the way, he would resort to "being a centaur." He was planning to be away from Venice not more than eight days. At Easter time they would journey together to Ferrara. Powle also reprimanded Kyrton for carelessness in dating his letter, for it was dated 17 March although not received until 22 March. Powle complained, "either you write with a 'post' date or the post was lazy." In closing he remarked that the Taylers' daughter commended herself to Kyrton, and Powle added, "I write this to sweeten your mouth after my bitter accusations" and requested that he be numbered "among the chiefest" of Kyrton's "poor friends."

Secretary Walsingham had asked Powle to write his opinion of a contemplated peace to be concluded with Spain, and in Powle's usual methodical and thorough style he had drafted a thoughtful and detailed reply in which he listed the arguments in favor of a peace and those against one (237:26r–31r), the latter far outweighing the former. On 26 March 1588, when Powle wrote his actual letter to Walsingham, his thirty-third, he summarized his views as follows:

Although Hannibal had used the argument to Scipio that a sure peace was better than a hoped-for victory,[25] Powle felt that a peace with Spain at this point would be unwise, for it would require yielding to an enemy nation Holland and Zeeland, the keys to England's gates. Furthermore, he assessed the strength of Spain as much overrated. Powle set forth his reasoning that, despite his many preparations for war, King Philip earnestly desired a peace for various reasons: in his advanced age he was "disposed toward quietness"; Spain's relations with Portugal were intricate and their nobility were not co-operative; Philip would be dishonored if he were unable to set forth his Armada, which had been so long in preparation; and he feared overthrow if the confrontation with Her Majesty's forces actually occurred. In addition, there was the possibility of the Turks' sending forth

Sir Francis Walsingham (1532?–1590) Principal Secretary. Line engraving by Passe? National Portrait Gallery, London.

their galleys either for Malta, Naples, or Sicily, and there was the factor of Maxmilian's imprisonment in Poland, with his release to be at Philip's own expense. There were huge expenses for Philip in the Low Countries. Spain's "Indian mines," which were to provide "nourishment" for all these funds, could be intercepted or withheld by means of Sir Francis Drake. Spain had a great circuit of territory but was lacking in manpower and funds.

Although nothing was being more tossed about in Spanish mouths than the name of the Imprese for England, Powle did not believe that the wisdom of the Spanish council or the king's aged blood would acquiesce to it or take on any enterprise with so many disadvantages as an encounter with English forces at sea and an attempt to land in England. Powle concluded that the world was falsely dazzled by the king of Spain's greatness, that although he had a fountain of gold in his Indies, it was unable to feed all the rivers that required nourishment. Huge sums were owed. His kingdom in Sicily was "pawn for the use of money." The Fuchers owned many towns both in Spain and other parts of Philip's dominions. He was almost "out of credit to levy money" if the Indies failed him. Therefore he had to defend his Indies coasts with his ships, and these ships were "slender for resistance in comparison with her Majesty's 'armada' for so it should be rightly termed."[26]

Although Powle misjudged the decision of the Spanish king and council to send forth their Armada, Powle was correct in his estimate of Spain's naval and monetary weakness. When the Spanish Armada finally set forth with high hopes in May 1588, its disastrous defeat tolled the knell of Spain's supremacy.*

On 6 April, Powle again wrote to Kyrton, chiding him about misdating his letters, for it seemed odd to Powle that his own letters always arrived in Ferrara the same day as written whereas Kyrton's arrived in Venice four days after they were dated from Ferrara. Powle was eager to hear how Kyrton's suit was progressing. He warned the young man to be circumspect in what he wrote, for unfriendly eyes might read his letters en route. Powle included news of the prince of Condé's death by poison to the great grief of the king of Navarre, for Condé had been a strong bulwark of the Huguenot cause. Powle wrote of the arrival of Queen Elizabeth's commissioner at Ostend on 20 March and of the peace treaty to be signed at Antwerp. The duke of Medina

---

*See pp. 97–98.

Sidonia had departed the twentieth of the previous month, some said to Algiers, others to Ireland, but no one knew for certain. Powle believed that he was not removed but lay in wait as a bar to Sir Francis Drake if he should make a stronger attempt on the Indies, as he had three summers in succession. Powle was expecting letters the next day from Master Rodwey from Frankfurt. If these contained any news, Powle promised to acquaint Kyrton with it.

In Tanner manuscript 169, folio 35r, is a portion of the thirty-fourth letter that Powle sent to Sir Francis Walsingham and the Privy Council. It is dated from Venice 20 April 1588 (N.S.; 10 April in England) and contains the following:

> Not four days since as I came from *Verona* in the company of a young gentleman of Naples that was going into Flanders as he told me, supposing me (whom he thought to be French) to have a place in the spoil of England, I heard this discoursed on, that the *Armata* being now in a readiness to go forth, and the Duke of Parma being furnished with all things necessary for the *Impresa*, there wanted nothing but to *reducesse certi piccioli impedimenti* [reduce certain small hindrances] that the King of Scots had in his own country, by reason of his preachers, which he forthwith would take order in to perfect the whole enterprise, the resolution between whom and the king of Spain was to settle him in her Majesty's seat, and after to give him his daughter, the Infanta, in marriage, and for a dowry to give her the kingdom of Portugal. These great matters of moment the Neapolitan had begun and ended with one mile's riding. Many other such fabulous reports and dreams I daily hear, which I do not acquaint your Honor with because, as there is a brainsick folly of such as conceive them in their idle thoughts, so there is a kind of offence in writing them, and the harmony in reading thereof is very harsh and unpleasant.   1588
>
>   St: Powle

In a brief letter to Walsingham dated 29 April (N.S.; 19 April in England) Powle advised that his last letter was 14 April (4 April in England), and since then his servant had arrived from England with His Honor's order for his return from Italy and the receipt of fifty pounds in sterling. Powle was therefore leaving with all speed, possibly that very day. He was going home via Hamburg and hoped to be in England by the end of May (State Papers, Venetian I:27). This letter to Walsingham was apparently signed with invisible ink that needed special treatment by the recipient to make the writing visible. Powle's signature is discernible only if a light is placed behind the paper so as to shine through it. The same applies to a few of Powle's letters now in the State Papers.

6
Home

Stephen Powle returned to England to find that in March 1587/8 a grant of arms had been made to him by William Dethick, garter king of arms. The escutcheon was of blue, gold, and silver with gold lions passant gardant in two of the quarterings and at the top a unicorn passant with blue horn, beard, and tail and gold hoofs.[1] The deed read in part: "Stephanum Powlum generosum Londinen armis ac sanguine clarum . . . perspicuis parentibus ortum" ("Stephan Powle, gentleman, of London, distinguished in arms and blood . . . born of eminent parents"). The coat of arms had been awarded in absentia, since Powle did not reach England until late May or early June.

On 29 June 1588 he wrote to Burghley from his father's house in Maiden Lane, giving the lord treasurer a report of Italian events just before Powle's departure from Venice and of news he had gathered en route home. He had met several captains along the way who had confided in him, imagining that he was an Italian from Verona. They said that they expected only "lean war" in the Low Countries because the fat had already been gleaned by others in their many years' warfare. But the captains were hoping for booty from England, although they were skeptical of success unless aided by Scotland and by English traitors. Concerning Powle himself and his sudden return, he explained to Burghley that it had been commanded by Secretary Walsingham's letters because of the increasing danger of the situation. It was a command for which Powle had been very grateful because he had heard that "the small portion of land" his father had once purchased was then for sale, "being wrought therunto by my stepmother."[2] The land being entailed, Stephen had an interest in it. He also understood that his father's office (clerk of the Crown), which was the mainstay of his father's livelihood, was likewise in danger of being sold for a small sum of money, to his discredit and his son's undoing, since Stephen had no other maintenance from his father, who would be unable to allow Stephen anything more after the money was spent. Stephen wrote that in the case of both of these situations he had hoped

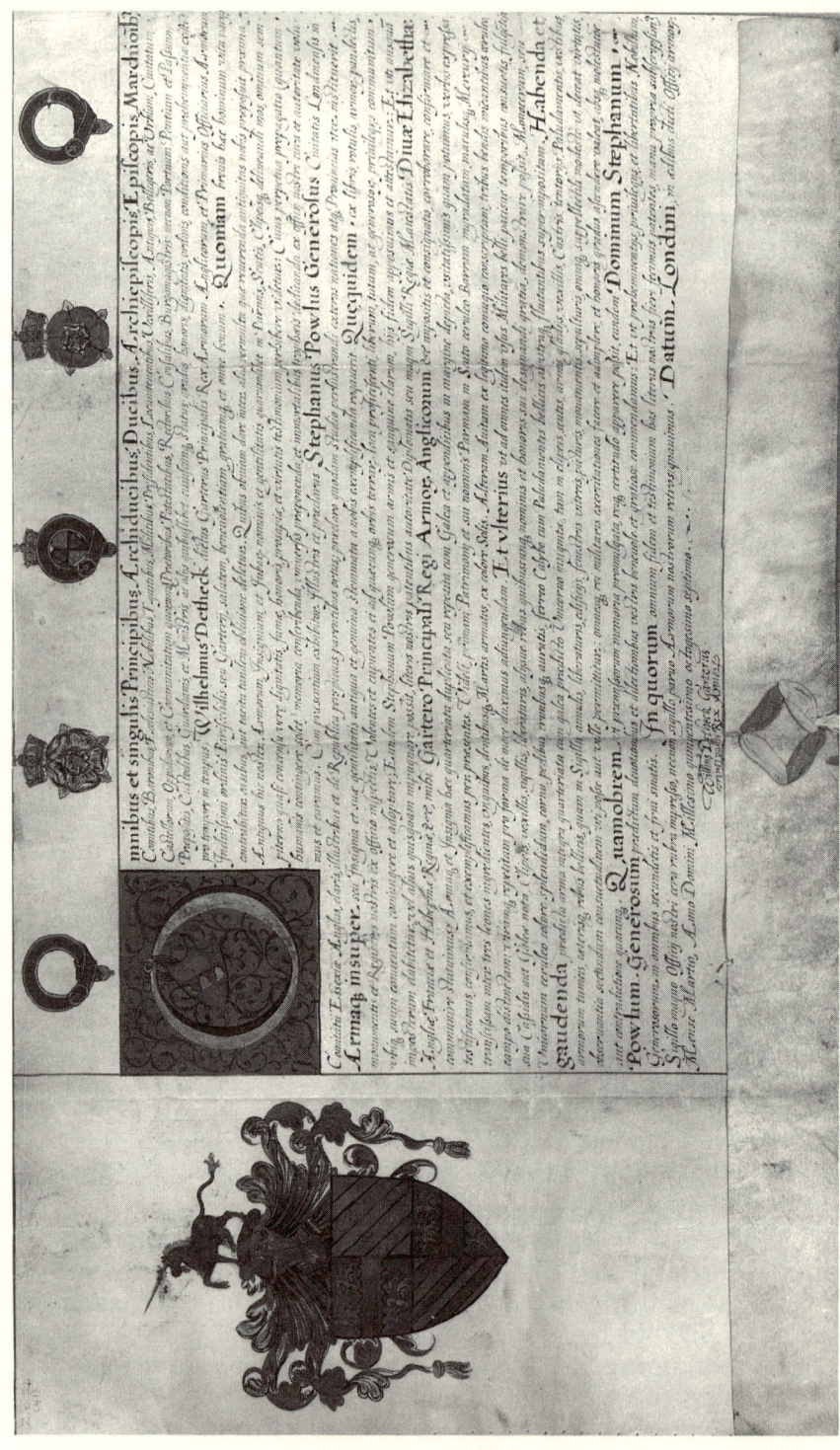

Stephen Powle's escutcheon, received in 1588. Folger Shakespeare Library, Washington, D.C. Z.c. 22 (41).

to work some prevention by my humble and dutiful entreaty at my return, but the land was sold and the entail cut off by fine three months before I came home, without order for my maintenance.[3] And in order that the Office be surrendered in consideration of some money, there be now some persons dealing with him.[4] For which cause, Right Honorable and my gracious good Lord, I presume to renew the suit made almost two years since by my father to your Lordship in my behalf. Of the which, although in my own opinion I am unworthy and for my past service have no ways deserved, yet because upon that motion then made I conceived some comfortable hope of the next vacant place in the Clerkship of the Council, and for that my employment by your Honor's means these 16. months in Italy hath in some measure augmented my experience. Moreover, my father's estate decaying, whereby I am utterly unprovided of all means to live, therefore, I am urged by these spurs to importune your Honor with this most humble petition, upon whom I depend as on my Lord and Master. And whose creature I want to be in some place, by that means to show with what devotion I have always served you. But if in the meantime those places being already furnished with men of greater sufficiency, the next place might be long before it fall, my most humble petition is it will please your good Lordship to be a mean to her Majesty to bestow on me the £150 a year her Highness gave me at my remaining in Italy or what other thing else soever your Lordship shall think convenient for my having no other help nor means besides your Honor's fatherly[5] provision to hold up my head even almost one day. (169:39r–40r)

Shortly thereafter Powle's desperate pleas were partially answered: he was given fifty pounds in connection with the wardship of Master Joye of Wiltshire (see p. 100), and Michael Hickes chose Powle "to succeed him" as a secretary to Lord Burghley (309:82v–83r).

By 17 June Queen Elizabeth's attempts to negotiate a peace with the duke of Parma were no longer feasible. King Philip's Armada had set forth from Lisbon the end of May; it arrived in the English Channel on 21 July. Within nine days a combination of English pluck, ingenuity, and unusual weather conditions brought about a decisive defeat of the fearsome but unwieldy Spanish vessels. Some were badly damaged when the Lord Admiral Charles Howard set adrift six blazing fireboats that tossing around in the near gale winds wreaked havoc on the closely ordered Spanish fleet with further destruction being inflicted by the crews of the more maneuverable English ships. By 30 July a badly battered Spanish flotilla withdrew from the Channel and headed northward, with Howard and Sir Francis Drake in pursuit. Eventually the pursuers withdrew as the Spaniards reached the North Sea, where bad storms continued to spew damage on the surviving vessels.[6] The fear that England would be unable to withstand a Spanish onslaught had proven unjustified. Powle and his countrymen could now breathe a sigh of relief.

In September 1583 the English Ambassador to Scotland, Robert Bowes, was eager to return to England and asked to be relieved of his duties. Perhaps it was he who later recommended Stephen Powle for the post in Edinburgh. Bowes and his wife had become acquainted with him there and had entertained him early in 1583.* In the summer of 1589 Powle was informed that he had been appointed ambassador to Scotland "with a provision of £500 yearly besides the allowance of sundry other particulars." Part of this he received immediately, and he would have had the rest upon employment "if the King of Scots' sudden departure into Denmark to his young Queen had not altered their occasions and counsels" (309:83r). In the autumn of 1589 James VI had left for Denmark, and on 24 November he and Anne of Denmark were married in Oslo.[7]

Although Powle never became ambassador to Scotland, he continued in government circles as one of the secretaries to Lord Burghley. Among the copies of letters that are preserved is one in Italian written 12 July 1590 by Lord Burghley to Signor Giacomo Filliasi, chief councillor of state to the grand duke of Tuscany (309:88r). Powle noted in the margin of his copy that this letter was to be a means to the duke "for peace and amity betwixt her Majesty and the King of Spain, written in English by the same Lord Treasurer and translated into Italian by me and sent into Italy under mine own handwriting and the Council's appointment."

In March 1589/90 Powle had married a young widow, Mistress Elizabeth Woodhouse Hobart (or Hubburt) of Waxham, Norfolk.[8] She was the daughter of a first cousin to Queen Anne Boleyn. In later years when thanking God for his blessings, Powle wrote (309:83r) that God's goodness caused Doctor Gooche[9] to "moyen" a marriage "between me and Mistress Hobart even miraculously and against all likelihood." At the time of Powle's wedding his purse was augmented by the loan of fifty pounds from Baker, the queen's surgeon. Powle was about thirty-four and his wife thirty-three when they were married in February 1589/90. On 15 December twin sons were born, but tragedy was to follow: Elizabeth Powle died nine days after the birth, one of the twins (Thomas) succumbed in early February of 1590/1, and the other (Stephen) survived barely eleven months (until mid-November).

---

*See p. 55.

On the wall of the chancel in the Church of Saint Margaret at Barking, Essex, is an alabaster tablet with a black marble panel inscribed in Latin that can be translated:

> Sorrowful Stephan Powle did dedicate this to the perpetual remembrance of his never to be forgotten wife Elizabeth Powle, who was in religion zealous, in conversation discreet, and by integrity of life sincere. She lived thirty-four years, made happy two husbands, bore five children, left in the world two sons, Thomas and Drew Hobart. The ninth day after the birth of twins, Thomas and Stephan Powle, she died, betwixt whom she lies buried the twenty-fourth of December 1590.

Above the inscription are two shields of arms with quarterings of Hobart (or Hubburt), Woodhouse, Cole, Hare, Powle, Tate, and Sandford.

In Powle's Commonplace Book (169:189v–190v) are poems of his in Latin and in English commemorating his wife and trying to accept her death as God's will. A typical one of the poems is the following, written as though to him from his wife in her new abode in heaven:

> This is a sacred show of grief, these be your holy rites
> Which heavy hearts do yield as due unto departed wights
> But when my hearse did mourn in black and coffin placed in ground,
> There was no cause these vaulted walls with planing sheets should sound.
> For though I late were happy wife unto my dearest Powle,
> And sailed in calm contenting seas with body joined in soul
> And now by just decree of him whose doom commands to die
> I yielding to that conquering power, now underneath do lie.
> Yet nevertheless I sailed aloft and breathe most fresh delight
> And hand of hallowed, blessed saints, a full contenting sight.
> You served on earth below; I reigned on high above the sun
> And far remote from earthly soil my lands where I do wonne.[10]
> You dandled be my fickle toys, and fond delights do please
> And all your prospects be nought else but endless wavering seas,
> But mine be starry joys which shine most clear from clouded moon,
> The mightiest monarch I behold in his most stately throne.
> O wished sight, O greatest gain, O everlasting wealth,
> O rich reward, O glorious life, O never ending health!
> Here hymns divine, here sweet conforts, here ever pleasing voices,
> Here all the blessed quiet of heaven still sings, triumphs, rejoices.
> Thus I embrace the highest good
> You worldlings all learned this:
> Fear God, obey his reverent hosts.   Eccles. 12.13.
> These were my steps to bliss.
>
> FINIS

7
Interlude: Recovery from Tragedy

Powle was stunned by the tragedy, and he sought comfort in his strong Calvinist feelings. On 10 March 1590/1 at Clay-hall in Essex, where he was temporarily living, he wrote a "Meditation" as a "thanksgiving to the Almighty for all his spiritual and temporal blessings wherein is briefly set down the whole course of his life, made early in a morning before day and begun almost at midnight." It was written on the words of the psalmist: "Media nocte surgam ad confitendum tibi Domine" ("In the middle of the night I shall rise up in acknowledgment to you, O Lord") (309:81r).

As Powle reminisced about his life, he contemplated the many spiritual mercies that God had bestowed upon him. As to the death of his dearly beloved wife, he was unable to speak, but he concluded that it must have been the judgment of the Lord, a judgment sometimes secret, sometimes clear, but always just.

Shortly after Elizabeth Powle's death, Michael Hickes, patronage secretary to the lord treasurer, had reminded Burghley of Powle's financial plight, had recommended his suit for the reversion of his father's two offices to Master Doctor Herbert, and had moved Her Majesty for Powle. In addition, Master George Coppin had offered Powle a note of wardship for Master Joye of Wiltshire[1] and the lucrative wardship was obtained (309:83r).[2] Powle closed his "Meditation" with a feeling of gratitude to God, for

> these thy mercies past assure me of mercies to come. I will not therefore shut up this meditation but will leave it unperfect and unfinished, because thy mercies shall never be ended but will always live, and shroud myself under the expectation thereof until such time, as being ended, I live forever with thee in heaven, where I will with thy blessed Angels *misericordias tuas in aeternum cantare* [sing of thy mercies eternally]. (309:83 r&v).

Shortly after this Powle "retired into the North to shun thereby the sorrowful remembrance of her (whereof methought every place was an adjuvant)" (246:3r). He resided for a while at Gretham in the bishopric of Durham. Possibly he held some office at Durham Cathedral, for in the "Meditation" penned in March 1590/1, he wrote of his gratitude that Master Dethick had "preferred" him "to his [Dethick's] father's liking for an office in Durham."

While Powle was at Gretham recovering from his grief, he visited a young gentlewoman, Mistress Cordell Maye, whom he had "long ago known as wise, godly, and modestly pleasant." She was "honorably married" and had borne a child but since its birth was "metamorphosed into folly, impiety, and pensive, yea despairing sadness." Powle diagnosed this as due in part to "the weak idleness of her brain after childbirth," partly because of "the melancholy aspect of her abode," the ancient house at Auckland of her father Dr. Hutton, bishop of Durham (the rooms were large and dark and the location solitary and deserted), but chiefly because she was prepossessed by consideration of her "weighty sins (as she believed)" so that she was "almost swallowed in a gulf of despair." Her friends (no mention is made of her husband) had tried unsuccessfully to "use persuasive conference" with her to overcome her "agonies of mind." To Powle, however, "she gave more attentive care" because of "their many years of familiar acquaintance." Therefore, as much for his own good, since he was thereby strengthening his own faith, as for her comfort, and because he had found it difficult to talk to her since she was never unaccompanied, Powle composed and sent a lengthy written discourse. It was delivered by his servant, Daniel Simpson. Some time later Powle wrote in his Commonplace Book:

> It pleased God to give effectual success to these my endeavours; for within a short space after, she saw her own blindness, acknowledged her own imperfections and recovered her former health, and since that time hath ever (as I hear) by the favour of the Lord so continued. (246:3r).

In the discourse sent 20 January 1591/2, Powle explained that with maladies of the mind as with infirmities of the body, the first step to recovery is to have the will to be cured, the second is to have faith in the sufficiency of the physician, and the third is to be precise in observing his prescribed order of diet and his other directions. Powle addressed his patient as "My most worthy to be regarded Charge" and signed the discourse "Your carefull and lovinge Governour, Stephan Powle," for when he had first known her, she had called him her "Governour" (Powle occasionally wrote his name with an "a"). In the discourse Powle provided her with optimism, assuring her of his confidence that she would return to complete health, and he prescribed religious faith and pleasant readings such as Philip Sidney's *Arcadia* to dispel her melancholy.

Within the next year or two Powle had returned to London, had met, and by the end of November 1593, married Margaret Turner Smyth,[3] a wealthy widow with a large estate inherited from her deceased husband (169:208r; MS. Lansdowne 75:132). She had borne ten children, six sons and four daughters, and was sole executor of the will of her late husband, Thomas Smyth, esquire of Surrey and Smyths-hall, Blackmore, Essex. The will, dated 15 February 1590 (1591 in modern dating) referred to the testator's illness and was witnessed by the testator's father, Thomas, and by his son John. All Smyth's lands, tenements, and goods were left to his wife Margaret to dispose of "as she promised" him.[4] The text of the brief will is in her seemingly agitated handwriting and appears to have been a hurried one. For three years (before and immediately after his marriage to her) Powle employed his legal skills to aid her in maintaining her inheritance of Smyths-hall and of more than five hundred pounds yearly (309:53r) in the face of apparently unjustified claims by the brother and son (Francis) of Thomas Smyth's deceased first wife, Blanche.[5]

At the death on 9 January 1604/5 of Margaret Powle's mother, Christian Turner, to whom she, as the only child, was sole heir,[6] she was further to acquire Crepping-hall and Lamarsh-hall in northern Essex. These estates had been purchased by Christian Turner in 1594 from Edward de Vere, earl of Oxford.[7]

On 20 June 1594 Powle had begun a long letter to his friend John Chamberlain, who had previously scorned marriage but had recently informed Powle that he now acknowledged that perhaps it was a wise step. Powle recalled their debates on the subject when in 1590 they were in France together at Saint Denis visiting the ancient monuments of the French kings interred there.[8] At that time Chamberlain had termed marriage "a servile yoke," "a banished liberty," and "a marring of our flourishing age" (the latter alluding to a false etymology of the word *marriage*). However, now that Chamberlain had become "reconciled to the Church of assured truth" and closer to worldly married happiness, Powle was sending him a few practical suggestions to guide him. Powle advised how to lay the groundwork for a good marriage: the best age to marry (Powle advocated about thirty-five as the optimum age for a man, although for a woman it would be all right to marry as early as eighteen); how to marry by the ear as well as the eye, that is, according to what one heard about the young lady from trustworthy sources as well as what one observed for oneself; and the importance of equality of social station between the husband and the wife-to-be (one should not be noble if the other was base) and near-equality in age. He emphasized that harmony is not produced by disparate elements. At this point in the letter Powle apparently tired, for he noted in the margin:

> This imperfect discourse was begun and composed in two hours at my house of Smyths-hall the 20th of June 1594[9] and shall be finished when I feel myself well disposed.
> I meant to have sent it to my good friend Master John Chamberlain. (169:206v)

Chamberlain's marriage plans evidently never materialized. According to a letter of Stephen Rodwey's (Lansdowne MS. 88:41r), at one time Powle tried to encourage a match between Chamberlain and Powle's cherished niece, Jane,[10] daughter of his sister Dutton, for by April 1592 Jane had been twice widowed.

We do not know the age of Powle's second wife at the time they married, but she probably was about forty, as she had already borne ten children the oldest of whom, John Smyth, was born in 1570.

After this second marriage, Powle's financial difficulties became a thing of the past. He soon purchased a London home in Chancery Lane next to the office of the six clerks and, by 1601, a small rural retreat at Mylend, northeast of London.

8
Early Years in Chancery

It took a few more years for Powle's career to blossom. In November 1593, when he was about thirty-eight, he had written to Michael Hickes (patronage secretary to Burghley) begging him to procure Her Majesty's signature on a bill for Powle to be treasurer's remembrancer by Burghley's appointment (Lansdowne MS. 75:132). It was an office concerned with fixed revenue and the recovery of debts and had originally been requested by Powle four years earlier. Whether or not he ever obtained it is uncertain, but by April 1596 he had secured a far more important post, that of deputy clerk of the Crown, because his eighty-three-year-old father relinquished the duties of his office at that time.

Clerkship of the Crown, which was an important and exacting office, entailed attending on the lord keeper (or lord chancellor) at all times, either in person or by deputy, and preparing for the great seal, all commissions for the queen's service filing election returns, and on the first day of every Parliament attending the House with a list of members of the new Parliament, as well as administering the oaths to the lord keeper of the great seal, to the master of the rolls, and to other officials, filing and recording proceedings before the court of claims, and enrolling them on the coronation roll. It also entailed the writing of pardons and writs of extent upon recognizances.

In the mid 1590s, Thomas Powle, while still clerk of the Crown, had been accused of neglect in the enrollment of commissions, of irregularities in writs and warrants, and of cheating the queen as much as thirty pounds at a sealing. It seems likely, however, that the malfeasance, if there was any, was not Thomas Powle's but that of Roland Watson, then deputy clerk of the Crown and controller of the hanaper, which was the financial department of the Chancery.[1] Whatever the case, it became obvious that there had been considerable carelessness, that no proper calendar of pleadings had been kept, and that the Chancery administration needed to be cleaned up and put in healthy order. Despite the unsavory accusations, Thomas Powle, in recognition of his many years of loyal service to Queen Elizabeth, remained nominally the clerk of the Crown in Chancery (a title he had held since 1569) although now, because of his advanced age, the actual work was being handled by others. Roland Watson, the deputy suspected of corruption, died in 1595, and in early 1596 Lord Keeper Puckering appointed in his place Stephen Powle, who had a reputation as an able and conscientious clerk.[2] Although Stephen's title was deputy clerk of the Crown, he assumed substantially the full duties originally assigned to his father. The State Papers for 5 April 1596 give as an example of his conscientiousness his reply to a query of the lord keeper in regard to the proper procedure for provisioning the Tower of London. Powle's carefully worded reply from the Crown office began as follows:

> I have searched the rolls and books of the office but cannot find any signed bill, recorded for the commissions of provisions for the Tower, and my Clerk, who has written in the office for above thirty years, does not remember any such especial warrant from her Majesty, but that the commissions have passed the Great Seal only by authority of the Lord Keeper or Lord Chancellor, but at the request of the Master of Ordnance. The like commissions for her Majesty's ships do usually pass at the instance of the Lord Admiral. (State Papers 12 257/11)

During Stephen's tenure he gradually achieved some order in what were until then haphazard and negligently kept records, and he made careful copies of many of them in the legal section of his Commonplace Book (MS. 168).

Puckering died later in April, and shortly after Thomas Egerton was appointed lord keeper. Powle had a role to play in the installation and wrote his father (168:88v) describing the impressive ceremony of the delivery of the great seal to Egerton. Afterward Egerton attended the queen in the Privy Chamber, and Powle recorded the poignant scene. Elizabeth had remarked, "I began first with a Lord Keeper and he was a wise man I tell you, and I will end with a Lord Keeper." Burghley remonstrated, "God forbid, Madam, I hope you shall bury four or five more." But Elizabeth protested, "No, this is the last." With that, she burst into tears.[3]

Stephen Powle continued in the Crown office through the period of the Essex Rebellion (309:205r), and Powle's Commonplace Book (MS. 168) supplies many details about it: copies of letters from the queen and from the lord keeper (168:191r), Essex's answers, proceedings in his trial (168:119r), and the warrant to the lord keeper for "executing an Earl on the hill" (168:11v). The second part of the Commonplace Book (MS. 169) has accounts of the death of the earl of Essex, of Sir Christopher Blount, of Sir Charles Danvers, and others of the rebels (169:74v, 143r; see pp. 217–19).

At the end of January 1596/7 the office of clerk of the Crown in Chancery was sold by Thomas Powle to George Coppin (then an assistant in the Crown office) but the sale was not to take effect until Thomas Powle's death. Coppin took office for life on 27 August 1601.[4] The purchase price has not been ascertained, but the annual fee was sixty pounds (State Papers 385 262/20), and by the time Sir George Coppin died in 1620 the office was said to be worth between seven hundred and eight hundred pounds a year.[5]

By 1597 "Old Tom Powle" was becoming much less active physically, although he managed to attend to his duties as senior six clerk. He was now residing with Stephen and his wife[6] at their home in Chancery Lane, next to the offices of the six clerks. Stephen had arranged for a door to be cut through to the adjoining building so that his father could reach his office from home without having to go outdoors (309:52r). On 22 January 1600/1, five months before his death at the age of eighty-eight, Thomas Powle surrendered "the room, place, and office" of his six clerkship to his son (168:119r), who, despite the harsh treatment he had received in his youth, had become the mainstay of his father's old age. Stephen's stepmother had either died by this time or had separated from his father.

The six clerkship was an especially lucrative office and ordinarily sold for about £6,000. However, when it passed from father to son, the fee was only a portion of this. The minimum income received from the normal functions of a six clerk were, even as early as 1594, more than £750 a year.[7] Six clerks were Chancery attorneys who received and filed all bills, answers, replications, and other records in causes on the equity side of Chancery. As occasion required, they certified to the court the state of proceedings in various cases. They also made out warrants and patents for ambassadors, sheriffs, and other officials. Each six clerk was assisted by about ten underclerks.[8]

Shortly after July 1602 the six clerks (Powle, John Evelyn, William Totyll, Richard Wilkinson, Francis Hubert, and John Clapham) wrote to Lord Keeper Thomas Egerton suggesting the advisability of discontinuing the practice of having a separate controller of the hanaper, for, as they explained, his duties could easily be handled by whichever six clerk was then acting as riding clerk. This would prove more efficient and less costly to Her Majesty than having a controller of the hanaper (168:146v). The riding clerk was a rotatable office assigned to each of the six clerks in turn for a period of one year. Powle served as six clerk from August 1601 until 1607.[9]

9
Family Life

As for Powle's private life, his marriage to "Margareta," as he called her, seems to have been a reasonably happy one. Although in his Commonplace Book he paraphrased portions of Jerome's "Invective Against Women as the Champions of Luxury" (169:66v–68v), he appended a refutation at the end:

> I will answer this enemy to nature as Aristotle did that philosopher who railed against the principles of nature, women, because all sorts of women be the very nurses of nature: "*Iste canis rabiacus multa dicit, sed nihil probat* [This raging dog speaketh much but proveth nothing]" or rather I will not answer at all this Paradox proclaimed to the world by gross ignorance itself, against the shining virtue of unspotted women, according to the direction of the wise Solomon: "*Ne respondit stultu secundum stultitiam suam*" ["Answer not a fool according to his foolishness"]. Proverbs 26/4.

In the margin Powle added:

> In the commendation of women, amongst many proofs: the four elements being male or foemina (according to Seneca), the female part is allowed the best. All sciences, all muses be women.

At the end Powle inscribed:

> The rest of this imperfect discourse shall be finished when I find myself disposed thereunto.
>
> 24 Martij: 1607

His notes cite examples of Margareta's homespun wisdom. In March 1609 he wrote that "Mia consorte diceva che":

> Lovers must woo like turtle doves that never woo but once; embrace like ivy: straightly, and die when the thing embraced dieth; kiss like cockles: which is so to proportion their affection that the same be not fitted to any but to one love.

Shortly after he met her (probably late in 1592), after quoting some lines from a Westminster tomb, he wrote in his Commonplace Book:

> I learned this of Mistress Smith, widow, whom I hope to marry, likewise this:
> for the cramp, the party or any attending by is to say "Margareta Smith" or the name of the party "The yoll the yoll give thy qwitbendy tatrayammatry 3 times over." (169:231r)[1]

Powle's Commonplace Book contains a number of practical remedies for common ailments. On 6 August 1611 his notes include "My wife's medicine *ad purgandas renes, et ad aperiendum passaginis contra calculum renibus*" ("to purge the kidneys and to open the tubes for passage of the stone") and, on 2 September 1611, "My wife's medicine against fatness and pursiness" (169:89r). The directions for this are as follows: "Take a handful of fennel and rooted bruised licoras. Steep them in beer or white wine all night and then drink the same every morning cold for one week or longer till it be loathsome unto you." "Fatness" (and perhaps gout) were health problems for Powle himself, as he also quotes other advice for these ailments, some from his mother and some from Walter Ralegh. One of his troublesome health problems in later life, in addition to obesity, seems to have been a weakness of the eyes, for two letters of 1618 from his physician, the versatile Thomas Lodge, well-known writer of pamphlets, verse, and plays, gave him some rather curious advice on how to strengthen his eyesight and how to lessen fatness. It is doubtful that Lodge's recommendations proved of much practical value (169:191r).*

Margareta had a number of children from her first marriage, and Powle seems to have readily adopted them as his own, since by the time of his marriage to her she was probably beyond safe childbearing age. In 1598 he helped the eldest son, John Smyth, write a love letter to the young lady he was wooing (see pp. 215–16),[2] and in 1620 he arranged for his wife's granddaughter Kate Smyth to become an attendant to Lady Mary Cheyney (169:198v), widow of Powle's stepbrother and a gentlewoman whom Powle esteemed highly.

However, Powle's closest family ties seem to have been to his "saintlike"[3] sister Dutton and her daughter Jane and grandson Rawleigh, born 15 April 1586 (and perhaps named after Powle's

---

*See partial transcript of letter on pp. 162–63.

famous Middle Temple roommate). He was the son of Jane's first husband, John Bussy of Katha, Lincolnshire, whom she married circa 1585 and who died in 1589 at the age of thirty.[4]

On 27 May 1597 Powle wrote to "Mine only to be beloved Niece," Jane. She had apparently chided her uncle for not having written her recently, for she was curious about what was going on in Chancery now that Stephen had become deputy clerk of the Crown. He apologized and added that he believed the delay in "procuring the reversion of the office"[5] was not an oversight but a means for his ensuing good, for

> having been busied these three years in calming the waves of a troubled estate in our land [some of his wife's relatives had made claims against her inheritance], I hope to have settled myself thereby in the haven of an assured inheritance of more than five hundred pounds yearly revenue, of which my endeavours (if it so please God to dispose the courses of the world) you or yours may be hereafter partakers. Beside in the meanwhile, I have obtained some petty offices of profit,[6] but yet of far greater credit, and more fitting my contentment who have shunned always to be *Huomo di Roba longa* [a long-robed man, that is, a judge or barrister in the law courts]: This Term[7] business hath so imprisoned my thoughts and actions that I remain confined and in a manner chained to certain limits, so that I am no ways free to dispose of either; which causeth mine absence from my dearest friends by letters. But if I be once enlarged, you shall find me a continual reviver, supporter, and awaker, by my scribbled lines of that good will which I hope shall never die, decay, nor so much as sleep in you.
> May 27, 1597.
>
> > Your loving uncle,
> > S.P.
> > (309:53r)

There is a letter to his niece in which the tables are turned: Powle scolds her for her remissness as a correspondent. After the death of her first husband, John Bussy of Lincolnshire, she had married John Fuller, Esq., of Bishopshall in the parish of Stepney, Middlesex County. He was a wealthy justice who died in 1592 (PROB 11, 79, fol. 355r). He made Jane his heir and executor but stipulated that she use some of his wealth to build two almshouses, one for poor men and one for poor women. As a justice, he had become aware of how hard it was for the destitute to avoid imprisonment.

Having thus been twice widowed in the last fifteen years, Jane had recently married Sir Thomas Mansell III of Margam and Penrice in Glamorganshire, Wales.[8] Margam, where Jane and Sir Thomas were living, was a residence of great splendor situated in beautiful woodlands at the foot of high hills about a mile from the sea. After the dissolution of the monasteries, Margam, then an abbey, had been purchased from Henry VIII by the grandfather of Sir Thomas, Sir Rhys (or Rice) Mansell. He had made extensive additions and had converted the abbey to a handsome home.[9] In Margam Abbey Church the marble tombs of many of the Mansell family are still extant. A prominent one has three reclining marble figures surmounting a table-type tomb. On it the effigy of Sir Thomas lies between that of his first wife, Mary Mordaunt, and of Powle's niece, whom Sir Thomas had married in late 1599. On the wall behind the tomb is a marble plaque commemorating Sir Rawleigh Bussy and his wife, Dame Cicelly. It states that he died at the age of thirty-seven in 1623 and that his mother was Jane, grandchild of Thomas "Pole" of London, clerk of the Crown in Chancery.

Stephen Powle's letter to his niece from the Crown office, 30 November 1599, complained that she still had not answered his last letter, which had been written a year ago. He might have taken it to heart if his heart had not for the past seven years been steeled "with many other crossing discontentments." Jane had objected that his last letter was in a secretary's hand, not his. Powle explained that it was to relieve his niece of having to read his own scribbled lines. He then reminded her of how eager he was to see her and begged her to come with her husband, Sir Thomas, to visit Powle and his wife in London, for now he could bid her welcome to his own house (in Chancery Lane). Now that his estate was settled and "all storms passed," he could "rest in a calm haven" and devote his time to his friends. This was to say "now I am wholly my self . . . all that I am, I am yours."[10] He bid her "look for no news especially of matters of state in these queasy times, for common occurrents would be frivolous and weighty ones would be dangerous to commit to an uncertain delivery." He closed with his and his wife's commendations to her and Sir Thomas and signed himself "Your loving uncle to be commanded" (309:52r&v).

There is another letter of his to his niece dated 21 February 1600 (1601 N.S.) from the Crown office. His niece had evidently asked him about the happenings of the Essex Rebellion but he was closemouthed, saying that he had enjoined his tongue to continual silence in matters of state.

For many have had cause to repent them of words uttered, but never of the same concealed. I write this because I being as it were in a rich fair of news, in regard of the place where I dwell in here and offices I hold, do endeavour to make my profit of the sight of other men's interchangeable markets, and neither buy nor sell any commodities myself, and (like those that sit in a specious theater) do feed my thoughts by observing other men's acting on the stage, which sometimes present Comedies of follies to laugh at, and sometimes Tragedies of sorrow to lament and pity, and never willingly play any part myself. This week past hath afforded us some examples of the latter: for not long since a number of giants (for their monstrous intentions, but pygmies for their weakness and power) laying hill upon hill, that is adding treacheries to treasons, and endeavouring thereby to mount up into Heaven to pluck Juno from her seat (as in the Poet's Metamorphosis) have been discovered by the favor of God, and worthily overthrown by the sentence of the law, the circumstances whereof I refer to Master Thomas his report.[11]

Therefore my good Niece, let me entreat you to pardon my not particularizing of the same . . . and let my present lines be only the ascertainer of you that I live in health, that I long to see you and my good sister your Mother, and that I affectionately love you both; moreover that my father is in health and remaineth with me in my house in London, out of whose Chamber in the Six Clerks into my dining room I have made a door for his more ease, as my Sister can inform you.

As a postscript he chidingly added, "I can acquaint you with nothing more than I wrote in my last till my wife hath received an answer from you to her letter" (309:51v).

Although Powle was careful not to reveal to his niece any inside information about the circumstances of the Essex uprising, he was well aware of the drama and the historical importance of what he was witnessing and kept records and comments among his private memoranda, for as a clerk of the Crown in Chancery he was responsible for putting in motion royal orders and attending to various details of legal procedure. Among his manuscripts are accounts of the events that preceded and followed the earl's trial. The story of Robert Devereux's downfall is well known, but Powle has added an occasional sidelight or descriptive detail and his account of Essex's speech on Tower Green at the time of his execution includes a number of phrases not in the official report as given by Dr. William Barlow, bishop of Chichester.

10

Recording the Essex Rebellion

Robert Devereux, second earl of Essex, had shown considerable pique and insolence toward the queen in July 1598, when she refused to accept his choice of George Carew as lord deputy in Ireland. At this time the lord keeper, Sir Thomas Egerton, wrote a friendly letter of advice to Essex, urging the hot-blooded earl for his own good and that of England "not to contend and strive" but to "yield and submit" to his sovereign. Egerton wrote (309:48r&v),

> have you given cause, and yet take a scandal unto you? then all you can do is too little to make satisfaction. Is cause of scandal given to you? yet let policy, duty & religion enforce you to yield; sue and submit to your Sovereign, between whom and you there can be no proportion of duty when God requireth it as a principal duty & service to himself and when it is evident that great good may ensue of it to your friends, yourself, your Country, and your Sovereign, and extreme harm to the contrary. There can be no dishonor nor hurt to yield, but in not doing thereof, dishonor and impiety. The difficulty my good Lord is to conquer yourself, which is the height of true valour & fortitude, whereunto your honorable actions have ever tended. Do it in this and God will be pleased, her Majesty I doubt not well satisfied, your Country will take good, your friends comfort by it, and yourself (I mention you last for I know that of all these you esteem yourself least) shall receive honor, and your enemies (if you have any) shall be disappointed of their bittersweet hope. I have delivered what I think simply and plainly; I leave you to determine according to your wisdom.

Three days later Essex wrote in a reply an eloquent but stubborn and self-dramatizing letter (309:48v-50r), in which he refused to give way to authority. Following are excerpts from his long letter to Egerton:

> Your Lordship should rather condole with me than expostulate. . . . There is no tempest to the passionate indignation of a Prince at any

Robert Devereux, second earl of Essex (1567–1601), c. 1596 after M. Gheeraerts the Younger. National Portrait Gallery, London.

time so unseasonable as when it lighteth on those that might expect a harvest of their careful and painful Labors. . . . Do I ruinate mine honor because I leave following the pursuit or wearing the false mark of the shadow of honor? Do I give courage or comfort to the foreign enemies because I reserve myself to encounter them, or because I keep my heart from baseness (though I cannot keep my fortune from declining)? No! No! I give every one of these considerations his due right, and the more I weigh them the more I find myself justified from offending in any of them. As for the last two objections, that I forsake my country when it hath most need of me and fail in the indissoluble duty which I owe my sovereign, I answer that if my country had need at this time of my public service, her Majesty that governeth it would not have driven me to a private life. . . . The indissoluble duty which I owe unto her Majesty is only the duty of allegiance which I never will nor can fail in. The duty of attendance is no indissoluble duty. I owe her Majesty the service of an Earl and of a Marshal of England, yet I have been contented to do the service of a Clerk, but can never serve her as a Villein or slave. . . . I can never yield myself to be guilty, or this imposition laid upon me to be just. . . . Have I given cause (you ask) and take a scandal? No, I gave no cause to take up so much as Fymbra his complaints, for I did *totum telum corpore recipere* [receive the whole weapon in my body]. I patiently bear and sensibly feel that, that I then receive when this scandal is given me, nay, when the vilest of all indignities are done unto me. . . . Cannot princes err? Cannot subjects receive wrong? Is any earthly power or authority infinite? . . . I have received wrong. I feel it. My cause is good; I know it. And whatsoever come, all the power on earth can never show more strength and constancy in oppressing me than I can show in suffering whatsoever shall or can be imposed on me.

The curious allusion to "Fymbra" seems not to have been noticed by Essex's biographers. In 86 B.C. Gaius Flavius Fimbria had joined the Roman army on the invitation of the Consul L. Valerius Flaccus to help fight Mithridates in Asia. Flaccus was a poor commander and a harsh disciplinarian, whereas Fimbria was a man of ability whom the soldiers respected. Upon a certain occasion there was a dispute between Fimbria and the quaestor of the army as to quarters, and Flaccus decided the dispute against Fimbria, who as a result was incensed and threatened to return to Rome. Flaccus took him at his word and installed another man in his place. Thereupon Fimbria impatiently watched for an opportunity to stir up a mutiny among the soldiers and used this occasion to take command of the army. Flaccus fled, and Fimbria pursued his former commanding general, discovered him hidden in a well, ruthlessly cut off his head, threw it into the sea, and left the body unburied. The allusion to Fymbra (or Fimbria) is thus to a deed that was said to be the vilest act recorded in Roman history.[1]

Essex apparently felt that he had given even less cause for complaint than Flaccus and yet a weapon had been thrust into his body. Essex was likening Elizabeth to the unduly angered Fimbria, whose complaints and preposterous actions were far out of proportion to the cause.

The letter, with its inference that princes can err, was a dangerous one, for it was considered treasonable to question the rectitude of an anointed sovereign. Although it was written privately to Egerton, it somehow surfaced in later years, when distrust of Essex was beginning to become overt. For the present, however, Essex made his peace with Elizabeth, at least temporarily, and was chosen as lord deputy to go to Ireland and subdue the rebel leader Hugh O'Neill, earl of Tyrone.

Essex set forth confidently with a sizable English army, but instead of proceeding directly against the wily Irish leader, as he had been instructed to do, Essex foolishly decided first to crush a number of minor chieftains. This resulted in a year wasted in minor skirmishes throughout Ireland. By the end of this time, the once-powerful English army had become weakened by disease and halved in numbers, with the result that it no longer had the strength to rout Tyrone.

When these facts were reported to Elizabeth, she became increasingly irritated and wrote to Essex from Nonesuch Palace. Powle in his Letter Book (309:91r–93v) transcribed her letter, captioning it "The Queen's letter sent into Ireland to the Earl of Essex and the Council there 14 September 1599 touching her dislike of his proceedings in those wars." The following passage typifies the tone of the letter:

> Right trusty and well beloved Cousin and Councillor, . . . Having sufficiently declared unto you before this time how little the manner of your proceeding hath answered either your direction or the world's expectation and finding now by your letters by Cuffe[2] a course more strange (if strange may be) we are doubtful what to prescribe you at any time or what to build upon by your own writing to us in any thing. For we have clearly discerned of late that you have ever to this hour possessed us with expectation that you would proceed as we directed you (but your actions always show the contrary) though carried in such sort as you were sure we have no time to countermand you.

Elizabeth was also indignant that Essex had created eighty new knights in Ireland, although after his creation of numerous knights at Cales (Cadiz), he had been warned that this was improper procedure and demeaning to the order of knighthood.[3]

Essex, however, could brook no criticism and, becoming more and more dissatisfied with his unsuccessful role as lord deputy of Ireland, he decided to return home immediately, although Elizabeth had warned him not to do so without her consent. He hoped that by making a direct appeal to Her Majesty, her joy at seeing him would make her overlook his disobedience.

Instead, his sudden entry into London with a band of followers caused the queen considerable alarm, and she determined to discipline him by confining him to the custody of Lord Keeper Egerton. After a period she relented somewhat and allowed the young earl to remain in his own quarters at Essex House under house arrest. Essex, however, continued to sulk and consume himself with indignation. Nor did he condescend to apologize for his actions, but instead behaved as though he were the wronged party. Long emotional strain and dysentery had weakened his constitution, and he soon became seriously ill. Although she did not restore his liberty, the queen sent her own physicians to minister to him. In Powle's Letter Book (309:50v) is the copy of a letter written at this time by Essex's servant Anthony Bacon to Lady Russell, Essex's aunt, thanking her for a medication that she had sent to the invalid earl. Bacon wrote, "his Lordship willed me to assure you that he would not receive such an excellent preservative from any Lady's hands in England in whose special kindness he reposed more confidence and to whose virtue and worth he was more devoted."

Some historians have attributed Essex's severe fevers after 1591 to malaria, but his biographer, Robert Lacey, believes that tertiary syphilis was a possibility and a plausible explanation for the strange disintegration of Essex's personality in later years.[4] His alternations among fear, anger, melancholia, and sly plottings could also have resulted in part from his enforced and unnatural sequestration from the life of the court and the popular acclaim on which he had thrived and, in part, from the anxious worry when Elizabeth failed to renew his patent for the monopoly of sweet wines, on which his income depended.

As Essex gradually regained physical health, he and his supporters conceived a plan they hoped would restore him to power. In Tanner manuscript 76, folio 62r, is "A Relation of what passed at Essex House and in the City of London February 8th Anno Domini 1600."[5] This document is not in Powle's hand but may have been one of the records collected by him, for some of the other entries in this volume concerned or referred to Powle.

Well known is the story of Essex and his followers' poorly organized march through London streets, of the failure of what appeared to be an attempt at insurrection, and of the consequent trial of Essex and Southampton at Westminster Hall for high treason, of both defendants having been found guilty, and of Essex's immediate condemnation to death.

Powle kept copies of all documents, which, since he was acting clerk of the Crown in Chancery, were his function to engross and deliver. Among these copies are frequent marginal notes by him, some of which point out shortcuts and irregularities of procedure that were taken to push through Essex's trial and execution with all possible speed.

Following the insurrection of 8 February and the subsequent trial, Essex and Southampton had been imprisoned in the Tower of London. Powle listed the names of the fourteen commissioners for Oyer et Terminer[6] to indict the earls in Middlesex (168:116r). The same commissioners also sat in London "differing only in this that the Lord Mayor William Ryder was added and named first in the Commission." According to Powle, "the Indictment was in one day in Middlesex and London and Westminster and Guildhall."

The next step, on 18 February (114v, 115v), was the *breve de certiorare* to both Middlesex and London to the commissioners to certify and to remove the record of indictments before Thomas Howard. Next to the copy of this is the following marginal comment by Powle: "Note that there was a Constable of the Tower for the time appointed, my Lord Thomas Howard, nevertheless the writs were diverted by direct commandment of the Lord Chief Justice [Sir John Popham] to the Lieutenant [Sir John Peyton] only."

Lord Thomas Howard had served under Essex at Cadiz and, although he had been marshal of the forces against Essex on 8 February, evidently was opposed to a speedy execution. Perhaps the memory of the execution of his father, the duke of Norfolk, for "treason" in 1572 also had evoked his compassion for Essex. By the *breve de certiorare* the indictment against Essex was removed from a lower to a higher court and thus out of Thomas Howard's jurisdiction. Here Powle noted other irregularities:

London. Breve de Certiorare. Not directed to all the Commissioners but only to those that did sit at that time on the indictment in London. The Lord Mayor [William Ryder] and Aldermen were not named in the writ although they sat at that time by especial commandment of my Lord Chief Justice [Sir John Popham] and Master Attorney [Sir Edward Coke] for what reason best to themselves known. (fol. 115v)

On folio 114v is a copy of the *venire facias,* also dated 18 February, for the lieutenant of the Tower to bring his prisoners to be arraigned before the lord steward. Thomas Sackville, Lord Buckhurst, who had presided at the trial had received a commission to be lord steward for the purpose of arraignment, whereby the prisoners were sentenced to be hanged, drawn, and quartered.

Because the prisoners were noblemen there followed a warrant (fol. 110r) from the queen to the lord keeper (Sir Thomas Egerton) to alter the execution from hanging to beheading and to direct writs thereof.

On 20 February the queen signed the warrant of execution (110v), which this time specified that Essex be beheaded on the green within the Tower rather than on the more public Tower Hill. Next to Powle's transcript of the warrant he commented upon the unusual procedure of bypassing the signet office. His marginalia are these:

> Note that this was engrossed in secretary hand, perused by the Lord Chief Justice, signed by the Lord Keeper, then passed the privy seal as appeareth by the Teste[7] overslipping of the privy signet office[8] in that the warrant signed was sealed by the privy seal and then delivered to the Lord Keeper who kept the same secretly for her Majesty's judgment, never mentioning nor noting the same.

One possible explanation of this procedure is that Elizabeth had signed the warrant reluctantly and wanted to allow for the possibility of countermanding the order in case Essex should offer her a satisfactory plea or apology.

Powle's marginalia emphasize the irregular and hurried way in which the warrant had taken shape and been kept secret and the way some officials at court pushed Essex's execution through with speed and some deviousness.

The original of the execution warrant (recently found among the Ellesmere papers)[9] has a large signature of Elizabeth[10] above the document, which, as Powle noted, is in secretary hand rather than by the usual, more time-consuming engrossing in a formal Chancery hand. It was sealed with only a wafer seal. Appended to the warrant is a note by the lord keeper that the execution took place on 25 February.

There had been fear in court circles of an outburst of sympathy for the handsome, thirty-four-year-old Essex and of resentment at the sentence because of his popularity among the general public. Apparently to avert this, some of the usual procedures were bypassed. The execution took place six days after the trial and was conducted in as private a manner as possible on the green within the Tower of London, and Essex himself was skillfully persuaded by his chaplain, Abdy Ashton, to make a full confession of his crimes so as to receive God's mercy and forgiveness. It was important that the adoring public be convinced of Essex's guilt.

On Tanner manuscript 169, beginning on folio 143r, is a report by Powle (an eyewitness account) of the earl of Essex's behavior, speech, and prayer at the time of his execution on 25 February 1600/01. Although an official version (also an eyewitness account) by Dr. William Barlow, bishop of Chichester, was later put into print together with his sermon on the conspiracy, it does not have all the details of Powle's diligent recording.* The latter makes vivid the sense of spectacle combining gruesomeness with religious overtones. Essex played his part with consummate dramatic skill to exemplify the importance Elizabethans attached to "dying well."

In addition, Powle entered in his Commonplace Book detailed accounts of the deaths of several of Essex's fellow conspirators: Henry Cuffe on 9 March (169:71r); Sir Charles Danvers on 18 March (169:72r); and Christopher Blount, also on 18 March (169:74v). As deputy clerk of the Crown, Powle would have been present at these "ceremonies."

Henry Wriothesley, earl of Southampton, also condemned for treason, was kept in custody in the Tower during the rest of Elizabeth's reign but was not executed. He had shown great contrition and repentance during the trial, whereas the earl of Essex had remained proud and arrogant almost until his final hours. Perhaps for this reason and because Southampton was the

---

*See appendix E, pp. 217–19.

last surviving member of his family, it was thought that the queen was reluctant to let the line die out. When King James came to the throne, he pardoned Southampton, who had been an advocate of James's succession. The earl subsequently became interested and actively involved in the Virginia Company.*

---

*See chap. 14.

11
Suits, Paradoxes, and Slanders

Let us return now to a slightly earlier entry of Powle's in his manuscript books. On folio 83v of Tanner manuscript 309 is found a prayer of his "for prosperous success in a suit to the Lord Keeper" dated 19 January 1599/1600. After Lord Burghley's death in 1598, Powle had usually addressed his suits to Thomas Egerton. Here Powle prayed to God (a God who seems to have been a very personal one) that his recent plea to Egerton might be satisfactorily answered:

> I have long been a petitioner unto Thee for some stay of living whereby I might more devoutly serve Thee.... It might please Thee to give such success unto the words in those my former letters expressed ... to creep into my Lord Keeper's favor so far that he may allow of mine humble request therein; and secondly that I may be able effectually to perform the articled conditions therein contained, so that his Lordship's heart being before framed by Thy omnipotent power to an assent and I by mine own strength and friends' help enabled to go through therewith, I may be settled in some secure estate in this world to advance Thy glory by good example of life and after in the world to come be made partaker of Thy heavenly kingdom through Jesus Christ my only Saviour and redeemer. Amen.
> 19th January 1599. *Crown Office.*

Among Powle's other notes of this period are the only known contemporary copies of four paradoxes written, according to Powle, by Sir William Cornwallis the younger in 1600 in the twenty-second year of his age.[1] They are entitled: "That a great red nose is an ornament to the face" (169:132r); "That it is a happiness to be in debt" (133r); "That misery is true felicity" (134r); and "That inconstancy is more to be desired than constancy" (135v). Powle seems to have been on terms of friendship with the elder William Cornwallis, who was related to the family of Powle's first wife's first husband, Miles Hobart.

Preceding these paradoxes and starting on 169:92r is the copy of a long tract popularly known as "Leicester's Commonwealth." It details the supposed atrocities perpetrated by Robert Dudley, earl of Leicester. In the margin at the left of the first page is the following annotation written in a later hand of Powle's: "The L^d of Leycester his common-wealth copyed of yonge Sr William Cornwallys written booke by my red hedded madde manne."* "My red headed mad man" was presumably Powle's current servant-secretary, as the tract is written in a hand different from Powle's but similar to that used on many other pages of his Commonplace Book. One is tempted to speculate whether the authorship of this vicious diatribe (originally published in 1584) was in any way connected with a member of the Cornwallis family, who were strong Catholics and would have opposed Leicester's ardent pro-Protestantism. The tract's authorship has never been definitively ascertained, although its strong pro-Catholic bias suggests that it was the work of a member of the Catholic Court party. A modern edition of the tract, edited by Dwight C. Peck,[2] opts for Charles Arundell, who was then living in Paris, as the major author.

Powle made brief annotations in the margins of his manuscript to index the tract's contents. A somewhat longer marginal note of his is found next to the section dealing with the "poisoning" of Walter, first earl of Essex, by Leicester's surgeon, Doctor Bailey, who, according to the text, was "a cunning man" who used an "Italian receipt" to cause the "extreme flux" of which the victim died.[3] Powle made no comment on this but wrote of Dr. Bailey: "This was the physician I knew at Basel and he showed me a medal of the Queen and the Lord of Leicester together; who told me also the Lord of Leicester was burst and had a rupture. Anno Domini 1580" (169:100v).

A vituperative letter against Powle himself is found in Lansdowne manuscript 88, on folios 38r to 45r. It was addressed to Michael Hickes by Powle's erstwhile friend Steven Rodwey and was captioned (apparently by Hickes) "25 October 1601 Master Rodway's letter to me touching Master Stephen Powle about money owing Rodway." The letter mentions money owed by Powle to Rodwey's brother and "other ill things betwixt him and me."

Powle had apparently claimed that he owed Rodwey's brother nothing and that if Rodwey persisted in his attacks, the law

---

*See appendix B, pp. 185–86.

would be brought to bear upon him. Rodwey had then written to him requesting a meeting, and Powle had set up a time for him to come, but when he arrived at Powle's home, he was presented with a letter and informed by Powle's servant that his master was ill with a cold and would be unable to see him. Rodwey's complaint to Hickes continued with increasing anger:

> Thinking peradvanture after his [Powle's] old foolish vanity I would accept of his counterfeit kindness for good payment and that because he is somewhat raised from the beggary and despair I knew him so long oppressed with, I would the rather now esteem his friendship and acquaintance which to say truth I do not so much scorn as abhor. . . . He doth press me with such insufferable wrongs that appear greater unto him than they are. . . . It seems strange unto me if that were true, in so long time and with so good means, his heart hath failed him to revenge them, that have done many other wickednesses desperately enough. . . . It is manifest that whatsoever he doth charge me to have done or spoken or attempts about his wife or anything else, all that to have succeeded since the marriage of his niece.[4] . . . [It] was not that he made offer of his niece unto Master John Chamberlain and others; nor that I lost her after so long time and love and acquaintance with her. . . . He best knows that . . . before or since her marriage [he] made offer of recompense . . . at Smithshall to redeem his peace and my silence.

Rodwey said he was enclosing to Hickes some of Powle's "shrinking and weeping Letters," but they are not extant. At one point he referred to Powle as "so great a clarke and the agent of a prince." Rodwey did not explain what his brother's involvement was with Powle, but on folio 43r there is mention of arbitration between them and a demanded settlement of two hundred pounds. Master Kiddemister (Kederminster), one of the six clerks before Powle's time, seems to have been the arbitrator. Powle had apparently offered Rodwey's brother a settlement of sixty pounds at his father's house (for publicly defaming him?), but whether it was rejected or never actually given is unclear. Rodwey implied that Powle had borrowed money from many others without repayment (William Gent, Master Cooke, and Cousin Newcom). Rodwey said he would get Master Suthcours as his counsel in order to obtain justice. Much of Rodwey's anger may have been due to the fact that he had envisaged marriage with Powle's niece Jane and that Rodwey believed his relationship with her had been aborted by Powle.

A few years earlier (on 4 August 1598), when Rodwey was

seeking a passport to go abroad to meet a Master Paget and was having difficulty procuring it (perhaps because he was suspected of recusancy), he had written Principal Secretary Robert Cecil asserting his loyalty and giving "Stephen Powl" as a character reference to confirm how loyally Rodwey had behaved in 1588 when "at the risk of his life" he uncovered an Italian popish plot to poison Queen Elizabeth through the treason of Giraldi.[5] But he also mentioned that the reason he had not gone to the Continent sooner was that a lawsuit was pending between Powle and himself, thus undercutting the value of Powle as a character reference for him.

Rodwey's letter to Michael Hickes apparently was ignored; there is no record of a reply from Hickes. Rodwey's reputation at this time was not of the best, and there seems to be no documentation to substantiate his accusations. It is clear that Rodwey had become extremely antagonistic toward Powle, but the real cause may have been Rodwey's earlier unsuccessful wooing of Powle's niece. Rodwey seems to have felt that his efforts were thwarted because of Powle's maneuvering to see that Jane made the best possible marriage.

12
Lord of the Manor of Smyths-hall

When Stephen Powle married Margaret Turner Smyth in 1593 he moved into the great house of Smyths-hall at Blackmore and became lord of its manor and custodian of its estates.

Blackmore, about three and a half miles east of Chipping Ongar, Essex, is today a charming and idyllic little village seemingly tucked away from the outside world. In Powle's time it also probably had an idyllic quality, although it was far more important then. It is said to have derived its name from the nature of the soil. The parish of Blackmore, through which the river Jordan flows, comprised Copsechys, Fingreth, and Blackmore Priory, which included the manor of Smyths-hall. Philip Morant wrote that "The Priory is reported to have been one of King Henry VIII's Houses of Pleasure and was disguised by the name of *Jericho* so that when this Casanovan Prince had a mind to be lost in the embraces of his courtesans, the cant word among the courtiers was that he was 'gone to Jericho.'"[1]

Smyths-hall was situated south of the village on high ground about a mile from the church. Upon dissolution of the monasteries, the priory had reverted to the Crown, but in 1540 it was granted by letters patent of Henry VIII to John Smyth,[2] one of the king's auditors, and his heirs. He built the handsome manor house, which was given the name of Smyths-hall.

Among the traces of Powle's residence there is an annual certificate of residence of 23 January 1602/3, stating that Stephen Powle, esquire, was assessed and taxed twenty pounds for lands owned in Blackmore, where he "not only at the time of the said taxation but the most part of the year before was himself with his family and household resident, commorant and biding."[3]

The manor of Smyths-hall, of which nothing remains, was situated on what today is known as Wenlock Lane about a mile from the still extant, beautiful little twelfth-century Parish Church of Saint Laurence, which contains evidence of some of Margaret and Stephen Powle's benefactions to the community.

been stained or polluted with any gratuity. I loved your father as my good neighbour and your good mother as my countrywoman, and I esteem of you as a breath of that stock. But I love my God, my self and my reputation better than any friend or familiar. (169:147r)

The majority of justices were hardworking and conscientious; they had to attend quarter sessions of about three days duration with leading officials, one of whom would have been Powle. Records were kept by the clerk of the peace. Major crimes or more difficult cases were usually handled by the assizes, a kind of itinerant court, on which Powle also sat. Justices of assize were sent into the country twice a year to try civil and criminal issues in the counties in which they arose and return the verdict to Westminster. Those on which Powle served met in Essex at Chelmsford and at Brentwood in March and July. One wonders how Powle was able to handle these posts in addition to his demanding work in the Crown office. But perhaps he was preparing for a time in the future when he would retire from Chancery, give up his London home, and spend more time in Essex.

The work of a justice of the peace consisted of down-to-earth problems of law and order: "keeping the peace" whenever it was threatened. Men were brought before him on many kinds of charges: assault, trespass, petty larceny, sheep stealing, drunkenness, vagrancy, disrespect for the Sabbath. A justice also had the right to deal with felonies such as murder, rape, robbery, and witchcraft, but usually those accused of the more serious crimes were bound over to the quarter Sessions or, if they were accused of a major felony, to the assizes. Anticipating trouble involved preventing riots and public disturbances. Those whose episodes of quarrelsomeness threatened the peace were usually ordered to post a bond as surety; sometimes two friends were required to support him as sureties. There were few jails, and they quickly became overcrowded; therefore, it was easier to take bail. If a man were held for a crime, his bond was security for his appearance. A bond was also needed from the accuser to ensure his appearing to prosecute the case.

When a suspected wrongdoer was brought before the justice, he tried to draw him into confession, cross-examine him in such a way as to learn what accomplices he might have had, and lead him into an admission of guilt. Often the Justice would report to the quarter sessions that the suspect "will confess no more."

Much of the justices' time was concerned with the proper maintenance of bridges, roads, causeways, footpaths, and ferries.

Licensing of alehouses was also under the justices' jurisdiction. In addition, they were vigilant about preventing monopolists from forcing up prices. When grain crops failed and the price of bread soared, the justices were quick to inform the Privy Council.[5]

When Stephen Powle became a justice of the peace for Essex, his father had already served in that capacity for many years, but by 1597, due to his advanced age, Thomas Powle was rarely "pricked" for service.

On 12 and 13 April 1597, the Thursday and Friday before Easter, general sessions of the peace (that is, quarter sessions) were held at Chelmsford before Sir Thomas Mildmay and Sir John Petre, barons, William Smyth, Geoffrey Nightingale, Andrew Pascall, Stephen Powle, Thomas Mildmay of Barnes, John Sames, and Christopher Chibborne, esquires.[6] This may have been Stephen Powle's initial appearance as a justice.

Typical of the cases that came before him at quarter sessions were the following:

On 5 July 1597, recognizances (bonds) of William Symonds of Blackmore, yeoman, and John Worme of the same, butcher, for William Smith of the same, butcher, to keep the peace; defaulted. Taken before Stephen Powle and signed with wafer seal attached.[7]

On 5 September 1597, persons licensed to keep alehouses were listed with their names and occupations. Recognizances were taken before Thomas Powle and Stephen Powle, esquires, and signed by them with wafer seals attached.[8] Two justices were customarily required for the licensing of alehouses.

On 11 January 1598/9 there was a maintenance order by the court in the town of Horndon for two poor children, Ann and Elizabeth Aylett, whose father had fled. The grandfather John was deemed able to relieve them and was ordered to repair to Master Weston and Master Stephen Powle and to show cause why he should not keep the said children.[9]

On 3 September 1600, John Nobbes of Stondon, clerk, and John Kempe, of the same, husbandman, for John Comaunder, alias Demaunder, of the same, laborer, to appear and keep the peace. Taken at "Smythes-Hall" before Stephen Powle, esquire.[10]

On 1 September 1614 in the calendar of prisoners in the house of correction, now at the bar was Elizabeth Smytten, born at Ingatestone. Suspected of counterfeiting lunacy, she was committed by Sir Stephen Powle. The verdict was for her to remain in the house of correction.[11]

Powle continued to serve as justice in both quarter sessions and assizes at Chelmsford, Brentwood, and Blackmore until at least 1616.

In the quarter sessions records there is an inkling of one of the problems encountered in the administration of Smyths-hall Manor—theft by servants. On 10 August 1594, about a year after Stephen and Margaret Powle were married, Elias Pickerd, laborer and recently serving man, was arraigned at Blackmore quarter sessions for stealing from his late master, Stephen Powle, esquire: a salt with a cover of double gilt worth £3 10s, a "jest" salt[12] footed and topped with silver and double gilt worth 30s, a cover of a stone jug double gilt worth 18s and a bowl of silver double gilt with cover worth £6. Evidently the theft was not proved, for Pickerd was judged "not guilty."[13] It is not known whether a thief was ever identified.

The aging Queen Elizabeth had died at Richmond on 24 March 1602/3 and James VI of Scotland had been declared king of England as James I. A little over a year later Stephen Powle, esquire, as one of the six clerks of Chancery and a justice of the peace for Essex, was summoned by the king to Theobalds, former home of Lord Burghley and for nine years after his father's death in 1598, of his son Sir Robert Cecil.[14] On 8 July 1604 Master Stephen Powle of Essex became Sir Stephen Powle when the honor of knight bachelor was conferred upon him. With him in the group to be knighted that day were: Michael Hickes of Essex, Thomas Dacres of York, Arthur Dakyn, Oliver Butler and Edward Mansfeild of Yorkshire, Christopher Pigott of Buckinghamshire, and George Hayward of London. Powle's precedence was second in the group (after that of Michael Hickes).[15]

On 20 October 1608, possibly to replace some of the silverplate and other articles that had disappeared over the years or been stolen from Smyths-hall, Powle made a number of purchases from the goldsmith Henry Cheffnere: four gilt stopes,[16] three broad bowls, two round salts, two flowered cups with stands—all gilt—two Collidge pots,[17] two bowls, salt and beaker, and two broad bowls, full gilt, weighing about four hundred thirty pounds. Cheffnere asserted that the latter alone were worth one hundred pounds in open market, but he charged Powle only two hundred pounds for the entire lot (168:3r).

13
Country Squire at Mylend

By 1603 Powle had purchased an additional but more simple country home. It was northeast of London at Mylend (or Mile-end) in the parish of Stepney, Middlesex County. The vestry records of the Great Church of Saint Dunstan in Stepney list Sir Stephen Powle as a Mylend vestryman between 1603 and 1618.[1] According to Powle's notes, he lived between White Chapel Road and White Horse Lane in Mile End Old Town.[2]

Mylend had more knights and gentlemen than other sections of Stepney.[3] Some of the prominent residents of the Mylend area were: Sir William Dethick (garter king of arms), Sir Arthur Throckmorton (M.P. and diarist), Christopher Newport (admiral of Virginia), Elizabeth, countess of Rutland, and Lucy, countess of Bedford.

According to Hubert Llewelyn Smyth, in 1580 about seventy-five hundred persons resided in the parish of Stepney. During Elizabeth's reign there had been a great increase in the number of country houses built by London citizens in East London. "It was the oldest and greatest of the suburbs of London: the open spaces, hunting grounds and playing fields of her citizens . . . as well as the refuge of craftsmen seeking to escape the regulation of her guilds."[4]

Although Powle and his wife, Margareta, resided also at the sumptuous manor house of Smyths-hall, which she had inherited, Powle may have wanted a country home more convenient to London and on a simpler scale, as well as one that reflected his own personality rather than that of his wife's former husband. Although from the time of his second marriage Sir Stephen had spent much time at Smyths-hall and had attained considerable status in the Blackmore community, his favorite place of residence and contentment seems to have been his home at Mylend.[5]

Unlike those landed gentry who quickly became bored with life in the country when they were deprived of the excitement of court and city life, Powle genuinely loved his rustic retreat at

Mylend, for it offered those qualities of living that to him were genuine and meaningful, in contrast to the deceits and maneuverings of the court. He had apparently maintained an enjoyment of rural pursuits and a joy in the land since childhood. Furthermore, it gave him time and seclusion for the study and meditation that meant so much to him. It was perhaps his idyllic life there and at Smyths-hall that eventually inspired his literary friend Nicholas Breton's 1618 dialogue between the courtier and the countryman, for in 1618 Breton warmly dedicated *The Court and Country* to Sir Stephen Powle.*

Shortly after his purchase of Mylend, however, there may have been some minor conflicts between Powle's values and those of his wife, for on 24 October 1605 he sent to his good friend John Clapham, one of the six clerks, "a half hour's conceit" titled "Why a man is said to be the head of his wife, her Lord and Emperor. Why her better, *et per consequent* why he hath precedency" (169:4r). Powle listed divine reasons, natural reasons, and conjectural or probable reasons. One of the divine reasons was that a man and wife are as Christ and his Church, whereof Christ is the head; another was that Adam was the whole body and his wife but a rib. Among the natural reasons Powle gave was that philosophers believe a man is governed by reason whereas his wife is governed by passions, affections, and other emotions; reason must be lord and the passions servants. Among conjectural reasons was that the man must be an exemplar for his wife and therefore should exceed her in power, place, providence, and circumspection, as well as in stature and greatness. The foregoing were topoi of the age and probably would have met with Clapham's wholehearted endorsement. Despite Powle's strong words, however, he seems to have been a compassionate and easygoing husband.

In Powle's Commonplace Book, following the "half hour's conceit," are verses "used as a chimney piece." They pose the question of what is most to be feared by a man: the wolf who preys upon his flock? the fire that burns his house? or the adulterer who preys upon his wife and works his shame? The conclusion, as written by Master Clapham, was that the most important thing to guard against is the wolf: for a man to retain his flock is more valuable for him than to retain his wife or home, for both of the latter can upon occasion become weary burdens. However, al-

---

*See pp. 168–69.

though Powle was well aware of the financial comfort brought to him by his second marriage, it is unlikely that he would have termed money his paramount value.

On 9 January 1605/6 (169:16r) Powle penned "My midnight meditation," in which he mused about the vanities of life and of men and on the "sandy foundations" upon which they endeavored to build themselves "perpetual mansions." They "gape after earthly honor and riches, and never so much as cast their thoughts to the shining firmament of heaven, where be seated the stars which be the glittering ministers of the everliving God." On earth one finds nothing but storms, tempests, and whirlwinds. Our thoughts and actions should be determined by two things: primarily the glory of God and, then, the salvation of our souls.

Three years later he wrote another meditation, much altered, which he considered better. It had been placed on the second shelf of his numerous document books, but Powle believed it had been stolen or purloined, as was true of many of his other papers (169:16v).

On 20 March 1608 Powle wrote from Mylend to his cousin Mistress E. Crompton, who together with her husband (probably Thomas Crompton) and little daughter, Durk, had moved from Mylend to Staffordshire, perhaps for reasons of health or finances. Powle wrote of what wonderful neighbors they had been and how much he, his wife, and sister Dutton (who lived nearby in Buckinghamshire) bemoaned the idea of their leaving and that "no neighbour or kindred . . . could give us more content or comfort" and that he would be "exceedingly joyful to see you both returned to Sir Peputy."[6] Whenever Powle passed the house where they had lived, he grieved "that the saint is gone" and that it was thus "left unhallowed." He also wrote that he hoped by next Michaelmas, if not before, that they would have returned, as his cousin Crompton had expected. Powle had now finished his little buildings and, as he explained to Crompton, had added "to his further delight the purchase of Master Simpson's house and garden, all which together with the minster hereof shall be at your disposal to command and use."

Some time later Mistress Crompton returned to Mylend, at least temporarily, and Powle wrote, telling her how delighted he was and thanking her for her letter and her husband's gift "of a curious piece of workmanship by our good friend Master Phillipps" and a gift of silver slippers "from little Durk, my valentine." In Powle's Commonplace Book (169:78v), below his copy of this letter, is a later comment about Crompton: "A poor kinsman in alliance and an assured friend in love."

There is a record of Powle's service in the six clerks office in London from 1601 through 1607.[7] We do not know how long after this he continued to use his London home in Chancery Lane,[8] for no further mention is made of it.

On Tanner manuscript 168, folio iii^v, there is a memorandum telling of the freezing over of the Thames on 26 January 1607/8, "the frost having continued from a fortnight before St. Thomas Day till this present without any more than one day's thaw within all that time." Between the hours of eight and nine in the morning of 26 January, Powle and his servant Richard Hoskin,[9] together with Job Murcot and John Wriothesley, walked across the river from Parliament stairs to Lambeth Bridge. When they were three-quarters of the way across, Powle met a client of his, "an ancient gentleman suffering from a dead palsy and therefore being carried in a chair supported with four staves and borne upon eight men's shoulders." The old gentleman was on his way to Westminster to see Master Doctor Amy, a master in Chancery, in order to have his answer taken by oath in a suit between John Powle and his son, George Poole. One wonders whether they were relatives of Sir Stephen's? He also saw men on horseback crossing the frozen river over to Lambeth at Lambeth ferry.

There is an entry in Powle's Commonplace Book (168:v^r) of a few lines of Italian verse by the Essex poet Nicholas Breton written in his own hand and dated by Powle February 1610 (1611 in modern dating).[10] Breton was a frequent visitor in Powle's home over the years, for there are a number of other such entries in Breton's hand.

Breton was born about 1555 (according to a deposition found by C. J. Sisson) and thus would have been about the same age as Powle. Although Breton's life was one of financial adversity, he was of gentle birth, the son of William Breton, a wealthy merchant, descendant of the ancient family of Layer Breton in Essex, who died young and left his estate to his wife, Elizabeth, on condition she not remarry; if she did, the full inheritance was to be turned over to his two sons, Richard and Nicholas. Their mother did, however, marry almost immediately after their father's death and subsequently remarried the poet and writer George Gascoigne. Despite William Breton's will, Elizabeth Breton, with the help of the two stepfathers, managed to appropriate and squander the sons' legacy, and thereafter Nicholas's life became one of considerable monetary struggle, although Gascoigne's influence may have been of some value in guiding Nicholas into literary pursuits. In his youth he attended Oxford and may have met Powle there. From his early twenties until his death, about 1626, Breton's writings were prolific and varied: satire, religious tracts, pastoral, and romance, in both prose and verse. He was fluent in Italian and dedicated *A Merry Dialogue* (1603) to John Florio. Breton wrote with facility and frequently with an airy, mocking humor. His writings reflect his originality and the kindliness of his nature, which had weathered an unfair proportion of life's hardships. One senses that he and Powle relished each other's company.

On 10 July 1612 Powle penned a letter to his "dearest friend Andrew Melvyn,"[11] the brilliant but controversial Scottish Presbyterian scholar who was then public professor of theology at the French University of Sedan. The letter (169:89v) was on behalf of the son of Powle's Mylend tenant, Master Franke. Powle recalled the pleasant days he had spent under Melvyn's tutelage in Saint Andrews, Scotland, and apologized for writing in English rather than Latin or French, as he used to do with Melvyn; he had been long absent from France, and now he was a mere Englishman. Powle explained that Master Franke was a gentleman "of especial esteem in his Majesty's Court both in regard of his office and in daily attending the King in eminent place and of his own especial worth and virtue." Franke desired to have his eldest son well educated in religion and languages and felt that it would be helpful if Melvyn could "have a careful regard" over him during his sojourn in France.

Powle expressed his regret that he had not known of Melvyn's sudden departure from England the previous year but now hoped that the English king would recall him to England again.[12] Powle fondly remembered Melvyn's having once written him that they were "companions in the Latins, the Greeks, the Palestinians, and the muses."

Although Powle spent as much time as possible in the quiet, peaceful atmosphere of Mylend, he did not shirk the legal, administrative, or local duties he was periodically called upon to discharge, whether as justice of the peace, vestryman, or whatever. Shortly he was to take an active part in the newly formed Virginia Company.

14
Sir Stephen Powle as "Adventurer" in the Virginia Company of London

On the preliminary pages of Powle's Commonplace Book, Tanner manuscript 168, there are memoranda that between the hours of ten and eleven in the morning of 9 March 1608/9 he delivered to Sir Thomas Smith[1] of Philpott Lane, London, "Treasurer of the Voyage to Virginia," the sum of fifty pounds. In return, Powle received a note with the arms of England testifying to receipt of the money. The memoranda mention that Powle had been chosen to be one of the council of the Virginia Company expedition and that his name had been inscribed in the roll and book kept by the company (168:iv^v).

Sir Thomas Smith, one of the leading financiers of London and a man of proven integrity, had previously been an investor and administrator of the Muscovy and East India trading companies. Their offices, like those of the Virginia Company, were located on the ground floor of Sir Thomas's spacious house in Philpott Lane, at the corner of Fenchurch Street. Upstairs was a collection of some of the trophies the captains of his trading ships had brought back to England from various parts of the world. The captains themselves were invited to use his house as a temporary home when necessary and to utilize information on routes and resources compiled by Sir Thomas's friend, the geographer Richard Hakluyt, who became an active adventurer in the Virginia Company.[2]

Early attempts to colonize Virginia had been primarily individual enterprises, for instance, two Spanish attempts (by Lucas Vasques de Ayllon in 1526 and by Pedro Menendez in the 1560s) and Sir Walter Ralegh's ill-fated Roanoke Colony in 1585. Realiz-

---

The major portion of this chapter was delivered as a paper on 22 October 1985 at a meeting of the Columbia Seminar on the Renaissance at Casa Italiana, New York City.

ing that these efforts had been hampered by limited backing, in 1606 a group of wealthy merchants and prominent Englishmen decided to form a company that would endeavor to secure ample funds for purposes of colonization and trade in Virginia. The impetus probably came from Sir Walter Ralegh when, as early as March 1589, he assigned the rights and concessions he had received from Queen Elizabeth to Sir Thomas Smith, Richard Hakluyt, John White, Ananias Dare, and a group of merchants who Ralegh believed could further his aborted efforts to establish a permanent English settlement in America. Ralegh had spent forty thousand pounds of his own money on the Roanoke attempt and believed that many times this sum would be needed to further a lasting settlement. Hakluyt had pointed out in his 1584 "Particular Discourse Concerning . . . the Western Discoveries" that there were many possible benefits from colonization, such as converting of the natives to Christianity, setting up merchants who were in debtors' prisons because of bankruptcy, and the possibility of luring the large vagrant population of England to the New World to learn more useful trades there. But the 1590s were an inauspicious time to launch a fleet of sailing vessels to America, for the post-Armada period was one of continued Spanish forays on the seas until 1604, when King James concluded peace with Spain.

In the early seventeenth century, with the increased wealth of upper-class Englishmen who were eager to invest their money at a profit, the time was ripe for a more ambitious enterprise. James, perpetually in need of further funds, was persuaded that there was profit to be made in successful trading and importing and that an English settlement in America would enhance England's prestige. On 10 April 1606 he had therefore issued "Articles, Instructions, & Orders for the Government of Virginia" as a royal charter to the newly formed Virginia Company of London, under the treasurership of Sir Thomas Smith. A small group of wealthy and prominent Englishmen had formed this company for the purpose of establishing colonies in the New World and perhaps sending back to England certain desired Virginia products.

The new company soon dispatched to America three ships (the *Susan Constant,* the *Godspeed,* and the *Discovery*) under the command of Captain Christopher Newport. After a four-month voyage, Newport sailed through "Chesapeack" Bay and made the first settlement at "James-town."

The first charter soon proved to be too closely under control of the king and left little opportunity for individual initiative, thus making it hard to interest suitable emigrants. It was obvious that a more liberal charter was needed to draw desirable settlers, facilitate their emigration, and attract more investors. Therefore, in February 1609 a second and more adequate charter was obtained from the king. It had been carefully composed by Sir Edwin Sandys (a leader in the House of Commons), Henry Wriothesley (earl of Southampton), and Sir Francis Bacon (then solicitor-general). This second charter enabled the company to organize as a joint-stock company[3] and obtain more capital. Instead of direct royal control, there was now to be private control under a freer royal charter. Many new investors were attracted: noblemen, important merchants, and a number of the most eminent persons in England. They avidly bought shares of the company's stock, which had been issued at £12 10s per share (perhaps equal to about $1,500 today). Fifty-six London companies and 659 individuals signed this Second Charter on 20 May 1609. One of them was Sir Stephen Powle. These investors who remained in England but provided capital for the joint-stock company were termed "Adventurers"; the other branch of the Company were the "Planters" (soldiers of fortune, tradesmen, and sometimes vagrants or misfits in the community) who purchased one share of stock (or agreed to work off the sum as indentured servants) and signed up to come to the "New World." They had read the company's prospectus as set forth in the 1609 broadside "Nova Britannia" that the Planters

> shall have houses to dwell in with Gardens and Orchards, and also food and clothing at the common charge of the Joint-stock, they shall have their dividend also in all goods and Merchandises arising thence by their labors, and likewise their dividends in Lands to them and their heirs forever. (British Library C.13.e.1[63])*

The broadside had been written by Alderman Johnson, son-in-law of Sir Thomas Smith.

With the 1609 charter, the colonizing and commercial divisions were placed under one company whose full title now became The Treasurer and Company of Adventurers and Planters of the City of London for the First Colony in Virginia. Jurisdiction was under the treasurer and a thirteen-member council, who were to reside in England. Although these officers were nominated by the Crown, the company now had authority to replace

---

*See illustration on page 140.

❧ For the Plantation in Virginia.
Or
Nova Britannia.

Hereas (if God permit,) for the better setling of the Colony and Plantation in Virginia, there is a voyage intended thither by many Noble men, Knights, Marchants, and others, to bee furnished and set forth with all conuenient speed: And for that so Honorable an action pleasing to God, and commodious many waies to this Common-wealth, should be furthered and furnished with al meanes and prouisions necessarie for the same, wherein both Honorable and Worshipfull personages, doe purpose & prepare to goe thither in their owne persons: This is therfore to intimate and giue-notice to al Artificers, Smiths, Carpenters, Coopers, Shipwrights, Turners, Planters, Vineares, Fowlers, Fishermen, Mettell-men of all sorts, Brick-makers, Brick-layers, Plow-men, Weauers, Shoo-makers, Sawyers Spinsters, and all other labouring men and women, that are willing to goe to the said Plantation to inhabite there, that if they repayre into Phillpot Lane, to the house of Sir Thomas Smith, Treasurer for the said Colony, their names shall be Registred, and their persons shall be esteemed at a single share, which is Twelue pound ten shillings, and they shall be admitted to goe as Aduenturers in the said Voyage to Virginia, Where they shall haue houses to dwell in, with Gardens and Orchards, and also foode and clothing at the common charge of the Joynt stocke, they shall haue their Diuident also in all goods and Marchandizes, arising thence by their labours, and likewise their Diuident in Lands to them and to their Heyres for euer: And if they shall also bring in money to Aduenture in the Joynt stock, their shares both in goods and lands shalbe augmented accordingly.

And likewise al other that wil bring in Twenty fiue pound or more by the last of March, though they goe not in their persons shall be accepted for Free-men of the Company, and shall haue their Billes of Aduenture, as all other Aduenturers haue in the same Action.

London
Printed by Iohn Windet. 1609.

1609 Virginia Company broadside entitled "Nova Britannia." C. 18 e.1 tract 63, British Library.

any undesirable ones and to elect their successors. The name of Sir Stephen Powle appears in the second charter as one of "His Majesties Council for Virginia."

Powle and Walter Ralegh had remained on terms of friendship ever since 1574 when they were roommates at the Middle Temple, even though after leaving the Inns of Court they went their separate ways: Powle to government service and the law and Ralegh to the Elizabethan court. Ralegh's eagerness to promote the colonization of Virginia undoubtedly had aroused an eagerness in Powle to join in the 1609 venture. His background in political and legal service (as a government agent in the Rhenish Palatinate and in Italy and then as clerk of the Crown and one of the six clerks in Chancery) had given him experience that would prove useful for his new undertaking with the Virginia Company. Now he would be not only a financial participant but also an administrative one in an advisory capacity.

Powle wrote memoranda (168:iv^r) showing that about this time he also made a monetary contribution to the expedition to Guiana. The Guiana venture was organized quietly and, for fear that the Spanish would get wind of it, was customarily referred to as an expedition "to Virginia." Powle's notes were the following:

> 13 February [1609/10] being Tuesday, Sir Thomas Roe, our commander for the discovery of Guiana and Sir George Brooke (as I heard since) departed toward Dartmouth where our two ships and provisions for two pinnacles more bestowed in them lay at ready for his coming. Partners: The Earl of Southampton £800, Sir Walter Rawley £600, Sir Thomas Smith himself with his partners £1100 and myself £20, which may God bless. The two ships departed from Dartmouth the 24 of February 1609 [in modern dating 1610].

Ralegh, ever since his successful expedition to Guiana in 1595, had been urging further exploration of the area. Although his imprisonment in the Tower of London precluded his joining in person, he contributed the substantial sum of six hundred pounds. His long imprisonment had been due to spurious charges of treason, probably made as a result of Robert Cecil's devious fostering of King James's enmity against Ralegh and abetted by the violent rhetoric of Edward Coke, whose accusations dominated the 1603 trial. Antagonism to Ralegh seemed at this time to be relatively easy to stir up, since his extravagance of manner and dress and his frequent arrogance had made him many enemies.

There had been English enthusiasm for both Guiana and Virginia as promising business enterprises. However, on his return, Sir Thomas Roe reported that El Dorado was a myth and that whatever gold there was needed to be searched for, dug up, and smelted.[4] Nor did immediate bonuses emanate from Virginia. There the colonists endured hardships and reverses for some time, and it was not until well into its second decade that the colony began to prosper.

With the company's second charter it was empowered to allocate land within the area that might be settled. This was specified as extending two hundred miles north and south of Point Comfort (on Chesapeake Bay) and inland "from sea to sea and including all the islands within the coast of either ocean." The 1607 settlement had established itself at James-town, or James-fort, as it was more aptly termed, for it had been fortified with a triangular palisade for protection against the Indians or the Spanish. There were to be direct imports of English commodities, and they were to be stored in "Magazines," from which they could be sold to the planters in Virginia with proceeds remitted to the Adventurers in England. Profit was also anticipated from Virginia's exports. By January 1609 a number of Virginia products, such as timber (for ships' masts), pitch, soap ashes and potash (for making soap and glass), tar, and dyes had already been exported to England; sassafras and further products were to follow (after 1614 tobacco became one of the most lucrative).

With the capital raised at the time of the second charter, an expedition was launched on a grander scale than any of the previous ones. Nine ships set forth under the leadership of Sir Thomas Gates, although Powle reports only eight, since one returned to England almost immediately. Powle's notes of 15 May 1609 describe the departure of this expedition:

> On Monday in the morning our 6 ships lying at Blackwall weighed anchor and fell down to begin their voyage toward Virginia. Sir Thomas Gates being the deputy governor until the Lord Delaware doth come thither which is supposed shall be about two months hence. Captain Newport, Captain Sir George Sommers, and 800 people of all sorts went in these 6 ships besides 2 more that attend the fleet at Plymouth, and there be inhabitants already at Virginia about 160. God bless them and guide them to his glory and our good. Amen. (168:iv^r)

Powle, like many of his countrymen, was a religious Calvinist who turned frequently to prayer—not only in strictly pious moments but also when hoping for an auspicious outcome to a professional suit or a business venture.

This particular voyage, however, was not to be a fortunate one. At the end of November news arrived in London of disaster. When near American shores, the fleet had encountered a tropical hurricane that raged for three days and four nights. The ships were so buffeted by the storm that the flagship *Sea Adventure*, under the captaincy of Christopher Newport, which had on board Sir Thomas Gates and Sir George Somers, the leaders of the expedition, became separated from the rest of the fleet and was wrecked on a reef half a mile from the coast of the Bermudas, although without loss of life, for the men managed to wade ashore with most of the gear from the ship. With the exception of a small pinnace called *The Catch*, which went down with all hands during the storm, the balance of the fleet weathered the rough seas and managed, with difficulty, to reach the settlement at Jamestown.

But these new arrivals and the earlier settlers were without supervision or adequate guidance for some ten months until Gates, Somers, Newport, and their shipmates were able to reach the colony by building two seaworthy ships from cedar wood found on the Bermudas together with timbers and equipment retrieved from the wrecked vessel. Although the Bermudas had always been an area feared and avoided by the seamen of those days—who believed them to be islands of the devil and a prodigious and enchanted area surrounded by gusts, storms, and foul weather—the shipwrecked Englishmen found the area instead to be a real Garden of Paradise, affording them fruits, nuts, and berries, an abundance of edible fish, and fertile soil in which to plant the seeds they had brought from England.

William Strachey, one of the shipwrecked men from the *Sea Adventure*, wrote a long letter to England describing the storm, the shipwreck, and the benevolent lushness of the Bermuda Islands.[5] Shakespeare apparently knew of this letter and of a 1610 published report by Silvester Jourdain titled *A Discovery of the Bermudas, Otherwise called the Isle of the Devils*. They seem to have been sources for *The Tempest*, which is believed to have been written in 1611.

Meanwhile, the leaderless colonists in Virignia had been living in a disorderly and improvident fashion, allowing houses to decay, growing no crops, and consuming the products of former labors. Much of their efforts were spent in fruitless searches for gold and silver. (The popular 1605 play *Eastward Hoe!* by Chapman, Jonson, and Marston had passages extolling the natural and mineral riches to be found in Virginia.) When Deputy Governor Gates and the rest of the men from the *Sea Adventure* finally reached Jamestown, they found the men in a pitiful state, beset with illness and on the verge of starvation.

When London was apprised of the bad news, a dilemma resulted. If the colony were not to be abandoned, more capital had to be obtained immediately, but how? Many of the Adventurers had expected that profits from the first installment could be used to meet the second, and now they were unwilling or unable to pay. To handle this financial emergency, Sir Thomas Smith, as treasurer of the company, managed to borrow funds against the security of the unpaid calls. From money thus raised, the 1610 expedition, under Thomas West, lord DeLaWare, set sail to bring supplies and help to the colony. Powle described the preparations for departure on 6 March 1609/10:

> The Lord DeLaWare took his leave of all the company on Monday at Sir Thomas Smith's in Fillpot Lane, treasurer of the Virginia Company, and on Saturday following departed towards his house in Hampshire from whence he went to meet his ships at Southampton ready furnished with 20 boxes: and plants, seeds, and all other provisions of grain as were to sow and victual 1000 men for one year. He had three ships: one where himself was called the [   ],[6] a flyboat of 1400 tons and a pinnace of 120 tons. His style was Lord Governor and Captain of Virginia. He took shipping for that voyage the [   ] of [   ].[7] God bless his worthy endeavors. (168:iv^v)

Lord DeLaWare's timely arrival was a turning point in the welfare of the colony, not only for the welcome supplies and skilled artisans that he brought but also for the order, resolution, and outward dignity that he restored. Unfortunately, he became ill within the year and had to return to England. He was succeeded by Sir Thomas Dale, who soon realized that much of the sickness that had afflicted the colonists was due to the unhealthiness of the marshy, low-lying area of Jamestown. The solution was to move the main settlement farther up the James River, some twenty-five miles onto higher ground. This decision proved a wise one, and the health of the colonists gradually improved in the new settlement of Henrico, as it was called.

Dale was a harsh disciplinarian who enforced a code of laws termed "Lawes Divine, Morall, and Martiall," but he also brought about some wholesome changes. The earlier communal system of property ownership was replaced by the rewarding of private initiative, with small plots of land granted to deserving settlers.

The Reverend Alexander Whitaker, minister of Henrico, later wrote of the progress that had come about since the providential arrival of Lord DeLaWare:

> Since when the English colony hath taken better root and as a spreading herb whose top hath been often chopped off renews her growth and spreads herself more gloriously than before. . . . Let us be encouraged to try our helping hands to this good work, yea God's work.

This was part of an appeal in behalf of the colony entitled "Good Newes from Virginia, sent to the Council and Company of Virginia resident in England" from Whitaker in 1613.

It had become evident by 1611 that additional capital had to be procured in London—at least thirty thousand pounds would be needed within the next two years. All possible measures were tried: pressure was directed against delinquent shareholders, with less than satisfactory results; the Virginia Company sold its rights in the Bermuda Islands to a subsidiary company for two thousand pounds; and finally, a lottery was proposed.

In March 1612 a third charter was obtained from King James, which gave permission to establish lotteries. At the same time, more specifications were made as to the organization of the London Company and rules were liberalized about the holding of courts in Virginia: there were now to be no restrictions as to the frequency with which they might be held. Thus, a democratic forum for free discussion, although not yet for administration, was made possible.

In London a Great Standing Lottery was established at Saint Paul's Churchyard to raise funds for the colony. Broadsides circulated throughout England, proclaiming the event: tickets were twelve pence each; five thousand pounds in prizes were offered, and the drawing for prizes was to begin 29 June 1612. Although the announcement was met with enthusiasm, far more lottery tickets were issued than could be sold; sixty thousand unpurchased tickets were removed before the final drawing in order to give the public a fairer chance at the prizes. Receivers, auditors, and other officers had been appointed to conduct the lottery in such a way that no one would be defrauded or deceived. Most of the prizes seem to have been in merchandise

A Declaration for the certaine time of drawing the great standing Lottery.

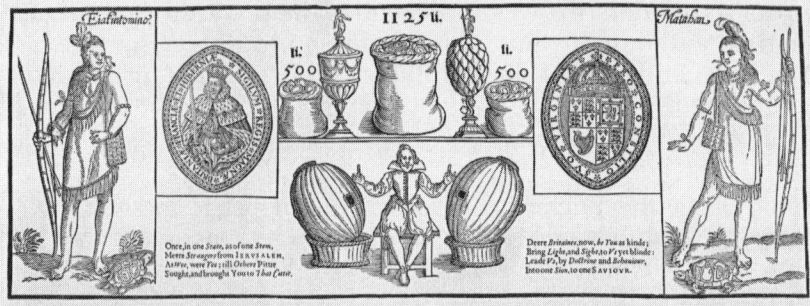

Once in our State, as of one Stem,
Meere Strangers from IERVSALEM,
As We, were Pie; till Others Pitie
Sought, and brought You to That Cittie.

Drere Britaines, now, be You as kinde;
Bring Light, and Sight, to V's ye blinde;
Leade Vs, by Doctrine and Behauiour,
Into one Sion, to one SAVIOVR.

It is apparent to the world, by how many former publications we haue manifested our intents to haue drawen out the great standing Lotterie long before this day: which not falling out as our selues desired, and others expected, whose moneyes are already aduenture'd therein. we thought good therefore for auoiding al vniust and sinister constructions, to resolue the doubts of al indifferent minded, in three speciall points for their better satisfaction.

The first is, for as much as the aduenturers came in so slackly with such poore and barren credits of moneys at the Lottery house for this twelue month past, that without too much preiudice to our selues and the aduenturers in lessening the blankes & prizes. We found no meanes nor ability to proceed in any competent proportion, but of necessity are driuen to the honourable Lords by petition. Without of their Noble care and disposition to further that publike plantation of Virginia, haue recommended their letters to the Counties, Cities and good Townes in England, whom we hope by sending in their voluntarie Aduentures, will sufficiently make that supply of helpe, which otherwise we should not in any reasonable time haue effected.

The second poynt for satisfaction to all honest and well affected minds, is, that not withstanding this our meanes of Lottery answered not our hopes, yet haue we not faded in that Christian care of the Colony in Virginia. to whom we haue lately made two sundry supplies of men and prouisions, where were doubt not but they are all in health and in so good a way with come and cattell to subsist of themselues. That were they now but a while supplied with more hands and materials, we should the sooner resolue vpon a diuision of the Countrey by lot, and so lessen the generall charge, by leauing each seuerall tribe or family to husband and manure his owne.

The third and last is our constant resolution, that seeing our credits are now so farre engaged to the honourable Lords, & to the whole State for the drawing and accomplishment of this great standing Lotterie. Which we intend shall be our last of all standing Lotteries for this plantation, that our time fixed and determined for accomplishing thereof, shall be if God permit, without longer delay, the 26. of June next being in Trinity tearme, desiring all such as haue vndertaken with bookes to solicite their friends, and all such as intend the prosperity of that worthie plantation, that they will not withhold their monies till the last weeke or moneth be expired, lest we be vnwillingly forced to proportion a lesse value and number of our blankes and prizes which hereafter follow.

And whosoever vnder one name or posie shall ad-

VVelcomes.

To him that first shall bee drawne out with a Blanke	100. Crownes.
To the second	50. Crownes.
To the third	25. Crownes.
To him that euery day during the drawing of this Lottery shall bee first drawne out with a Blanke	10. Crownes.

Prizes.

1.	Great Prize, each of	4500 Crownes
2.	Great Prizes, each of	2000. Crownes.
4.	Great Prizes, each of	1000. Crownes.
6.	Great Prizes, each of	500. Crownes.
10.	Prizes each of	100. Crownes.
20.	Prizes, each of	200. Crownes.
100.	Prizes, each of	100. Crownes.
100.	Prizes, each of	50. Crownes.
400.	Prizes, each of	20. Crownes.
1000.	Prizes, each of	10. Crownes.
1000.	Prizes, each of	8. Crownes.
1000.	Prizes, each of	6. Crownes.
4000.	Prizes, each of	4. Crownes.
1000.	Prizes, each of	3. Crownes.
1000.	Prizes, each of	2. Crownes.

Rewards.

To him that shall bee last drawne out with a Blanke	25. Crownes.
To him that putteth in the greatest number of Lots vnder one name or Posie	400. Crownes.
To him that putteth in the second greatest number	300. Crownes.
To him that putteth in the third greatest number	200. Crownes.
To him that putteth in the fourth greatest number	100. Crownes.

If diuers bee of equall number, then these Rewards are to be diuided proportionally.

Addition of new Rewards.

The Blanke that shall bee drawne out next before the Greatest Prize, shall haue	25. Crownes.
The Blanke that shall be drawne out next after the said Great Prize, shall haue	25. Crownes.
The Blanke that shall be drawne out immediately before the 2. next Greatest Prizes, shall haue each of them	10. Crownes.
The seuerall Blankes next after them shall haue also each of them	10. Crownes.
The seuerall Blankes next before the foure Great Prizes, shall haue each of them	15. Crownes.
The seuerall Blankes next after them shall haue also each of them	15. Crownes.
The seuerall Blankes next before the six Great Prizes, shall haue each of them	10. Crownes.
The seuerall Blankes next after them shall haue also each of them	10. Crownes.

uenture twelue pounds ten shillings or vpwards. if he please to leaue & remit his Prizes and Rewards, bee they more or lesse, the Lottery being drawne out, hee shall haue a bill of Aduenture to Virginia, for the like sum he aduenture'd, & shall be free of that Company, & haue his part in Lands, & all other profits hereafter arising thence, according to his aduenture of twelue pounds ten shillings, or vpwards.

Whosoeuer is besides with the payment of any sum of money, promised heretofore to be aduentured to Virginia, if hee aduenture in this Lotterie the double of that sum, & make payment thereof in ready money to Sir Thomas Smith Knight, Treasurer for Virginia, he shall be discharged of the foresaid summe he promised to haue been aduentured to Virginia, and of all actions and damages therefrom arising, and haue also the benefit of all Prizes and Rewards whatsoeuer in this Lottery, for the like sum which he shall bring in, and yet notwithstanding, if after the Lottery drawne, he list to remit al his said prizes and Rewards, he shall haue a bill of aduenture to Virginia for the said entire summe according to the last preceding Article.

And if vpon too much delay of the Aduenturers to furnish this Lottery. We bee driuen to draw the same before it be full, the purpose to shorten both blanks and Prizes in an equall proportion, according to that wherein wee shall come short, bee it more or lesse, that neither the Aduenturers may bee defrauded, nor our selues, as in the former, any way wronged.

The Prizes, Welcomes, & Rewards shall be paid in ready Money, Plate or other goods reasonably rated. If any dislike of the said Plate or other goods, he shall haue ready money for the same, abating onely a tenth part. Except in small prizes of tenne Crownes or vnder, wherein nothing shall be abated them.

The money for Aduentures is to be paid to Sir Thomas Smith Knight, Treasurer for Virginia, at his house in Philpot lane: or to such officers as shall be appointed to attend for that purpose at the Lottery house: or to such other as shall subscribe, for the ease of the Countrey be authorised, vnder the Seale of the Company, for receipt thereof.

The Prizes, Welcomes & Rewards being drawne, they shall be paid by the Treasurer for Virginia, without delay, whensoeuer they shall be demanded.

And for the better expedition to make out sum compleat, as well to hasten the drawing of our Lottery, as chiefly to inable vs the sooner to make good supplies to the Colonie in Virginia: Whosoeuer vnder one name or posie shall bring in ready money three pounds, either to the Lottery house, or to any Colleonor, the same party receiuing their money, for euery three pounds so receiued shall render them presently a siluer spoone of 6. shillings 8. pence price, or 6. shillings 8. pence in money.

Imprinted at London by *Felix Kyngston*, for *William Welby*, the 22. of Februarie. 1615.

rather than in cash. Thomas Sharplisse, a London tailor, drew the first prize of four thousand crowns "in fayre plate."

Between 1606 and 1613, the company had spent £36,624 in establishing the colony. In 1613 a trial shipment of tobacco was sent to England. John Rolfe had procured seed of the sweet-smoking West Indian tobacco and had grown and cured it successfully. It took readily to the Virginian soil and was much more to Englishmen's taste than the native weed grown by the Indians. Although the smoking of tobacco was frowned on by King James, the colonists realized that it could be a lucrative crop for Virginia and it was soon widely cultivated. In 1604 James had written a diatribe against the weed, titling it *A Counterblaste to Tobacco*, but later he was not above accepting the revenue it produced.

There were still to be financial problems with the London investors, for out of a membership of nearly one thousand Adventurers, more than half had long considered the project unachievable and had failed to pay the full amount of their shares. Between 1614 and 1616 many had abandoned the enterprise, leaving it to a small group of determined believers to support it. One of the steadfast group was Sir Stephen Powle, who continued to serve on the council and to contribute financially by buying additional shares. He contributed at least £187 10s[8] and perhaps more of which there is no longer an extant record.

From about 1614 the company had been gradually allowing settlers the opportunity of working their own land rather than having to produce for the public stock. With this incentive, there was more enthusiasm for hard work. In 1616 a division of land was made with fifty acres available for each share of stock owned and an additional fifty acres to be granted as soon as the company had expanded its area of settlement. Each grant could be further increased according to the number of persons transported to it. This land dividend was an important return on a shareholder's investment, for, according to William Robert Scott's *The Constitution and Finance of English, Scottish, & Irish Joint-Stock Companies to 1720*,[9] on the basis of the par value of the shares, the cost to the shareholder was only 2½ to 5 shillings per acre. With the introduction of extensive private land ownership, conditions in the colony improved, for now individual owners took over responsibility for their estates. Whether or not Powle received any grants of land in Virginia is not known, for few records of this period are extant.

Tobacco was being widely planted. It had proved so profitable that it had become the colony's chief crop. By 1617, twenty thousand pounds were exported from Virginia and this amount doubled the following year.

By the beginning of 1619 most of the early problems had been overcome, and the Virginia Company was at last on the verge of success; the colony now produced a trade estimated at almost a hundred thousand pounds annually. In a letter of John Rolfe's to London, he wrote that 1619 had been the colonists' most plentiful year. The next couple of years saw continued growth in the settlement. But, as progress was made, internal struggles developed for control of the company. Serious dissensions and Sir Thomas Smith's illness brought about his retirement as treasurer and the rise of Sir Edwin Sandys, a strong parliamentarian and an inspiring speaker who, unlike Smith, was strongly opposed to King James's efforts to dominate the colony. Early in 1619 Sandys presented to the company the outline of a new and far more liberal charter, usually referred to as The Great Charter. It provided the basis for a less authoritarian, more representative form of government in the colony. On 30 July 1619 the first American legislative assembly met in the little church at Jamestown. Popularly elected burgesses gathered there with the governor and council of the colony, and on the first of August gave their approval to The Great Charter.

Meanwhile in London, the company wrestled with the problem of finances. It continued to hold successful lotteries: prizes were given and a substantial profit was made for the company. However, in mid-1619 tradesmen began complaining that the excitement generated by the lotteries was a deterrent to business and industry. As a result, on 8 March 1621 the king issued a proclamation ending the lotteries, and on 21 March they were officially suspended by order of the Privy Council, thus depriving the Virginia Company of a major source of income. Fortunately, by this time twenty-nine thousand pounds had been raised to finance further supplies and recruits for Virginia.

The company now turned its attention to encouraging families to emigrate to the colony, preferably honest laborers with wives and children. Since there had been a dearth of women in the settlement, in 1620 the company sent over ninety "young maids to be wives." Each young woman's passage was to be paid by the colonist who subsequently married her. The experiment was continued for some years, and it helped to strengthen the fiber of the colony, as did the emigration of families.

But Sandys, feeling that still more workers were needed to plant adequate crops and help with the lucrative cultivation of tobacco, urged more settlers to come to Virginia. However, the sudden increase in would-be colonists proved more of a detriment than an aid, for there were not yet adequate facilities to receive them. There was insufficient housing, and what existed was poorly built and of a temporary nature, nor were there enough food supplies for the new arrivals. Nevertheless, large numbers of would-be settlers were crowded onto boats that were scantily equipped with food and supplies. When the passengers arrived after their lengthy journey most were weak, ill, and inadequately nourished. Thus, instead of providing a boost for the colony, they became an added drain on it. To make matters worse, the healthier settlers were quickly acquired as servants by the few wealthy landowners who needed them to cultivate their own tobacco fields.[10] Because of the quick monetary return from the raising and shipping of tobacco, the planting of corn and essential food staples tended to be neglected.

But Sandys had many ambitious plans for the colony, including diversification of products and industries and even the founding of a college, and he was not easily discouraged. He was confident that the colony could soon be put on a firm financial footing so that funds would not have to be continually drawn from the now nearly depleted company treasury.

But on Good Friday morning, 22 March 1622, came a shattering blow: a ferocious massacre under the leadership of Powhatan's brother, the treacherous Indian chieftain Opechancanough. A period of peace between the Indians and the settlers had existed during the last years of Powhatan's reign, after the 1614 marriage of his daughter, the Indian princess Pocahontas, to John Rolfe. But Powhatan died in 1618, and thereafter his vindictive brother awaited an opportune time to try to drive the English out of the land. Fortunately, Jamestown had been forewarned by a friendly Indian youth and was armed. But elsewhere, for 140 miles on both sides of the James River, 347 persons of all ages were slaughtered by tomahawk, club, and scalping knife. Plantations and a new iron foundry at Falling Creek were wiped out; there was devastation everywhere. When the English recovered, they reacted with vengeance. Indians in turn were ruthlessly slain; their villages and corn were burned to the ground.

Great as was the loss of life in the massacre, far more settlers lost their lives from ensuing epidemics and other disease. George Sandys, brother of Sir Edwin, estimated that during 1622–23, five hundred to six hundred colonists succumbed to sickness. There were deaths from typhus, typhoid, cholera, and dysentery, and some from malaria. Infection was frequently brought from England, and it spread rapidly on the crowded sailing ships. There was also unhealthy overcrowding in the colony's reed huts. In fact, according to Wyndham Blanton's *Medicine in Virginia in the Seventeenth Century*,[11] the mortality figures for the entire period from 1607 through 1624 were staggering. In February 1625, only 1,095 settlers were alive in Virginia of the 7,549 who had come to the colony, that is, not many more than one in six survived.

A new financial threat arose over the tobacco contract. King James now insisted that all tobacco come first to English ports, where customs duties could be levied on it, and these taxes recently had been raised considerably. By now, the tobacco trade was the main source of the colonists' revenue; sixty thousand pounds had been exported in 1622, despite the massacre. Tobacco had proved to be Virginia's most valuable product because of the ready market for it in England and Holland. In the 1609 second charter, King James had exempted the London Company "from all taxes and impositions forever upon any goods or merchandise . . . either upon importation to Virginia or exportation thence into our realm of England . . . except only the five pound per *centum* [five pounds per hundred pounds] for custom . . . according to the ancient trade of merchants." This charter was replaced by that of 1612, in which the tax exemption was granted for only another seven years, thus expiring in 1619. Now in 1622 large custom duties were being imposed on tobacco, and the king insisted that taxes first be paid at an English port before the tobacco could be shipped elsewhere.

A struggle to prevent such restrictions was led by Sir Edwin Sandys, Henry Wriothesley, the earl of Southampton, Nicholas Ferrar, Jr., and their followers, who were supported by the colonists and were known as the Patriots' Party. They were opposed within the company by Alderman Johnson, Sir Thomas Smith, Nathaniel Rich and Robert Rich (earl of Warwick) whose faction was called the Court Party. The Court Party members were bitterly opposed to Sir Edwin Sandys's leadership because of personal grudges against him and because of his economic policies that they felt had been unsuccessful and were causing the bankruptcy of the company.

King James had been irritated by the displacement of Thomas Smith and the rise of Sandys, for he feared that with this change of treasurership he might lose control of the colony. He named several men of the Court Party who would be acceptable to him as treasurer but was violently opposed to Sandys, who had so frequently attempted to thwart him in Parliament. Although the colonists, who by now had some voice in their own affairs, refused to choose anyone on the king's list, they made the concession of selecting Southampton rather than Sandys as treasurer. However, the original governing council of thirteen members had grown in size to unwieldy numbers, and the company was now so split by factionalism that it could no longer function in a unified way.

By 1623 the king, whose hope for a quick financial profit from the colony had proved unrealistic and whose distrust of democratic institutions had probably been increased by the wily Spanish minister, the conde de Gondomar, was incensed and requested the London Company to surrender its charter. When they refused to do so, the king demanded that all records of the company and its operations immediately be turned over to the Crown to ascertain whether it was being properly run. Detailed, carefully kept records were reluctantly surrendered to him.

Questioning the right of the company to have jurisdiction, a legal order of *quo warranto*[12] was issued by Sir James Ley, lord chief justice of the king's bench. The legal arguments used by the chief justice were that the company's charter was in general an unlimited vast patent. In particular, the company had been given a power to transport to Virginia as many of the king's loving subjects as were desirous to go there; consequently, by exercising this liberty they might eventually carry away all the king's subjects into a foreign land. Alexander Brown, proposing political reasons for the dissolution, suggested that perhaps the Crown foresaw that the colony could become a place of refuge from royal tyranny and would finally shake off the yoke of the mother country.[13] Wesley Frank Craven demurred with this view and believed that the decision to dissolve the company was purely an economic one: the London Company was near bankruptcy and was being torn apart by internal squabbles; the colony itself was in a desperate economic condition; and the Crown, in trying to protect the colony from being burdened with the company's debts, decided that the current charter should be abrogated and a new one instituted.[14] Probably, as Thomas Wertenbaker concluded,[15] both these motives played a part in James's decision.

It seems likely that in bringing matters to his attention, the Court Party had hoped to oust Sir Edwin Sandys and continue the company under other leadership, for they were well aware of the king's dislike of Sandys. Instead of this happening, the outcome was the official dissolution of the Virginia Company and the designation of Virginia as a royal colony. On 27 March 1625, King James died suddenly and his successor, Charles I, who had been more favorably disposed toward the company, promised to grant a new charter, but this never materialized. Fortunately, however, by this time the colony, under its general assembly and burgesses, was strong enough to survive without dependence on England and ultimately was relieved to find that, contrary to expectations, there was less jurisdiction by the Crown than there had been by the very paternal company.

It is difficult to get a clear picture of the company's final years because of the internal factionalism, with its charges and countercharges between the Patriots' Party and the Court Party, and because the company records turned over to the Crown subsequently disappeared. They were either lost or destroyed. Susan Myra Kingsbury, who edited the Library of Congress manuscript and painstakingly gathered materials for four folio volumes of extant Virginia Company records, observes that it is generally believed that most of the company records were deliberately destroyed by the Crown, that James wished to destroy evidence of inefficiency during the martial government of the first decade and evidence of the comparatively prosperous condition of the liberalized second decade. The king's position was that conditions in the colony would have been better had the original system of government by a council of thirteen in England and an absolute governor in Virginia been continued instead of the later popular government, with so many voices. However, Kingsbury believes that it is conceivable that the lost records may still turn up.[16]

Because Nicholas Ferrar, deputy treasurer of the company, foresaw the possibility that the company's records might be destroyed by the Crown (on 9 January 1622 James had deliberately torn out of the Commons Journal the page on which was written the important protest of the Commons that they had and by right ought to have freedom of speech),[17] Ferrar and the company auditor, Sir John Danvers, quickly managed to have copies made privately of the voluminous records.[18] The copies were given to the earl of Southampton, last treasurer of the company, for safekeeping. When the king learned of these copies, he demanded that Southampton turn them over to him, but the earl refused, saying that he would as soon part with his life as with the records of his honor. The earl died of a fever in the Netherlands later in 1624, but the records were supposedly preserved by his family.

However, most of those prior to 1619 disappeared; the remaining documents (acts of the general courts from 8 May 1619 to 17 June 1624) were later acquired by Thomas Jefferson and were bequeathed to the Library of Congress after his death.

When one seeks a fair evaluation of the latter half of the Virginia Company's existence (from 1616 until its demise in 1624), one is puzzled by two conflicting versions. The view had been held for many years that with the retirement or possible dislodging of Sir Thomas Smith, the company became more and more disorganized and ceased to function in a businesslike manner. This may, however, have been a view fostered by the Crown. It is echoed in the *Generall Historie of Virginia, New England and the Summer Isles*, written by Captain John Smith in 1624. John Smith resided in the colony for a year and a half from 1609 to mid-1610 as a vigorous but at times questionable governor. In 1610 he was removed from the office and sent back to England by the company. His lengthy history glorifies him and his exploits and manages to echo many of James's sentiments, for it was published under the auspices of the Crown. Since there is a paucity of early historical sources for Virginia, its considerable detail would be of great value had its author been more objective. Unfortunately, it has been shown to contain a number of factual errors.[19]

The notion of a deteriorated colony after Thomas Smith retired is strongly refuted in an interesting and impassioned document drawn up by Sandys and Ferrar and titled "A Discourse of the Old Company."[20] It was written in 1625 between mid-April and mid-May in answer to the Privy Council's request for suggestions as to how the colony should then be governed. It gives a brief history of the settlement, showing that at the end of twelve years (in 1618) a rule of harsh martial law was changed to one of justice, including land ownership by the settlers and an assurance of individual liberty.

The "Discourse" asserts that thenceforth the colony began to flourish. In 1621 "three hundred French and Dutch families made request to the state in that year that they might plant in Virginia whither not long before, condemned persons had refused to go even with pardon of their lives." Despite calamities such as widespread disease, a massacre by Indians, difficulties with the tobacco contract, and struggles with a malicious faction within the company, "the plantation had managed to prosper beyond belief and almost miraculously."[21] It was obvious that what was best for the colony was the maintaining of rights for the individual and a voice in the settlement's affairs. In the words of the "Discourse" the colonists "had grown into an opinion that they were the happiest people in the world, . . . the old Adventurers renewed their zeal, and great numbers of new ones came daily to contribute large sums." Although the language of the "Discourse" sounds a bit overblown, the facts are probably essentially true, for we do know that after the dissolution, the colony was healthy enough to survive on its own, and it seems likely that original Virginia Company records disappeared because they gave evidence of conditions to which the Crown was unwilling to admit.

According to Scott's work on joint-stock companies, surprisingly little money had been spent to establish the colony: less than £46,000 in Smith's time and less than £16,000 thereafter. But, despite the great strides that the Virginia Company had made after so many years of struggle and discouragement, it was not to enjoy the fruits of its labors. King James's arbitrary interference had brought about the disintegration of the company and the loss of its more than £100,000 of stock. Nevertheless, its members had the satisfaction of knowing that the young colony it had so long tended and believed in was at last on a firm footing. In addition, the company had left an important legacy: the form of popular government that had been introduced under Sandys[22] during the company's last five years.[23]

One would like to know what Sir Stephen Powle thought of these final years, for he was still listed as an adventurer at the time of the company's demise in May of 1624. Powle was a very circumspect gentleman and the only inkling of his feelings comes from the inclusion of copies of three letters near the end of his Commonplace Book. These suggest that later in life he pondered on the misused power of a king.

One of the last entries in Tanner manuscript 169 was made in the late 1620s, after the accession of Charles I. On folios 201r–5r are translations of three lengthy French letters written between Pierre Du Moulin (1568–1658) and Jean Louis Guez de Balzac (ca. 1597–1654).

Moulin was a French Protestant divine who had come to England to assist King James with his *Regis Declaratio pro Jure Regio*, which was an answer to a speech made by Cardinal Perron. James's work was translated into French by Moulin and published in 1615. Moulin was rewarded with a benefice in Wales, a doctor of divinity degree from Cambridge, and a prebend at Canterbury. From 1620 to 1628 he was back in France as professor of theology at Sedan.

Balzac was a noted writer of flowing French prose who was one of the original members of the Académie Française. He became disillusioned with the French court and, while still young, went into retirement, where he continued his writing and kept up an active correspondence with his friends.

The first of the three letters is from Moulin, thanking Balzac for the manuscript of his book *Le Prince*, subsequently published in 1631, which was a political analysis written in two parts: the first dealt in general with kings and rulers and the second praised the current French king, Louis XIII. *Le Prince* is the point of departure for the subjects that are discussed in the letters: the qualities of a just ruler and the question of whether fealty is owed to an unjust or tyrannical sovereign. Moulin's strongly expressed view, which is at odds with that of Balzac, is that one must live in a state of law even if the laws are bad ones, for a state of anarchy is insufferable.

Courteously differing from Moulin, who was many years his senior, Balzac writes, "Were I a Swiss . . . I would by no means change my liberty for the best Master in the world but since God has caused me to be born in chains, I will carry them cheerfully, and being neither cumbersome nor heavy, I will not hurt my teeth trying to bite them asunder." He is grateful that the rule of Louis XIII has been a mild one: "Our King will not put a yoke on the consciences of his subjects. Nor does he desire to receive by force that which cannot be obtained by persuasion." Balzac says of Moulin that "Never man knew the art . . . of supporting ruin with greater strength," but Balzac realizes that "it is most dangerous to go about to change evil things." However, he seems to be implying that were he given enough provocation, he might well incur the danger.

The last of the three letters is from Moulin and includes the following vehement statements:

> I am of this opinion that in civil causes it is more expedient for a people to have an evil Master than none at all.
>
> Peace and prosperity will always be found more stern and durable in a Monarchy than in any other State.

An English translation of these letters was first published in 1636 by A. S. (Gent.). I have found that it varies in numerous small respects from that given in Powle's papers. The reasonable conclusion is that the Commonplace Book translation was made by Powle himself a few years before his death in 1630, when he was about seventy-five. We know that he had an excellent knowledge of French, Italian, and Latin.

I believe that Powle's interest in this correspondence might well have stemmed from his musings on the high-handed way in which King James had dissolved the Virginia Company and perhaps on King Charles's subsequent autocratic rule over England.

One does not know whether Powle agreed with either of the Frenchmen's views, for the Tanner manuscripts give no positive answer. Stephen Powle was an altruistic and thoughtful man who believed firmly in the importance of establishing a thriving English colony in America. He was also a prudent man who had faithfully served two monarchs, Elizabeth and James, and although his notes show that he sometimes disapproved of the acts of others at court, his loyalty to the monarch seemed never to waver. However, the fact that he felt the two Frenchmen's controversial letters worth translating and keeping suggests that in later years Powle, like others of his countrymen, had begun to question royal prerogative.

15
Later Years at Smyths-hall and Mylend

Despite Powle's involvement with the Virginia Company and his various official duties, he was keeping up with family obligations and his usual busy life at Smyths-hall. There is a letter of 23 November 1611 to Powle's niece, the Lady Mansell, in which he referred to the recent sickness and recovery of his nephew Rawleigh Bussy, whom he termed his heir. Powle sent his "kind commendations" to him, his mother, his sister Mary, and to "little Kate," who presumably was Rawleigh's daughter (169:89v). He had married Cecily Mansell, the daughter of Anthony Mansell of Llanthrithen, a brother of Thomas Mansell III.

In February 1613/14 Powle wrote from Blackmore to his "dear cousin Master Lassells, esquire of De Thorpe" telling of his wife Margareta's slow recovery from a long and lingering illness: "a fervent fit of double quatern ague," which together with "occasions of the King's service" had kept Powle at Smyths-hall. He was hoping, however, soon to be able to return to the peace and quiet of Mylend, although, since his wife as yet neither ate nor slept properly, there was still fear that she might develop consumption (169:146r). Apparently, Margareta Powle recovered in due course, for there are no further references to her illness.

Among other memoranda of this period are various "medical" prescriptions for Powle from Sir Walter Ralegh. Some relate to urinary problems and others concern difficulties with the eyes. Lady Ralegh, too, seems to have been on terms of intimacy with the Powle family, for Powle mentions a New Year's gift from her to Powle's sister Dutton in January 1612/13 (169:140r).

Several items among Powle's notes at this time deal with land transactions he had made. Typical are the following: in March 1613/14 a seven-year mortgage that he held was extended by him for seven years more, until Michaelmas 1620 (169:139r); during 1614 Powle and Walter James sold to Thomas Lord Darcie a large tract of land "well over a thousand acres," including the manors of Beaumont, Oldhall, and Newhall in Essex, together with various other manors and parks.[1]

On 8 June 1614 Powle wrote to his nephew Rawleigh Bussy bemoaning the fact that, except for "good sister Powle" (presumably his middle brother's widow) and his own sister Dutton, who lived in Bucks County, Powle had "neither kindred nor alliance" living near him now that Rawleigh and his "brood" and his mother, Jane, were living in the "remote country and mountains of Wales." However, Powle was delighted to hear of Rawleigh's recovery from illness and hoped that the young man would soon get to London so that they could see more of each other (169:141r).

Among other communications of this period is a medical prescription dated 27 August 1614, from Sir Walter Ralegh, which purports to be helpful "for the preservation of the sight" (169:142r). A 1616 letter reveals that Powle had been having trouble with his vision (169:147r); this is further confirmed by Powle's handwriting, which had become larger and more irregular in conformation. Another "medicine" for the eyes follows, as does one for the toothache.

Earlier that year Powle had written a love letter for his servant Dick Hoskyn, who was enamored of Kesie Franke, daughter of Powle's tenant at Mylend, Dr. Franke (169:142r). By this time Powle must have been quite adept at this literary form, since he had previously written such letters for James Butts (169:46r, 53r, 54r) and at least one for John Smith, Powle's stepson (309:46r).

On 169:177r, next to the date 1 December 1617, is found the sad note: "My good sister Dutton[2] died Sunday morning about one of the clock after midnight . . . at Master Revell's house in Fleetstreet, London." There follows a letter dated the same day to Master Francis Mansell, brother-in-law of sister Dutton's daughter, Lady Jane Mansell. In it Powle expressed his acute grief at the departure of his "most dearly, dearly, dearly beloved sister." Powle had been "struck dumb with sorrow," and he referred to his sister's "shutting up her godly life with a saintlike death." A second letter to Francis Mansell follows, dated 2 December 1617, in which Powle suggested that if his sister Dutton had made no will, it would be wise to take an inventory of the goods found in her trunks, for if they were of any great value, it was likely that they were left in her custody in trust.

On 21 December Powle wrote a letter "to the right worshipful and virtuous Lady Savage," "sent to her by her nurse." It shows his skill and integrity in handling a delicate situation:

Honorable Lady   I am very sorry that my good Sister Dutton's death is the cause of your perplexed discontent at this time and so much the rather for that as I have heard her say, and I assure myself thereof, that you (reposing confident trust in her) had left in her custody of your jewels, plate and money amounting to a great value. I was long before and at the time she died at my house in Essex. And I hear it is given out that she never mentioned either by message to me, or by word of mouth to others about her anything of the great trust you reposed in her concerning that business; which I hardly believe because I have known her these 40 years to have had a tender heart and scrupulous conscience; and therefore I will never be persuaded that she did dispose of that great mass of wealth found in her trunks (being none of hers) to any, but to will it to be directed and delivered to you to whom (in my opinion) it did of right belong. Because Sir John Savage, your worthy husband, (as I heard her say) had given you these parcels of plate and jewels belonging to your chamber and person in the nature of Paraphernalia (as the Civilians[3] used to call them) to make show of the due belonging to a Lady of your birth and worth and that money you had he gave you leave to take (if [he] died before you) to uphold your estate with and your daughter and her children whom Sir John so entirely loved.

This much I thought meet to testify (under my hand) to acquaint you with the uttermost of my knowledge hereof and withall to comfort you: that God will never suffer any to wrest these your jewels, plate, and money so injuriously from you. For I know that if Sir Thomas [Mansell] or my niece be possessors of them, both of them be good Christians, honorably minded and of upright conscience. I commend my service to your good Ladyship and commit you to his protection who is best able to relieve and preserve you.

Smithshall this 21. of December 1617

> Your Ladyship's poor friend to be commanded,
> St: Powle

(169:177v)

By the same messenger Powle sent a letter to his niece, Lady Jane Mansell, which stated that her husband's brother, Francis Mansell, and her servant, John Rowe, had already apprised her of Powle's grief at the death of her worthy, saintlike mother and he was therefore the more bold

> to press you with the true consideration of her estate left behind her which could not be of any value and much less so great as the now found mass of much wealth found in her trunks [of] £ 200 amount. She acquainted me with the trust and confidence the Lady Savage (her Cousin) did repose in her, and of certain jewels, plate and money

she left in her custody.... The jewels and plate she said Sir John had given her as things belonging to her chamber and person being a provident Lady and of good birth and worth.... The money, she said, he gave her leave to retain (for he thought her to be well moneyed) for the upholding her estate with her daughter and grandchildren, if he died before her. Now (my dear Niece), the distressed Lady is informed that this her estate is sent down into Wales and therefore she importuned me to acquaint you with the true circumstances of this her most important business, which I have accordingly done. And therefore assuring myself of your conscionable and Christian mind (who know my sister's, your mother's, estate to have been but mean) I do not doubt but that you will farther her to her right by causing these her goods, if they be carried into Wales, to be restored to her. This with my best and most hearty commendations to your best beloved self, Sir Thomas Mansell, my nephew Rawleigh and all yours, I commit you to his protection who is best able to preserve you.

Smithshall. 21 Dec. 1617

Your Loving Uncle to be Commanded,
S Powle

(169:177v–178r)

Apparently, Lady Savage's property was returned to her, for no more is heard about it. But Powle's niece shortly wrote him "a very passionate letter grieving that no one grieved with her," assuming that he was busied about nothing but his estate and was free from all outside concerns. This caused him to write her a lightly scolding reply, pointing out that although it was natural for creatures to touch their own wounds tenderly and to feel their own pains or discomforts with intense anguish and sorrow, it was wrong to assume that others had no griefs or worries. He assured her that despite the suit by Master Only, the legalities of her Lincolnshire lands[4] (about which she was so unnecessarily perturbed) were in good order. Touching himself, he protested that

> although I have (I thank the Almighty for it) a convenient estate, money, plate and other necessaries to advance my reputation, and friends (according to the account of the world) many, yet I have sundry secret gripings at my heart which I hold not wisdom to discover to any, for we live not now in an age of commiseration. And therefore I repute it discretion, safety and a mean to uphold estimation in the world to turn the red side of the apple outward and the

white side of the plaice.[5] And for this cause, I desire . . . to live a retired, private, contemplative life, setting behind me all those gorgeous glitterings and to be seated far from the eye of the envious or the malice of the wicked. . . . I speak little in company and write less to my absent friends whereof you taxed me in your last letter. But I would not give my private meditations on this subject for all the kingdoms of the earth. It may perchance comfort you to see others bleeding with the like wounds that you do, for I constantly affirm that there is nothing in this life but thorny cares, corrosive crosses and hateful unkindnesses which like hot burning fevers consume the very marrow of the mind . . . yet nevertheless I wish you long to enjoy the benefit of life, for I know it is desired of all other creatures to have a lasting continuance. But, for my part, I hold that life happiest that is the shortest. . . .

By reason of the Term's business, having no more leisure to prosecute this invective position further, I here end with my dearest commendation to your best self and good Sir Thomas Mansell. (169:65r&v)

Powle was busy with his work on the council of the Virginia Company and as justice of the peace in Essex and perhaps in other legal capacities. At Exeter College, Oxford, there is a three-page tract completed on 26 February 1617/18, titled "A problematical discourse of the Judges' Robes and Habits begun long since by Sir Steven Powell knight and lately perfected."[6] In it, Powle explained the reasons for the shapes and colors of the caps, gowns, and coifs that judges wore and why they sat on the highest parts of their seats. The reason given for the latter was "to resemble . . . the great judge of the whole world . . . sitting on the imperial ark of God's throne, the rainbow." The reasons for the various articles of attire were also emblematic. For instance, judges' caps were square to remind them that they should be quadrate men imbued with the four cardinal virtues: justice, prudence, temperance, and fortitude.

In addition to his legal work, Powle spent time caring for his estates in Blackmore and Mylend, and he also bore some responsibility for his eldest stepson's estate in Wakes Colne, Essex, for there is an Essex quarter sessions record for Epiphany 1615/16 as follows:

"Chappell Bridge" in the highway in Chapel, over the river flowing from Earls Colne towards Colchester, before and since 25 June, is ruinous and broken so that horses and carts cannot cross without great danger, and Stephen Powle of Blackmore. gent. in the right of Margt. his wife, and John Smyth of Wakes Colne, gent. by reason of

his tenure of his manor of "Creppinge *alias* Creppinge hall" in Wakes Colne and Chapel ought to repair it.
Jury panel for the body of the County brought indictment for the above. (Q/SR 212/50)

In Michaelmas 1617 the bridge had still not been repaired (Q/SR 219/33), as Powle had evidently argued that the faulty bridge should be repaired by the men who constructed it. There is another quarter sessions record shortly thereafter, stating that the charge was respited. It could not be ascertained who had built the defective bridge, but Sir Stephen Powle had agreed to repair it (Q/SR 224/24).

There is a letter to Powle dated 20 August 1618 from his physician Thomas Lodge (169:191r). Powle had possibly met Lodge in the early 1590s when he frequented the King's Head Tavern on Chancery Lane,[7] a few doors away from Powle's home. The author, playwright, and future physician shortly thereafter found it wise to leave England because of increasing debts. While in France he studied medicine at Avignon and became a qualified physician. In 1602, on his return to England at the age of forty-four, he was granted a doctor of medicine degree from Oxford. By 1609 he had become one of London's six most prominent doctors.[8]

In 1618 Powle complained to him of obscurity and dullness of the eyes and of obesity. Lodge prescribed for both. He conjectured that the weakness of Powle's eyesight was the result of "untimely study after meat" and "feebleness of the visive spirits." To remedy this infirmity he recommended a well-ordered diet, moderate dry air, moderate sleep (but not during the daytime), "keeping the body soluble, feeding on light meats and those easy to digest and such as to attenuate and moisten, and abstaining from wine." He suggested that, if the stomach was weak, a little Mathiolus Cinammon Water would be helpful, as would rubbing the legs and thighs frequently, and not reading or writing immediately after dining. He cautioned that "wrath, cares, vehement perturbations and fears are dangerous, especially after eating." As for therapy he wrote:

> since I know your nature alienated from them, I dare not enjoin you to phlebotomy, purges, sternutations,[9] and such like though the method of Physic requireth the same, only this as an easy and facile medicine you may use:
> Take eyebright, fennell, and calandine; boil them with a red cock in

fennel water adding a whole mace or two and take that broth in the morning and evening.

For a local medicine to put into the eyes mornings and evenings he advised:

> While the fennell riseth into a stalk, cut off the head; in the hollowness thereof put sugar candy till it be filled. Leave it till it fall into a liquor. Put this moisture into your eyes mornings and evenings and let the event praise itself.

The other "accident" Powle complained of was "fatness." This, Lodge explained, was either natural or accidental. The natural, which he conjectured was Powle's type, might be somewhat eased but not eradicated. To ease it, one must abstain from much sleep or too much sitting. For, as Aristotle said, "sedile facit pinguedem" ("a seat makes fatness"). If one ingests fat and well-fed meats, this furthers the evil. Appolonius, the son of Hierophilus, fattened those who were lean by the use of salty things. Therefore, the opposite should help to reduce fatness. Exercising and purging once a week were two excellent remedies.

Lodge had urged Powle to lease his house at Mylend to a Master le Groate,[10] had "remembered" Powle to "his Lord" (perhaps Sir Thomas Edmondes, ambassador at Paris), and was eager to do Powle any office he could. The letter (169:191) was signed

> Your worship's unfeigned
> Thomas Lodge

Another communication of the same date from Lodge[11] followed, in which Powle was advised about a preparation "for cleansing the passage of the water" (169:192r).

On 169:205r&v is found a curious letter "sent to Sir Walter Ralegh not long before he suffered." It is anonymous and was apparently transcribed by a servant of Powle's, Francis Saunders.[12] Whether or not it was composed by Powle himself is not known, but the fact that it bears no comment by him suggests that it was in accord with his sentiments. The letter basically is advice on humbling oneself before God and on how to meet death. The following are quoted from it:

> Brave, knowing yet ignorant Rawleigh. . . . From thy first beginning thou madest thyself the center of all thy thoughts and actions. For

which now thou livest unpitied, therefore I pity thee, that thou hast drunk a deep draught of Fortune's pleasures . . . so of her bitter portion of sorrow . . . Each man oweth a death, thou two: one to thy Maker another to thy Prince. Pay one then th'other is cancelled . . . Many envy greatness, riches, liberty, friends, most some of this, thou none. Oh Rawleigh, by the missing of this thou hast easy and smooth steps made to the dwelling of Death . . . death to thee hath (or should have been) thine eating, sleeping, discoursing companion. . . .

The letter concluded with the following:

If thou wouldst know who it is that writes thus to thee, A Stranger (yet a thankful one for delivering thy high Deified abilities to the world) yet . . . one that grieves that so many of thy perfections by thine imperfections should thus untimely be extinct. Yet thou hast built thee a monument. . . . The History of the World[13] . . . Wherefore victoriously wear in Death what thou didst win in Life for I shall never see more Rawleigh.

                Farewell:

If this letter was indeed from Powle, it may seem a strange "consolation" from one who was Ralegh's friend; however, it is likely that the writer was primarily interested in the salvation of Ralegh's soul.

On 169:192v Powle transcribed a love poem supposedly written by Ralegh to Queen Elizabeth "in the beginning of his favor." Starting on the same leaf is a copy of Ralegh's letter to his wife the night before he first expected to be executed. However, Powle noted, "he did see her again & they were together for a month or more after this was written." After a short reprieve, Ralegh was executed in Old Palace Yard, Westminster, on 29 October 1618. His remains were buried in the Church of Saint Margaret, Westminster, where Powle himself was interred twelve years later.

In Powle's Commonplace Book, Tanner manuscript 169, are several poems by his longtime friend, the poet Nicholas Breton. On folio 43r is "A passionate Sonnet made by the King of Scots upon difficulties arising to cross his proceeding in love and marriage with his most worthy to be esteemed Queen." In the margin Powle noted that Breton was in Scotland at this time (1589) and Powle believed that the verses were actually written by him in the person of the king. On folio 147r is a ten-line Latin poem captioned by Powle "Master Bretton's verse." It is dated June 1616 and begins, "Tempus adest, et tempus abest, fugit annus et annis" and ends, "Non valeo, fueram, non ero, tempus abest." Two other short sets of amusing "Verses by Nic. Breton" (folio 173v) are dated 27 October 1617 and are as follows:

> I and U: A placed alone is but an idle word:
> E parce E spells nothing but itself:
> I yet alone, may lovely thoughts afford:
> But O, alas, doth play the frowards elf:
> to prove the reason of this Riddle true:
> not A, nor E, nor O, but I and You.
>
> My Witch: Your eyes bewitch my wit, your wit bewitched my will.
> Thus with your eyes and wit you do bewitch me still
> and yet you are no witch whose spirit is not evil
> and yet you are a witch, and yet you are no devil
> Oh witching eyes, and wit where wit, and eyes may read
> a witch and not a witch, and yet a witch indeed.

In 1618 "Nicholas Breton, gentleman" published in London a prose dialogue entitled *The Court and Country, or a Private Discourse betweene the Courtier and Country-man; of the Manner, Nature, and Condition of their Lives*. Its dedicatory page reads:

To the Worshipfull and worthy
Knight, the favourer of all good
Vertues and Studies Sir STEPHEN
POLL, of *Blackmoore in Essex; and*
to his worthy Lady Health, Honour,
and eternall Happinesse.

Worthy KNIGHT,

Being well acquainted with your true knowledge of the Honour of the Court, and the Pleasure of the Countrey: your judiciall Observation in your Travels abroad, and your sweet retyred Life at home: Finding my Service indebted to many of your undeserved bountiful Favours, and willing, in some fruites of my Labour, to shewe the thankefulnesse of my Love, I have adventured to present your Patience with a short Discourse in the manner of a *Dialogue*, betweene a Courtier and a Countriman, touching the Lives of either: What Matter of worth is in it I will leave to your

discretion to consider of, with my bounden Service to the honour of your Commaund, hoping that either heere or in the Country it will be a pretty passage of idle time, with some matter of mirth to remove melancholy. And
so in Prayer for your health, and your good Ladies, to whom, with your selfe, Dedicating
this short *Dialogue,* I rest

Yours, humbly devoted to be Commanded

NICH. BRETON.

Breton's dedication to Stephen Powle is a very personal one.* The likelihood is that the two men were well acquainted. Powle's Tanner manuscripts contain at least four instances[14] of brief insertions of light verse by Breton, except for 169:43r, they are probably in Breton's own hand.

In *The Court and Country,* Breton's analyses of the courtier's and countryman's life and the vindications of each tallied well with Powle's feelings. One imagines the two men had at times discussed the pros and cons together.

Like Breton's pointers in "Necessary notes for a Courtier," Powle had learned that the successful courtier must "guard against envious ambition, malicious faction, palpable flattery and base Pandarism." He well knew the values of humility and civility, love of virtue, and loyalty to the sovereign. Qualities that had proved important for a courtier were "a sharp wit, a quick apprehension, a smooth speech, and a sound memory." Hopes for advancement came with "prayer to God, diligence in his service, respect of persons, and judgment in affections"; he should ever be wary of "wanton eyes, glib tongues, hollow hearts, and irreligious spirits."

Breton's dialogue likewise points out the values and virtues of the countryman, which Powle so well appreciated in his later years. As Breton's Countryman put it:

---

*Compare perfunctory dedications to Stephen's father, Thomas Powle, by William Hayward and T.E. on pp. 188-89.

My mind to me a Kingdom is: so that the quiet of the mind is a greater matter than perhaps many men possess. Then for wealth, Godliness is great riches to him that is content with what he hath, which many great men sometime perhaps have less than meaner people. . . . Love God above all, and thy neighbor as thyself: which if you do in the Court as we do in the Country, Envy would work no hatred, nor malice mischief: but love in all persons would make a palace, a Paradise. . . . We reverence learning as well in the Parson of our parish, as our schoolmaster, but chiefly in our Justices of the Peace, for under God and the King they bear great sway in the Country.

We can surmise that Breton's dedication implied his genuine affection and respect for Stephen Powle and his admiration of his virtues and abilities.

In later years Powle's great love was for the country as a place of pleasure and peace of mind and as a provider of solitude for study and contemplation.

On 18 August 1620, Powle received a letter at Mylend from Francis Hubert, who was then living at Gray's Inn. Hubert had been one of the six clerks during part of Powle's tenure and had now "retired himself to a private obscurity." With the letter Hubert had enclosed a recent literary opus, whether verse or prose is not indicated, and had begged Powle to read it and pass judgment. Hubert apologized profusely because he feared the work would prove "a Monster wanting brain," and he asserted that it was "a *Posthumus* born after the death of his father's happiness." Hubert apparently was then in financial straits and was asking Powle for some sort of help—"the ingredients or the quantity" are not specified. Neither the enclosure nor Powle's reply is extant.

On 15 March 1619/20 Powle wrote from Mylend to Master Lucas, a neighbor in whose household Lady Margaret Powle's granddaughter, Catherine Smith, was then employed. Sir Stephen apologized for the "importunate love" that had developed between young Catherine and Master Lucas's son without his father's "privity." Catherine, likewise, had concealed the situation from Powle and, as he explained, had "rejected two especial matches of great worth which he had procured for her." Powle, however, seemed more than willing to forgive the young lady provided she had Lucas's pardon for her delinquency in duty to him "as her best father" (169:195v). But Lucas did not grant his forgiveness.

On 19 August of the same year, with the hope of placing his granddaughter in a congenial household, Powle wrote to the Lady Cheyney, widow of his stepbrother, Sir Francis Cheyney of

The Court and Country,
OR
A briefe Difcourfe Dialogue-wife fet downe betweene a Courtier and a Country-man.

Contayning the manner and condition of their liues with many Delectable and Pithy Sayings worthy obferuation.

Alfo, neceffary Notes for a COVRTIER.

Written by *N. B.* Gent.

The Country-man. *The Courtier.*

Printed at *London* by G. ELD for *Iohn Wright*, and are to be fold at his fhop at the Signe of the Bible without *Newgate*, 1618.

z

Title page of Nicholas Breton's *The Court and Country*, 1618. 8670759, British Library.

To the Worshipfull and worthy
Knight, the fauourer of all good
Vertues and Studies Sir STEPHEN
POLL, *of Blackmoore in Essex; and*
to his worthy Lady Health Honour,
and eternall Happinesse.

Worthy KNIGHT,

Eing well acquainted with your true knowledge of the Honour of the Court, and the Pleasure of the Countrey: your iudiciall Obseruation in your Trauels abroad, and your sweet retyred Life at home: Finding my Seruice indebted to many of your vndeserued bountifull Fauours, and willing, in some fruites of my Labour, to shewe the thankefulnesse of my Loue I haue aduentured to present your Patience with a short Discourse, in the manner of a *Dialogue*, betweene a Courtier and a Countriman, touching the Liues of either: What Matter of worth is in it I will leaue to your discretion to consider of, with my bounden Seruice to the honour of your Commaund, hoping that either heere or in the Country it will be a pretty passage of idle time with some matter of mirth to remoue melancholy. And so in Prayer for your health, and your good Ladies, to whom, with your selfe, Dedicating this short *Dialogue*, I rest

Yours, humbly deuoted to be Commanded

NICH. BRETON.

Dedication to Powle of *The Court and Country,* 8670759, British Library.

Drayton Beauchamps in Bucks County (169:198v). Sir Francis had died at the age of about seventy in 1620, after making a harsh will[15] that left his widow in an unfortunate position. It bequeathed "to my well beloved wife who hath always been careful of me and of my health in the time of my several visitations with sickness" merely her own wearing apparel, linen, jewels, rings, books, and other items she had brought with her to the marriage—and, in addition, all his milk cows. But even these bequests were given on condition that within one half year after Sir Francis's decease she "shall give good and reasonable home and security to my executor hereafter named to live in my said house." He named his nephew Frauncis Cheyney his executor and heir and further specified that if there were contentions or differences between his wife and nephew Frauncis for any matter whatsoever, they "may be reconciled by four indifferent knights or gentlemen of worth." He entreated his friend William Tothyll (formerly one of the six clerks) to be overseer of his will.

Powle's letter (169:198v) to Lady Cheyney was addressed to "My only yet best sister," for Sister Dutton and Sister Powle had now died. He was anxious to ascertain Lady Cheyney's health and to hear whether she was free from vexation by her nephew, Master Frauncis Cheyney, "betwixt whom and you I have heard by Master [   ] there was like to grow some variances." Powle offered for her "entertainment" as an attendant his wife's granddaughter, Mistress Catherine Smith, "the most especial person next my wife, yourself and my niece Mansell's brood that I esteem in the whole world." Mistress Smith, he wrote, had an income since the recent death of her mother of twenty pounds annually and the possibility after the decease of her unmarried brother of a portion of two hundred pounds in land. Powle hoped "hereafter God will make me able to visit you at Drayton Beauchamps." He signed himself, "Your only brother to love and command."

Powle also tried to assist other members of his wife's family. He wrote a letter (169:195v) from Mylend for his wife's younger daughter, Kate, on 11 May 1620 to be sent to the lord bishop of Norwich, telling about the young man to whom she was affianced. When his father discovered the couple were about to marry, he peremptorily severed their relationship and forbid them to see each other again. The lord bishop was being asked to intercede in Kate's behalf. Perhaps the young man meanwhile submitted to his father's decision, for Powle noted that the letter was never sent. Two years later, in 1622, Kate received some wittily sarcastic verses from a young Master Wilson of Wakes Hall, Essex (169:199v):

> Beware fair maids of musky coursive[16] oaths:
> take heed what gifts and favors you receive:
> let not the fading gloss of silken clothes
> dazzle your virtues or your fame bereave,
> for lose but once the hold you have of years,
> who will regard your fortunes or your face.
>
> Each greedy hand will strive to catch the flower,
> when none regards the stalk it grows upon.
> Each nature seeks the fruit still to devour,
> and leaves the tree to fall or stand alone.
> Yet this advice fair creature take of me:
> let none take fruit unless they take the tree.
>
> Believe not oaths, not much protesting men,
> credit no vows nor no bewailing songs,
> let Courtiers swear, forswear, and swear again.
> Their hearts do lie ten regions from their tongues,
> for when with oaths they make thy heart to tremble,
> believe them least, for then they most dissemble.
>
> Take heed, lest Caesar do corrupt thy mind
> Or fond ambition sell thy modesty.
> Say thou a king, thou ever curteous, find
> he cannot pardon thy impurity.
> Begin with kings, to subject then wilt fall
> from lord to lackey and then last to all.

That Powle had these verses copied into his Commonplace Book suggests that he shared their sentiments and admired the clever lines. His extant notes tell us nothing more about the fate of his stepdaughter or stepgranddaughter.

On 24 June 1620, Powle wrote from Mylend to his niece, the Lady Jane Mansell, at Margam in Glamorganshire, Wales (169:88r), thanking her for her recent calm and peaceful letter after the many stormy and warring thoughts she had had. As for himself, having "given over the world," he had become settled in the possession of calmness and was living in the expectation of peace. He had at last found a way of life that he had long desired.

He had recently conferred with Sir Thomas Mansell and had helped him to arrange the "conveyancing of the park."[17] Powle also had attempted to evaluate with his niece and Sir Thomas the three marriage proposals that their daughter Mary had received. Powle was inclined to prefer Sir John Kearns's son because of his suitable age, the properness of his person, his good education, and "convenient living." Powle expressed the opinion that children who are married to heirs whose parents are still living are like servants and "spend the flower of their time in complimental duties, in expectation of that which often times (being prevented by death or other crosses) they never attain unto (example hereof in my good sister your Mother and of sundry others). Therefore if some sure youth could be procured for her estated in present possession of land," this was preferable to being heir to double that amount.[18] In a later hand Powle noted in the margin: "Men nourished with hope change in suspense but live not. Hope prolongeth more than it satisfies. While they consult at Rome, Sagunt[um] doth perish."

At the end he added:

My nephew Rawley hath been with me and my wife since his coming up hither.... We are both exceeding glad to see him so ripe of judgment in his young years, and sure a complete young man for personage and behavior. I end with this music which I know is most pleasing to motherly ears.
        Your only uncle to love and to command,
        Stephen Powle

(169:88r–89r)

Sir Rawleigh Bussy (he had been knighted at Bromham, Bedfordshire, 1 August 1618) fulfilled his early promise and developed into an outstanding young man. He and his wife, Cecily Mansel, a niece of his stepfather's, had four sons and four daughters, but Rawleigh was to die at the early age of thirty-seven, on 10 October 1623. His death seems to have devastated his mother, who died several months thereafter "of a broken heart," so it was said in family annals.

Within less than a year after the Bussys' pleasant visit to Mylend, Lady Margaret Powle died. We do not know the circumstances but the Blackmore Parish Register[19] recorded that she was buried there on 28 April 1621. The effigy on her tomb sculpture is that of an elderly woman (she would have been at least in her midsixties).[20] It is to be seen at the east end of the south aisle in the Parish Church of Saint Laurence, Blackmore. There stands the prominent altar tomb of Thomas Smyth (who died ca. 1592–93, at the age of seventy) and of Margaret Smyth Powle, his wife. Their recumbent figures are those of a fine-looking, bearded man in armor and a rather stern-faced woman in long, close-fitting dress with ruff. The base of the tomb has alabaster pilasters, between which originally were the kneeling figures of four sons and two daughters. Most of these figures have long since crumbled away, although a few fragments are still to be found in the bell tower.

It may seem odd that Lady Margaret, Powle's wife of over twenty-seven years, was entombed with her first husband but one recalls that at the time of Sir Thomas's death she made certain promises,* one of which may well have been to erect a tomb for him in which she too would eventually be buried. Perhaps, too, she wanted to be with her deceased children. Whatever the reason, Powle apparently carried out her wishes.

After his mother's death, John Smyth (who was then living in Wakes Colne, Essex, at Crepping-hall, a small estate given to him by his grandmother, Christian Turner[21]) came into possession of Smyths-hall. But that he ever took up residence there is unlikely, as he died unmarried at the age of fifty, shortly after his mother's death; his will was probated 8 June 1621.[22]

As for Powle, perhaps he stayed on at Smyths-hall a bit longer to put the estate in order for his younger stepson, Arthur, who came into possession of it on his brother's death. Or perhaps, if Mylend was then vacant, Powle may have retired to the home there that he had earlier referred to as his "place of contentment."[23]

One is tempted to speculate about his state of mind at this time. What might have been some of the "secret gripings" that he kept hidden from the world and to which he alluded in a 1617 letter to his niece?† Now that he was getting on in years he may have had regrets that, despite his substantial achievements, many of his early ambitions were unrealized. Unlike his literary contemporaries, he had no great works to pass on to future generations, nor had he any living children of his own. However, he undoubtedly found solace in his studies, in religion, and in the fact that he had been a good public servant who had been true to his principles and had endeavored to do well whatever work was assigned to him: whether in conscientiously providing astute foreign intelligence to his London masters in the pre-Armada years, or in punctiliously carrying out his office of deputy clerk of the Crown with integrity and thoroughness, or in serving in a

---

*See p. 102.
†See p. 160.

public-spirited way as a wise and upright justice of the peace.

Besides, he had financially bettered himself in the world and had become a learned and able and caring man whom his family and most of his contemporaries respected.

In his later years, with his eyesight failing, he might have felt that his active days were over and that there was time now only for reflection and the joys of meditation. But Powle's life proved not to be yet over. There was still to be another chapter—although a brief one.

16

"Indian Summer"—A Third Marriage

After Margaret Powle's death in April 1621, Sir Stephen may have taken up year-round residence at his home in Mylend. However, after more than twenty-seven years of married life, perhaps he became lonely, for in May 1623 he married again. His new wife was a lady he probably had known for many years. On folio 6v of Tanner manuscript 76[1] there is inscribed in a large, seemingly joyous hand (apparently that of Powle's current servant-clerk) the following:

1623.
this 8 of may Mr Powle & my lady Wygmore was
mared att Ringingtown
this 3d xx of may Mr Powle and myself went to Milend[2]

There seems to have been no English town called "Ringingtown," but the Church of Saint Margaret, Westminster, which was famous for its beautiful bells, was a popular place for weddings and may well have been known familiarly as "Ringingtown."

At the time of this third marriage, Powle would have been about sixty-eight years old. Lady Anne Wigmore (or Wygmore) was the widow of Sir Richard Wigmore, whose May 1621 funeral Powle referred to in Tanner manuscript 168, at the bottom of folio v^r. Wigmore had in 1594 been constable of the castle and steward of the manor assigned to the earl of Essex;[3] in 1603 he became a captain and received a knighthood;[4] and in 1608/9 he had been made marshal of the field to King James. In the latter office his duties were "to see that the King not be attended by any but his own followers, nor interrupted and hindered in his sports by strangers and idle lookers on."[5] Powle's notes imply that he had a distaste for Wigmore, whom he would have known as a sporadic investor in the Virginia Company of London. After mention of Sir Richard's funeral,[6] Powle quoted a passage from Master Michael Wigmore's sermon on that occasion:

> All worldly pleasing delight is but *vinus horae hubris in sama* [wine of the hour; arrogance in Samos].

One assumes that Powle's subsequent comment was descriptive of Sir Richard (at least in his later years):

> Gluttony and drunkenness having coupled: do spawn and bring forth chambering and wantonness.
> Ambr: *Libro primo de poenitentias,* cap. 14, sayeth, "Libido pascitur coniungiis: nutritus deliciis, vino ascenditur: ebrietate inflammatur" [Sexual desire is nourished by spouses, fostered by delicacies, it is increased by wine, it is inflamed by drunkenness]. (168:v^r)

According to Sir Richard's nuncupative will,[7] he left a ring to his daughter, Lady Mary Holland, a gelding to his son-in-law, Sir Thomas Holland, and the rest of his impoverished estate, which included only his Kingstreet house, to his wife, Anne.

In 1621 and 1622 the widowed Lady Anne Wigmore paid taxes on the Kingstreet home, which was in the Parish of Saint Margaret, Westminster, but by the spring of 1623 the local tax record shows that Sir Stephen Powle and his family and household were living at this location.[8] No descriptive accounts have been found as yet of Sir Stephen's and Dame Anne's life together, although on 19 November 1623, six months after they were married, Powle entered in his Commonplace Book a note captioned "My wife's medicine for pain." It was the following:

> Take a pint of malmsey and slice therein a red onion and let it boil till one quarter of the pint be boiled away, putting therein a slip or two of thyme and when it is ready to be taken off then put in sweet butter about the quantity of half an egg, to which when it is ready to be drunk, add thereunto (for the bettering of the taste) a good quantity of sugar. This must be drunk as hot as may be suffered as occasion shall serve, when the pain cometh on you. (169:139v)

We do not know whether this proved efficacious, but it sounds far more palatable than most of the other medications given in Powle's memoranda.

In 1625 the plague struck Saint Margaret's and fifteen hundred parishioners died. To avoid the infection, which was rampant, Powle and his wife removed some seventy miles away from London to the more healthful countryside of Bramford in Suffolk. The subsidy list notes that in 1625 Powle paid his taxes there and not at Saint Margaret's.[9] Mylend had apparently been

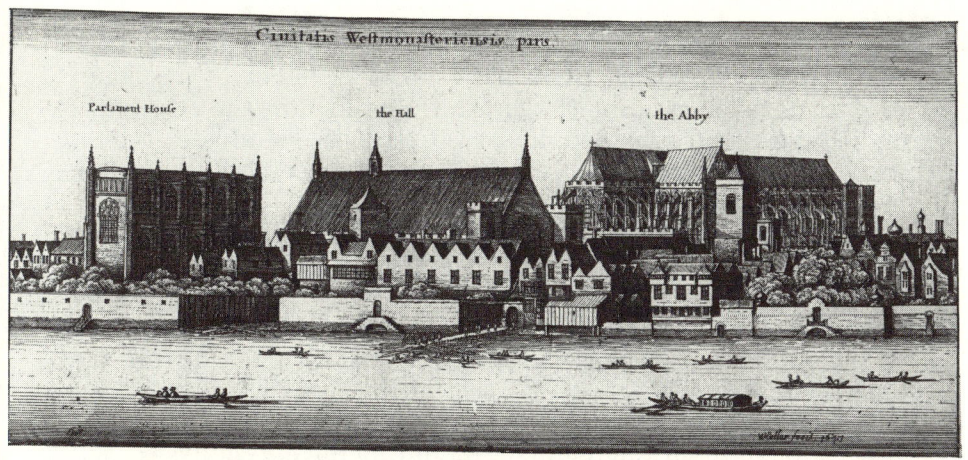

Two views of seventeenth-century Westminster by Wenceslaus Hollar. British Library 35302.1 & 3. In lower picture Church of St. Margaret is at the right.

sold some years earlier. By Easter week of 1626 Powle was again paying his taxes in Saint Margaret's.[10] By this time the worst fury of the plague had subsided. It was fitting that Westminster, which had been the center of so much of Powle's career, should become his home in his final years.

During Queen Elizabeth's time the old Palace of Westminster had become the administrative and judicial center that it subsequently remained. The court of Chancery had met there in the southeast corner of the Great Hall, the enormous hall whose handsome hammer-beam roof had been constructed during the reign of Richard II. It was the seat of the Crown and of all for which it stood, but it had been used chiefly as a court of justice, and many eminent Englishmen, including the earl of Essex, had been tried there. From the sixteenth century on, Westminster also became the permanent meeting place of Parliament.

Saint Margaret's Church was probably originally built in the twelfth century, but in its present form, with its beautiful interior, it dates from the fifteenth century. In April 1614 it became the official church of the House of Commons. Isaac Bargrave served as minister from 1622 during the period that Powle's residence was in Saint Margaret's Parish.

Kingstreet, where Lady Anne and Sir Stephen lived, extended from the Palace of Whitehall past Saint Margaret's Church and Westminster Abbey to the Old Palace Yard. William West, whom Powle had known in the Chancery office, also lived on Kingstreet.

Among the last entries in Powle's Commonplace Book were the three letters on royal prerogative referred to in chapter 14. The late 1620s evidently were for Powle a time for reflection on his busy life and its happenings and for rereading the letters and records he had accumulated during his lifetime.

In the parish register for the Church of Saint Margaret[11] are entries that state that "Sir Steephan Powell" was buried there on 26 May 1630 and next to his name is the marginal symbol ⊢╀┤ , which is found only next to the names of the more important parishioners. Less than ten and one-half months later, Lady Anne Powle also died. She was buried there on 9 April 1631. Powle would have been about seventy-five. We do not know the age of his wife.

Powle made no will, but there is an administration for him dated 26 April 1633.[12] The administrator was William Moonke, "Creditor of Sir Stephen Powle recently of Westminster, from and with the consent of Dame Anne Powle, recently a widow." It is not known whether the consent was given in a testamentary letter or orally before her death, which is unmentioned in the Latin of the administration document. William Monke (or Moonke) was the fourth son of John Monke of Herston, Sussex. As listed in the Saint Margaret's Parish Register, he had married Philippa Sleight on 1 August 1620 and had a daughter, Joan, born about a year later. What Monke's connection was with Powle has not been ascertained. Perhaps he and his wife were a young couple who lived in the area and with whom the Powles became friendly and to whom Sir Stephen had been financially obligated.

That Powle made no will is understandable, for Rawleigh Bussy, whom he had years ago referred to as his heir, had predeceased him by seven years, as had Powle's niece Jane; the rest of his immediate family had long since died. Lady Anne would have inherited from Powle without a will but, of course, she died within a year of his death.

POWLE GENEALOGY

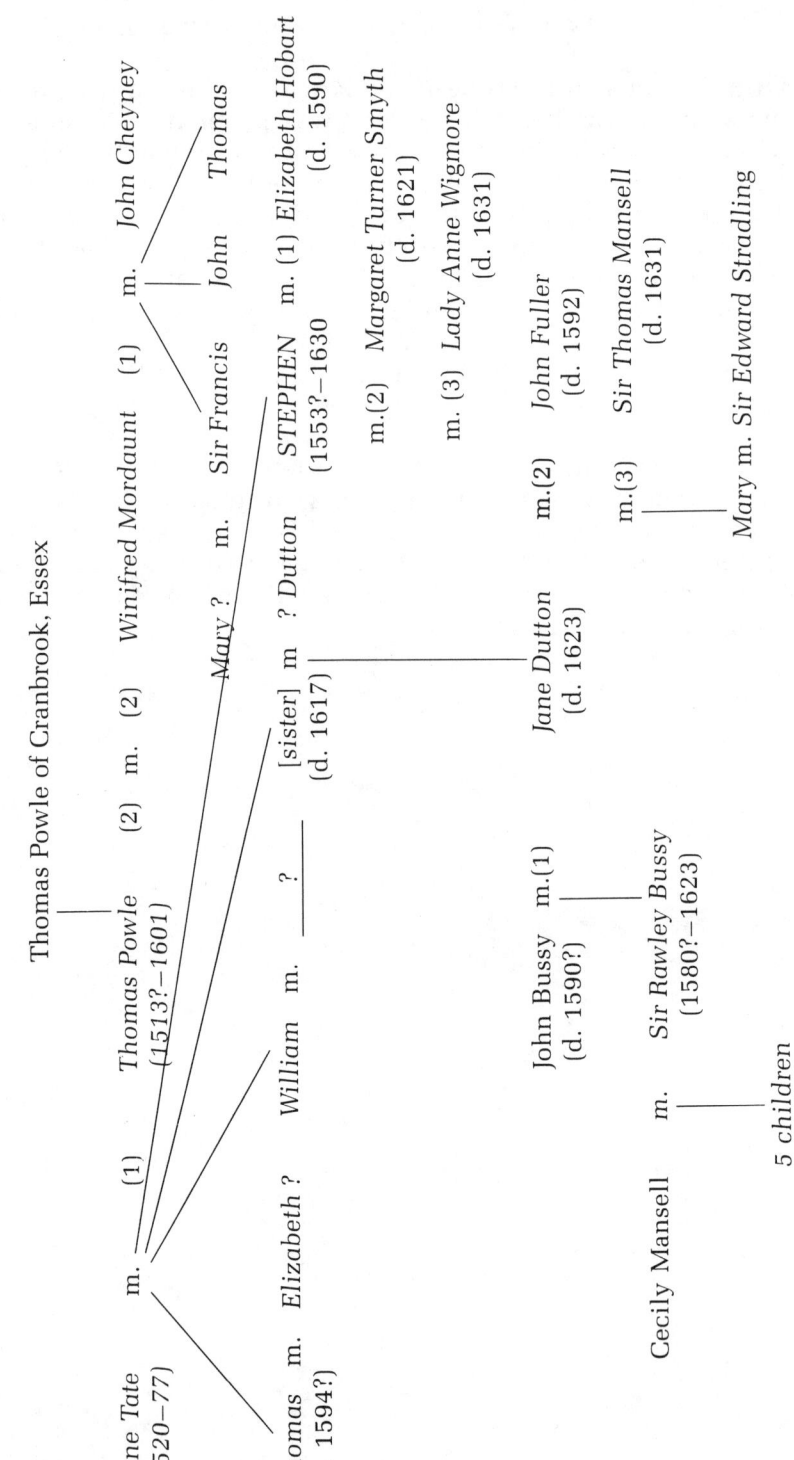

Appendix A: Catalogue of Manuscripts and Their Provenance

To calendar Powle's voluminous collection of manuscripts with their span of over fifty-two years is not always easy. As found today chiefly in the Tanner volumes, a great many of Powle's papers are chronologically jumbled. At times it is difficult to determine correct dating. Although Powle was usually very careful and accurate, there are a few instances when he apparently made a slip of the pen, perhaps due to haste or to confusion between English and Italian dates.*

Duplicates exist of a number of his letters. In his early years he made drafts[1] of the letters he wrote, and he kept these in his Commonplace Books, together with originals or transcriptions of some of the letters he received.[2] Often, as in the case of those written to his father, to Burghley, and to Walsingham, the final letters were preserved by the recipients,[3] with the result that we have these final copies as well as the drafts made. On the other hand, occasionally a letter to which Powle has referred is no longer extant, and sometimes there are pages missing from his long letters.

It is remarkable that so many of Powle's manuscripts have come down to us intact, for there is no evidence that he made any particular provision for their survival after his death. The likelihood seems to be that they remained for a while in the hands of his administrator, young William Moonke,[4] who died in Wokeingham, Berkshire, in 1659 (PCC Administrations, fol. 188).

A preserver and transmitter of Sir Stephen's records may possibly have been Henry Powle,[5] a collateral descendant who was born in 1629 or 1630 in Shottesbrooke, Berkshire, and died in 1692. Henry Powle became an important legal and political figure as speaker of the 1689 Convention Parliament and was influential in bringing William and Mary to the throne. He is reputed to have had considerable legal, historical, and antiquarian knowledge and, with the aid of John Bagford, gathered a large library of manuscripts and historical records, some of which later became part of the Lansdowne collection at the British Museum. One wonders whether he may have acquired and

---

*See Preface, p. 12.

assembled his forebear's sixteenth- and early seventeenth-century manuscripts, for they are likely to have been of great interest to him.

We come next to Thomas Tanner (1674–1735), bishop of Saint Asaph in Wales, also an avid antiquarian. He is known to have purchased through dealers and at auction a large number of the Powle manuscripts, which at Thomas Tanner's death were, together with other of his manuscripts and papers, bequeathed to the Bodleian Library in Oxford, where they are to be found today within large bound volumes of the bishop's manuscripts. Those relating to Stephen Powle include his legal notes and documents, personal memoranda, and many of his letters. Those of Powle's letters that were addressed to high government officials, such as Principal Secretary Walsingham or Lord Treasurer Burghley, have survived in the Elizabethan State Papers now at the Public Record Office in London and in the Harleian, Cotton, and Lansdowne manuscripts at the British Library.

Herewith is a brief summary of those manuscripts I have been able to locate. I trust that they will prove of some value to future scholars. Early letters (pre-1589) and Chancery records of 1595 through 1601 are nearly all in Stephen Powle's holograph; most of the later papers (especially post-1601) are copies from his drafts made by his clerk.

Summary of Manuscripts

Add'l MS. 37687G, fol. 41v. Grant of coat of arms to Thomas Powle, April 1556.

Cotton MS Nero B IX, fols. 134r–37r. Letter from Stephen Powle at Frankfurt on Main to Lord Burghley at the English Court, 2 April 1586, describing various occurrences at Augsburg, Heidelberg, and elsewhere on the Continent. In addition, it summarizes Duke Casimir's letter of "instructions," which SP was to deliver to the earl of Leicester in Holland.

Exon. MS. 88 (Exeter College, Oxford), fols. 55r–56r. Tract on the Judges' Robes by SP, 1618 (although begun earlier).

Harleian MS. 296, fols. 48r–49v. SP's newsletter to Secretary Walsingham from Venice, 7 November 1586 (N.S.).

MS. 6994, fol. 98r. From Walsingham to Burghley concerning news received from SP, 12 September 1587,

CH. 57.H.22 Mortgage of lease of Clay Hall, 1594.

Lansdowne MS. 50, fol. 11. Letter from Casimir to Burghley praising SP and his services, 1586.

MS. 88, fols. 38r–45r. Steven Rodwey's letter to Michael Hicks complaining about SP, 25 October 1601.

MS. 100, fols. 144r–46v. Young SP's account of his travels written to his father, 1580 (duplicate in Tanner MS. 309).

Rawlinson MS. D 913, fols. 68r–82v. Early letters to his father, brother, and friends, 1578–80. These are duplicated in Tanner MS. 309.

Salisbury (Cecil) MS. 63/24/25 Letter dated 4 August 1598 from Steven Rodwey to Sir Robert Cecil asserting that SP could vouch for Rodwey's loyalty to the English Crown while in Italy.

Vol. 3, p. 44 Note to the Privy Council from the six clerks (including SP) vouching for the behavior of Daniel Powell, one of their underclerks, February 1605/6.

State Papers, Domestic, Elizabeth, 1586–88. Newsletters of SP to Walsingham from Italy, December 1587 to April 1588 (State Papers 101/81)

State Papers, Venetian. Letter from Geoffrei Leatherio mentioning SP as addressee of letter to be delivered to John Chamberlain, 16 December 1588 (N.S.) (SP 99/1/28).

Tanner MS. 76, fol. 6v. Note about SP's 1623 marriage (probably written by his servant); fol. 7r. Knights made at the winning of Cales (Cadiz) by the earl of Essex in 1600. Listing of sixty-four names is in SP's hand; other folios list participants in Essex Rebellion and disposition of their cases, letters to and from earl of Essex, letter of Queen Elizabeth to Mountjoy, deputy of Ireland, speech of Egerton on the Star Chamber, record of Essex's trial, and poem about him by Henry Cuffe. The two last are possibly in SP's hand.

Tanner MS. 78, fols. 95r–107v. Copies of letters sent by SP to Burghley containing intelligence from Casimir's Court, 1585–86.

Tanner MS. 130, fols. 123r–128v, In dispraise of travel, written by SP in 1581 with quotations from various writers; 129r–131v, Description of city of Geneva, 1580; 132r–134r, Topographical description of Italy, 20 June 1581; 134–135r, Letter from SP in Paris to his brother Thomas, 20 June 1581 (duplicate in Rawlinson D913); 135v–37v, Description of the clock of Strasbourg (duplicate in Tanner 309).

Tanner MS. 168, 208 folios. First part of SP's Commonplace Book containing legal records connected with Powle's duties as clerk of the crown and other legal memoranda, notes relating to Virginia and Guiana voyages, lines of Nicholas Breton's in the poet's hand, legal procedures against the earl of Essex, and other notes and memoranda.

Tanner MS. 169, 236 folios. Second part of SP's Commonplace Book containing numerous letters, comments on Saint Jerome's view of women, a "passionate sonnet" received from Nicholas Breton purportedly by King James of Scotland but believed to be of Breton's authorship. Material relating to the earl of Essex (his behavior and speech at his execution and final speeches of his co-conspirators). Four mock encomia by Sir William Cornwallis, an early copy of "Leicester's Commonwealth," verses by Breton, later seventeenth-century notes by Thomas Tanner, and other miscellaneous memoranda.

Tanner MS. 231, 104 folios. To SP in Heidelberg (1585) from Adam Goraius near Cracow, Polonia. Includes brief notes of Goraius's on various areas (Spain, Portugal, Savoy, Muscovy, Constantinople, Venice, Pomerania, Silesia, Bavaria, Bohemia, and Persia).

Tanner MS. 237, fols. 26r–31r, Considerations touching a peace with Spain, written by SP for Walsingham; 31v–54v, Documents about the earl of Essex (post 1597) copied by SP.

Tanner MS. 246, 31 folios. "The Soul's Secret Meditation," a discourse of comfort written by SP to Mistress Cordell Maye at Gretham, Durham, in 1592.

Tanner MS. 309, 301 folios. Early letters and travel diaries (1576–88), coins of France, Scotland, Geneva, Basel, Strasbourg, and Lorraine (denominations and their values in English currency), copy of a letter from Burghley to SP, 1587 correspondence with John Chamberlain, and insertion of a letter in Chamberlain's hand. Also, some later letters and notes.

Tanner MS. 314, fols. 79v–97r. Letters from SP (1587–88). Duplicates of some in Tanner 309.

Other MSS include records of Middle Temple, Oxford University, probated wills and other legal documents at the Public Record Office, local records at the Essex Record Office in Chemlsford and at the Westminster Archives Library in London, and MSS of the Mansell family of Margam and Penrice in Wales.

Appendix B: Printed References to Stephen Powle

References in print to Stephen Powle are for the most part quite brief ones. W. J. Jones, in his *Elizabethan Court of Chancery* (Oxford, 1967) mentions Powle on pages 81, 131, 134, and 136 in connection with his appointment as deputy clerk of the Crown but makes more extensive references to his father, Thomas Powle, who held several important Chancery offices for a great number of years and about whose later slackness in office there was criticism. Pierre Lefranc in *Sir Walter Ralegh, Écrivain* (Quebec, 1968), pages 83n, 278, 406, and 680–81 refers to Powle as a friend of Ralegh's to whom the latter sent various "prescriptions" and from whom he received a letter of counsel. David Quinn in "Notes of a Pious Colonial Investor," *William and Mary Quarterly* 16: 551–55, quotes some of Powle's 1608–10 notes from Tanner manuscript 168 in connection with his interest in the Virginia Company. Conyers Read in *Lord Burghley and Queen Elizabeth* (1960; reprint, London, 1965), page 522, recounts in abbreviated form an incident related to Powle at the time of Thomas Egerton's investiture as lord keeper (see p. 105 above). In Douglas MacLeane's *History of Pembroke College, Oxford* (1897), pages 120 and 123, and in the *Dictionary of National Biography*, in an article on William Camden, there are references to Powle and his schoolmates at Broadgates Hall (later Pembroke College), Oxford. Alexander Brown's *Genesis of the United States* (1890; reprint, New York, 1964), 2:971, has a few biographical notes on Powle in connection with his interest in the Virginia Company of London. Powle's name appears in several lists of investors and of council members in this book, and also in Susan Kyra Kingsbury's *Records of the Virginia Company* (Washington, D.C., 1933), and in a 350-year Jamestown commemorative pamphlet by Samuel M. Bemiss (Williamsburg, Va., 1957), entitled "The Three Charters of the Virginia Company of London," on page 30, in connection with the second charter of 23 May 1609.

Leslie Hotson in his "Who wrote 'Leicester's Commonwealth'?" in the *Listener*, 16 March 1950, page 482, quotes from Powle's marginalia at the top of his Commonplace Book copy of the anonymously published work (169:92r). Hotson transcribes Powle's note as "by my red headed mad man" and so concludes that Powle knew who the author was. However, the complete marginal note as found at the top left of the original manuscript at the Bodleian does not support this conclusion, for it reads in full: "The L^d of Leycester his common wealth copied of yonge Sr William Cornwally[s] written book by my red hedded madde manne." The beginning of the note is faint and probably would not have appeared in a photocopy or other mechanical copy. In *Shakespeare by Hilliard* (Berkeley and Los Angeles, 1977), pages 25–26, in discussing the rage for device guessing and symbolism, Hotson refers to a 1587 letter of Stephen Powle to Walter Cope (78:105v, June 1586) to whom he had sent as a gift a German carving in ivory "to manifest my secret meaning therein." Powle elucidated, "Let the whiteness thereof signify my sincerity; the roundness in length, the perfection of my good will long to continue; and the degrees and stairs therein, the desire I have to mount higher in your acquaintance and favour."

John Walter Stoye in *English Travellers Abroad* (London, 1952) on page 95, discussing connections between England and the Huguenots, cites Powle's visit to Geneva, his later acquaintance with Andrew Melville in Scotland, and Melville's recommendation in later years of a suitable Protestant household for the son of one of Powle's friends who planned to visit France.* Deborah Jones, writing about Lodowick Bryskett's sister Lucrece, in Charles J. Sisson's *Thomas Lodge and Other Elizabethans* (New York, 1966), page 305, refers to a lease of East Ham marshes about 1594 to "one Paul" at the rent he had held it at before and in a footnote identifies "Paul" as "probably either Stephen Powle . . . or his father." It would more likely have been Thomas Powle who held land in that area.

---

*See page 136.

Appendix C: Funerary Monument of Powle's Parents

According to the 1633 edition of John Stow's *Survey of London*, pages 431–32, there was "a faire monument in the south wall of the Chancell, at the east end" of the Parish Church of Saint Dunstan's the West with the following inscription:

> Here-under lyeth the body of Thomas Powle, esquire, Clerke of the Crowne and one of the Sixe Clerkes of the High Court of Chancery, Controller of the Hamper,[1] Clerke of the Forest of Waltham, and High Steward to the late Queene *Elizabeth* of all her Mannors within the county of Essex. Hee had by his wife Jane Tate (descended from the line of honourable ancestors) five sonnes[2] and one daughter: who likewise is here with him buried. Both lived in the feare of God, and dyed in his favour: Shee in the 57. yeere of her age, the 24. day of November 1577. And hee, in the 88. yeere of his age, the 26. day of June. *Anno* 1601.

Stephen Powle *Esquire*, their only surviving sonne and successor to his father in the Office of one of the Six Clerks of the Chancery; in dutiful pietie, consecrated to lasting memory this holy monument.

> Corpus foetidum carcer,
> Mors libertas,
> Vita mare procellosum.
>   Sepulchrum portus,
> Mundus vaga peregrinatio,
>   Coelum Patria.
> Disce ergo mori,
>   dedisce vivere.[3]

Appendix D: Books Dedicated to Thomas Powle, Clerk of the Crown

Bellum Grammaticale a discourse of great war and dissention betwene two worthy Princes the Noune and the Verbe, contending for the chefe place or dignitye in oration. First made in Latin by Lord Andrew Guarna of Salerne, and after translated into Frenche, and nowe for the worthinesse of historie turned into English by W. H. [William Hayward].

London, Henrie Bynneman, 1569.

[tiny quarto]

On Aiii^v: "Epistle to the right worshipfull Master Thomas Powle Esquier, Clerke of the Crowne in the Queenes Maiesties honourable Courte of Chancerie, and one of the Six Clerkes of the same, William Hayward wisheth health with long life and prosperitie."

The Second part of the first Booke of the Myrrour of Knighthood: in which is prosecuted the illustrious deedes of the knight of the sunne, and his brother Rosicleer, sonnes unto the Emperour Trebetio of Greece: with the valiant deedes of armes of sundry worthie Knights . . . now newly translated out of Spanish into our vulgar tongue by R.P. [Robert Parry? or Richard Parre?]. London, 1599. Printed by Thomas Este.

APPENDIX D

To the right worshipfull Master Thomas Powle Esquire, Clerke of the Crowne in her Maiesties high court of Chancerie. By T.E. [Thomas Este?]:

> ... sithens custome hath made it to bee as a law in mens hearts observed, that they account books published not to have sufficient warrant except they bee dedicated to some worthie personage of authoritie, I am bolde to present unto your Worship this Booke entituled the *Second part of the Mirrour of Knighthood* done out of Spanish and now newly printed . . . .
> by Diego Ortunez de Calahora [earlier edition was 1582]

Appendix E: Transcripts of Typical Letters from and to Powle and Other Representative Pages from His Notebooks

To the Lord Chancellor Bromley before my travel 1579 (Tanner MS. 169:59v–60r)

Right honorable and my very good Lord,
Although it were my duty rather to approach your person myself than either to make these my letters the deliverers of my humble suit, or any other to be the sollicitor of my causes, yet the trial that all men have of the gracious favor you show to the meanest of your suppliants by what way soever they utter their requests and especially to those that be studied of learning as such, that thereby I have been emboldened most humbly to crave your Honor's favor by letter. Master Powle, my father, being one that dependeth wholly on your Honor the employing of whose life resteth at your commandment and the bestowing of whose liking is altogether at your appointment, I have on some occasion given by me (for which I am not a little grieved) turned his wonted favor into heavy displeasure, the which how burdensome it is unto the heart and mind of a natural son your Honor by wisdom doth understand and by the smart that I endure I have experience of. And for the recovery of the same I do most humbly beseech your Honor to bestow your grave persuasions with my father in my behalf, whereby in your Honor shall be manifested that wonted charitable mind which all men have noted in you, by returning a son to the liking of his parent, in my father the effect of that dutiful and serviceable good will he hath heretofore made you of in words, and I being disburdened (by your Honor's means) of that load of sorrow I am oppressed with, shall be bound always to pray for the continuance of your Honor with increase of all felicity and happiness.

        Middle Temple, London   5 August 1579
        Sent by Master Gibbes   Always at your Honor's command
        of that society.   S. Powle

* * * * *

To my loving Brother[1] Master Cooke. 1583. (Tanner 169:34v)
[Appended in later hand] This letter nor any of this kind were in any part satisfied, and yet I undertook mine own course being then very young.

My good Brother Cooke, I am well assured I should blush to deliver that by word which I do by writing at this present because I want in aid of you (amongst the rest) of my especiall well-willers. I know very well that hereby I take the course to discredit myself with my ordinary friends in which number I account not you my good Brother. But herein I must follow the example of those that being once over the shoes made after up to the middle in water, or of maskers that having once presented themselves to open view must of force deliver their suits to their Ladies though they refuse to hear it, using their personage they put on as a privilege for their presumption. For, having once made known unto you my father's hardness towards me, do now secretly acquaint you with my suit to yourself. I hope, Brother, the rather to be allowed in your judgment because my masking garments have never yet been shown in any public feast or private assembly, and the vizard I use is his absence, the hall I present myself in is your private closet, and in lieu of a Lady I court yourself, my good Brother, not in matters of Love but of luck. If I were a comedian, I might boldly write as they do on their doors, so I at the entrance of your sight into this Letter to make the matter more plausible *Never played before*, for I am but a young soldier in this kind of service and not *Miles Emeritus*. I hope therefore my brother Cooke will pardon these first oversights in that I hazard my credit with this rashness as it were to the battle because I promise never to offend in the like foolish hardy adventure again but rather will choose to lose my life in some more dangerous service elsewhere. But methinks I hear you say to yourself, "What of all this?" Well, Sir, you shall be satisfied in a word and that with preposterous rhetoric. For a long proem you shall have a short conclusion and no other part of Oratory interposed. You shall behold a monstrous shape that hath a great head and a little heel without any other feature or member of a body: a philosopher's supper with an egg and an apple without any more dishes. That is, you shall receive a poor beggar's presents that craveth of you not the loan but the *gift of five pounds* towards the furnishing of this my journey which I am shortly to undertake. These last words may seem to resemble wine mixed with wormwood that is good in the taste at first but unpleasant in the smack at the end, or the whole letter may be like a Scorpion that embraceth with claws before and stingeth with the tail behind because the first part of my letter is brotherly and the last over boldly written. But I know your forwardness to relieve such as be in want and I am sure you are acquainted with my necessity. I hope you will supply the one, and I give you a younger brother's word that I will remain thankful for the other. And when God shall make me able, I shall repay you. This is a simple pawn I confess to such a sum, yet I suppose with you it shall

carry that value I pledge it for, being the only jewel I am presently possessed with.
And thus I end with commendations to your own good self.

1583.
Your Loving brother to command,
Steph: Powle

To the right Honorable and his very good Lord and Master, the Lord High Treasurer give these. 12th June 1585. [Delivered] by Captain Hoorde. To the Lord Burghley from S.P. at Casimir's Court (Tanner MS. 78:95r).

Right Honorable and my very good Lord may it please your Honor to be advertised that I came to Heidelberg the tenth of April where I found neither that entertainment which your Lordship's favorable letters in my behalf requested, nor that welcome which my long and chargeable journey in some sort deserved. For when word was carried up to the Palsgrave's [Casimir's] lodging from the Porter's Lodge (for nearer I was not admitted) that an English gentleman had letters to his Excellency, he sent down to know from whom and being answered they were sent from Your Honor, he commanded by a second messenger that I should deliver them to one of his men and as for myself I should speak with his Excellency at some other time. I seemed somewhat unwilling to deliver the letters but yet upon that straight commandment I was enforced thereunto.

I presented myself two days after unto Master Vambolt, his chiefest favorite and gentleman of his chamber. For answer he told me that he had commission from his Excellency to let me understand that Your Lordship's letters were somewhat obscure in two or three places. Nevertheless, he conjectured the meaning and therefore he appointed me a place to serve him with his Pages, which in this country, Right Honorable, for a man to be a companion with is accounted a great disgrace, for besides that they be but boys for years they be very mean in apparel, rude in behavior and ignorant in all knowledge whatsoever that hardly an English gentleman would receive for lackeys. I seemed nothing to dislike of this entertainment although it did amaze me very much to see Your Honor's letters so slenderly valued and myself so meanly accounted of. I defer this long to acquaint Your Honor hereof because I hoped for a better success unto so hard a beginning. But I find it to be all one. Sithence my repair to this court, be never inquired of me either of England in general or of Your Honor's health in particular. I have been in "heaven." I have been given to understand that secretly his Excellency had knowledge that Your Honor did hinder his request to her Majesty for the expedition of Cologne [see p. 225, n. 2] whereby he thought himself much disadvantaged in honor for he hoped by the restoring of the Archbishop to have purchased to himself reputation and glory. For which causes seeing I am no ways accounted of by his Excellency and the expense of money consuming of [   ] tendeth to no other end but my loss, I have thought it best by little and little to discontinue this service. Nevertheless I will remain still in the University of Heidelberg presenting myself sometimes to his Excellency, attending always Your Honor's pleasure to command my service either here or elsewhere.

I have not imparted this my slender entertainment to either father or friend because I would not have any bring unto the small account the Prince made of Your Honor's letters. Moreover it would be a blot unto my credit at my return, whereof [   ] myself, your Lordship hath especial regard considering this the only patrimony I am presently possessed with.

To Master Vambolt, lord chamberlain to Duke Casimir. 22 December 1585. (Tanner MS. 309:62r).

Illustrissimo Signore,
    Havendo io riscuto hieri lettere d'Inghilterra con una dechiaratione nella lingua Inglese che la Regina a fatta della cagioni che hanno mossa la sua Maestà di recevere sotto la sua protettione Holland et Zelanda. Non poteva far did manco considerando il mio dovere alla Signoria vostra che di pregaria che me commandi ad interpritare gli punti principali, et cose piu rimarchevole in essa declaratione, se per sorte v[ostra] s[ignoria] non l'abbia ricevuta nella lingua francese. Per bisognandonni andare a Norimberga per certe mio facende straordinarie, la prego humilmente che si degni advertirne la Santa Altezza accioche mi commandi qualche seviggio in quella bande. Il quale farò molto fidelmente et fra tre settimana poi (piacendo a Dio) ritornare a Heidelberga. Ultimamente quando io fui in quella bande apportai lettere d'importanza dal luogo tenente di S[anta] A[ltezza] da Numarca tocanda le cose d'Amberga.
    Domattina overo inansi (si v[oster] s[ignore] la vuole) la mostraro per effetuare con opere che adesso offrisco con parolle. In questo mentre, presento a v.s. un par di quanti al'Inglese per un testimonio del mio affetionato animo ch'io porto verso di lei. Il Signore Iddio vi prosperi et feliciti et vi dia la sua gratia et favore perpetuo.

I went to Nuremberg immediately with Master Rodwey. The worst journey for snow in going and water in returning that ever I made in all my life.	Scritto inanzi che fui in Italia.

The following is a translation of the foregoing letter to Master Vambolt, Lord Chamberlain to Duke Casimir:

Most illustrious Sir,

Having received yesterday letters from England with a declaration in English giving the Queen's reasons for having taken Holland and Zeeland under her protection, I could do no less (considering my duty to your Grace) than to beg you to order me to interpret the principal points and the most important things in that declaration, unless your Grace has received it in French. Since I have to go to Nuremberg for some special business affairs, I humbly beg you to be good enough to let his Highness know so that he can ask me to serve him in those regions, which I shall do most faithfully and (God willing) return to Heidelberg within three weeks. The last time I was in those parts I carried important letters of his Highness from Numarca involving matters concerning Hamburg.

Tomorrow or sooner (if your Grace wishes) I will show you in deeds what I now offer you in words. In the meantime I present to your Grace a testimony of the affection that I bear you. May God bring you prosperity and happiness and may you live in his grace and favor forever.

I wrote later that I was in Italy.

To Lord Burghley at the Court from Frankfurt on Main, 2 April 1586 (Cotton MS. Nero B IX, fol. 134r–37r).

Right Honorable, my duty in most humble manner remembered. According as I informed your Lordship in my last letters dated the 27th of January, I am now returning homeward with his Excellency's letters to your Honor, to my Lord of Leicester, and to his Excellency's mother-in-law who is resident at Vianen not far from Utrecht in Holland. And by the way I am to deliver a letter and message unto Master Ségure, the King of Navarre's Ambassador[2] being at Frankfort on Main.

The Occurrants

10 Feb. The Fuchers of Augsburg, Sir Marco and Sir Giovanni, were at some discord among themselves and their cousins about the accounts with the King of Spain, because they importuned him with payment and he offended with the extreme usance of their money. And in the meantime Ferdinand, Archduke of Austria, hath taken some Signorial towns belonging to one of the Fuchers, under color of defending Sir Reymondo Fuchers who is his subject in respect of land holden of him and remaining at Isenbruch at his Court.

14 Feb. Duke Casimir by the assent of the old Duke of Saxony, Marquis of Brandenburg, and sundry other princes of Germany did send a messenger to the French King for license for their Ambassador to have access unto him; which was granted by letter likewise in most favorable

sort: that all France lay open before him to command therein as in his own dominions. This letter I did read by the mean of Erasmus Schregelius, one of his Excellency's most assured servants and counsellors. Whereupon there should have been an Ambassade of more than twelve honorable personages belonging to sundry princes had not the death of the Duke of Saxony been a hindrance thereof. Nevertheless they mean to continue their former Ambassade within these fourteen days viz: about the midst of April. And thereupon his Excellency himself advertised me that he had written to her Majesty by Zulker, his servant, to entreat her Highness to join with them by her Highness's Ambassade into France as speedily as her Majesty could.

The desire of the princes of Germany is to procure a peace by appointing the King of Navarre heir apparent by consent as well as by right to avoid the subversion of France by civil wars and thereby to cut off the endeavors of aspiring minds from obtaining their desires which otherwise being not prevented might serve as a precedent and ill example for their subjects to do the like if by force at any time a Dukedom or Crown might be obtained, which inconvenience, if he were not able to take order for, then they as his good neighbors would by common assent and joined forces endeavor to redress.

Monsieur Vambolt, his Excellency's gentlemen of the Chamber, was sent to the young Duke of Saxony immediately upon the death of his father, who returned answer that the young Duke was very forward and most willing to persist in his father's steps and that he was most entirely affected to his brother Duke Casimir.

There be two reasons that move the princes of Germany to endeavor a peace by hindering the proceedings of the Guisard in France and the King of Spain in the Low Countries and to aid those of the religion in France and to assist her Majesty in Holland: first, their own quiet and safety, for that they would be loath to have such an ill neighbor in Lorraine, Partois, and France as the Duke of Guise if his endeavors should prevail, and therefore the appointment of an heir by consent is the only means to have their desires satisfied in enjoying assured security; secondly, their profit and gain, for the King of Spain tyrannizing those in the Low Countries whose estates be upholden by the traffic of merchandise transported by the rivers of Rhine, Main, Neckar, Meuse, and Mosella and also through their towns and dominions by land to all their Marts and Fairs, the princes have their revenues greatly diminished by the de[lay] of this intercourse, because merchants dare not adventure their goods nor persons, and therefore the princes receive neither toll nor customs, whereas they hope her Majesty's clemency would be such that the traffic should no ways be hindered if her Highness were settled there in peaceable possession.

But yet the princes themselves wishing favorable success unto her Majesty's proceedings, the greater part do nevertheless wonder to what end her Majesty's enterprises will come in making head, as they term it, against the mighty and rich King of Spain, affirming her Majesty's forces small, her Majesty's revenues nothing in comparison of the Spaniards, her Majesty's men unexpert in many affairs by reason of long peace, her Majesty's captains without discipline by reason of their want of experience, and therefore never able to oppose themselves against the King of Spain's advised governors and well trained soldiers. Examples of the first they allege of Master Norris in Friesland four years since, of late at Nimegen and Grave and that the English men have never been able to bear arms against the force of the Spaniard in any conflict these two years. I have heard this spoken in most malicious sort in Heidelberg where his Excellency hath his residence. For confirmation of the other, they compare her Majesty's Little England to the great Indies of Spain.

Moreover, they see not any straight league of alliance that her Majesty hath with any princes of Germany unto whom all Europe hath recourse in matters of service, so that they imagine her Majesty presumeth too much on her own strength.

Right Honorable, concerning this last point, his Excellency in secret manner commanded Erasmus Schregelius (before named) to give me in Latin short instructions to impart unto my Lord of Leicester in my way homeward. The first whereof was:

1. Cudi in Anglos fabam.

His meaning is that the long continuance of the wars in France and Low Countries is thought to have proceeded from the aid the weaker part hath received out of England and therefore the Catholics do work means to move the princes of Germany for a contribution toward a defense of their frontiers because the English men first secretly and now openly have set foot in Germany, and therefore to be feared they will in time overrun it as the Goths and Vandals did in times past like a land flood overflow all Europe.

2. Germanos pontificos totos in eo esse ut sumptibus Imperii non tantum Bavarus redintegretur, sed arma quoque cum Hispanis in Anglos suscipiatur.
3. Verendum ut Hispanis malitiose res Gallicas componat et cum Rege et proceribus Imperii Ligam contra Anglos constituat.
4. In eum finem duo menses, in novissimis Comitiis Augustanis ordinibus in Belgio infestatis, decretis, iam wormatiae repeti; et in eam rem assensum esse in subsidium Bavari, (id est Episcopi Coloniensis) Comitis Emdenensis, et Wilhelm Juliacensis.
5. Haec tum consilia pontificiis turbata esse et eo nomine quoque ad Truxesium scriptum 10. Martij.

It may please your Honor to understand his meaning in these two last instructions. Amongst other decrees made at Wooches in March last this was one, that there should be a contribution granted (like unto that at Augsburg in the last Diet Imperial [in] 1582) by the whole Empire, to defray the two months' charges of defending those forenamed princes with Rutters and footmen against all enemies whatsoever, which being passed by the suffrages of the delegate ambassadors, Erasmus Schregelius (before named) being Ambassador for his Excellency could not hinder directly but in this sort following he did *interburare eorum consilia* (as he termeth it) which was to demand in the right of his master Duke Casimir (who is the chief in the circuit of the upper and nether Bavaria, and of the whole Palatinate) that the collection being gathered, his Excellency might have the honor of the distribution because he being neighbor unto some of them that stood in the need thereof was best able to judge and therefore was most fit to distribute and bestow it. This demand caused a stay of their absolute determination in this matter, so that as yet there is no collection made although the Catholic princes do daily labor therein. Hereof Erasmus Schregelius advertised the old Bishop of Cologne into Holland the 10th of March by a letter written in cipher.

The means for her Majesty to hinder their endeavors he putteth down in this instruction following:

6. Unde et Anglis haec consilia praevenienda:
    1) Aliquot principes primores ut D. Cassimirus; firmiter amplexandi.

I suppose he meaneth that his Excellency's pension should be renewed and that her Majesty do entertain a league with the Duke of Saxony, and by that means her Majesty hath the Marquis of Brandenburg because they join together in all actions with William Landgrave of Hessia and to use means by ambassadors that the Duke of Brunswick be a neutre [neutral].

    2) Administri eorum beneficiis afficiendi ut heros in benevolentia retineant.

His meaning is that some annual stipend be given to the chief favorites of these forenamed princes, as well to keep these Lords assured to her Majesty as also to procure their friends to aid them with horse and men in time of need. He named in the Palatinate the Baron of Done, the [ ] chief person of honor in his excellency's Court, Mr. Peutricke, a Colonel in the last voyage for the Bishop of Cologne and such a one whose counsel is much relied on by his Excellency, Mr. Vambolt, his Excellency's gentleman of his Chamber, and sundry other in divers places of Germany, as the Earl of Ortenberge in Bavaria, Colonel Severini in Westphalia, who offered to his Excellency the loan of 50,000 talars if he stood in need thereof and 200 horse to be at his Excellency's command this winter. He affirmed that the King of Spain did the like amongst the Catholic princes as with most of the Archdukes of Austria. Schregel

told me that himself in the last voyage of Collen [Cologne] furnished 200 footmen amongst his friends.
The manner of proceeding in the instructions:

3) Cogitandum primo de Religionis Unione.
4) Item de Regionum defensione.
5) Item de numero et mutuo auxilio eq[u]itum et peditum: sed in his caute procedendum.

And to that end these may be the better ordered to have always an ambassador in Germany amongst the princes as the King of Navarre hath Master Ségure and Master Clervant residing at this present at Frankfort.

6) Item Agente in Germania.

For although the King of Navarre hopeth altogether to have supply of money out of England, yet he must have his men out of Germany.
His Excellency looketh for an ambassador out of England and marveleth greatly that her Majesty hath deferred so long the sending of one considering he was advertised by three several letters of the coming of sundry. When any departeth from him, he is likely to have these instructions which I have sent to your Honor in this letter.
The French King hath brought up almost all the mart of horses and harquebusses: *vide* 200 horse and 800 harquebusses.
Because the King of Denmark's ambassador seeth that the German princes be long before they send their ambassadors, therefore it is thought that he will depart hence to M[   ] alone the first of April.
Master La Noue and his Lady came to Geneva about the 12 of March. The report continueth still that the Duke of Savoy will come down into the home countries and that the Prince of Parma shall be commanded to retire himself into Naples to be Viceroy there. And therefore the city of Geneva, although they stand on guard, yet they are not in fear to be besieged, as I was informed by letters from thence the 18th of March.
Monsieur de Beza, Oseander and Jacobus Andreas, the chief Lutherans of our age do meet at Mombelliard to dispute about the Ubiquity. They be both there but Monsieur de Beza is not yet come by reason of sickness.
The Bishop of Wirtzburg hath banished all those out of the dominion saving such that make profession of the Catholic religion. The Duke of Bavaria at München doth the like, and almost all the princes Catholic in Germany.
The [   ] of the Landgraves resident at Cassells delivered his opinion in private unto a gentleman of his bedchamber of my Lord of Leicester's proceedings in the Low Countries: which was that he thought his Honor dealt rigorously in displacing so many of the Estates in so short a time

in innovating their government, in putting down the arms of Spain as an absolute monarch, in defacing the monuments of the Prince of Orange, of the Archduke Mathias, and in general, in that his Honor doth exact so much of them in seeking to have the disposing of all their finances.

The Marquis of Baden was requested by my Lord of Leicester's letters to entertain a gentleman into his service, to give him occurrants of these parts, and to farther this request his Honor did write unto Duke Casimir to entreat that favor of the Marquis of Baden. Duke Casimir informed me that the Marquis refused to do it, because he would not be suspected of the Spaniard, so that the gentleman returned back in as secret manner as he might.

There be sundry libels written and printed in Dutch and French sounding greatly to my Lord of Leicester's dishonor. Master Ségure did first inform me thereof and wished that some English gentleman would be a suitor to the Burgomaster to inhibit the sale of them. He himself did buy as many as he could to burn.

After I had written thus much, Master Palavicino came to Frankfort minding two days after to depart to Heidelberg to Duke Casimir, and Master de Gitry in his company. The next day came Baron Done hither also who had been in Prussia, Saxony, in the Duke of Brunswick's country to confer with the Colonels about furnishing of Duke Casimir of horse at his appointment, whereof I will acquaint your Lordship at my repair to England.

This is all I am to impart unto your Honor at this present wherefore wishing to your Honor long life and perpetual happiness, I most humbly take my leave. From Frankfort on Main the 2 of April 1586.

Your Honor's most bounden servant,
Stephen Powle

Powle's Copy of Tichborne's "Elegy for Himself"

In Stephen Powle's Commonplace Book (Tanner MS. 169:79r) is a copy of Chidiock Tichborne's fine eighteen-line poem, next to which Powle has noted: "Poem of Chidiock Tichborne written by himself 3 days before his execution. I have the originall written with his own hand."

Tichborne was one of seven conspirators executed in the summer of 1586 for their involvement in the Babington conspiracy to kill Elizabeth and put Mary on the English throne. This poem presumably was found in Tichborne's cell in the Tower of London at the time of his death and was procured by Powle perhaps through his Crown office connections. He seems to have been fully aware of its literary merit.

The "Elegy" was later set to music in John Mundy's *Songs and Psalmes* (1594) and in at least two other musical collections. A modern copy of the poem is found in the Tudor period anthology *The Golden Hind* (ed. by Roy Lamson and Hallett Smith, New York, 1942), page 577, but this version differs from Powle's transcription in several words and in one completely changed line. Perhaps it was altered or "improved" for the sake of the music.

Following is the complete poem as transcribed in Powle's Commonplace Book. Changes made in the later version as found in *The Golden Hind* are entered above the line in italic. It is likely that Powle is reponsible for preserving the original lines of one of the most beautiful short poems in the English language.

Elegy for Himself

My prime of youth is but a froste of cares:
My feaste of joy is but a dish of payne;
My cropp of corne is but a field of tares
And all my good is but vaine hope of gaine:
       past
The daye is gone, and yet I saw no sonn:
And nowe I live, and nowe my life is donn.

My tale was heard and yet it was not told,
The springe is paste, and yet it hath not sprong,
My   *fallen*
The frute is deade and yet the leaves are greene
    spent
My youth is gone, and yet I am but yonge
I saw the world and yet I was not seene
My thread is cutt, and yet it was not sponn
And now I lyve, and nowe my life is donn.

I sought my death, and found it in my wombe
I lookte for life, and saw it was a shade.
I trod the earth and knowe it was my tombe
      was
And nowe I die, and nowe I am but made
My   *my*
The glasse is full and now the glasse is rune
And nowe I live, and nowe my life is donne.

To the Right Honorable Master Secretary Davison [principal secretary] 30 November 1586. (Tanner MS. 309:62r–63r)

Right Honorable, I humbly crave pardon for my importuning of you with a suit at this unseasonable time, and that by letter. Let necessity I beseech you excuse me in the one and my sickness in the other. May it please your Honor to be advertised that Master Robert Barnby, merchant venturer into high Germany and especially about Nuremberg, Augsburg, and Ulm, having sustained great loss of £4000 by the casting away of a ship about Yarmouth two months since that came from Hamburg, and also by the Dunkirk's pillage of two other ships (wherein he had to the value of £2500 in Italian commodities) this last summer; and moreover, having been fraudulently dealt with by his servants whom he put in trust to his great hindrance likewise. And because of all these grievous crosses that were imposed on him by the hand of God (which no man's wisdom could prevent or withstand) he is not able to uphold his credit (the which he hath greatly in recommendation) unless he may be permitted to enjoy his liberty to collect such debts as are due unto him by others. Therefore he doth most humbly beseech your Honor to procure her Majesty's protection for the space of one year. The which suit of his I am the more desirous to further by my humble and presumptuous request of your Honor's favor herein, both for that I can assure your Honor of my poor credit (which is all the jewels I am presently possessed of) he doth not seek the benefit thereof fraudulently to deceive any man of their goods but doth mean to make full satisfaction to every man's contentment; and also because a poor cousin of mine is interested therein as his partner, whose cause I in conscience tender. If it shall please your Honor to favor my suit in their behalf, your Honor shall not only do a gracious act in preserving him from ruin that is almost overthrown but shall find me as I am already in all duty to be your Honor's most grateful affectionate servant.

I had a suit of mine own to acquaint your Honor of, which was to entreat the employment of my poor service though unworthy into some foreign country when any occasion is offered, as I suppose there will be daily in these same troublesome times, and that which I want in sufficiency I will supply *fide et taciturnitate* [in trust and in keeping silent]: whereof my Lord Treasurer whom I attend on will render sufficient testimony if your Honor will at any time vouchsafe to acquaint him therewith. But the good will I have to prevent this present honest merchant's overthrow causeth me to forget mine own future private good and my duty to your Honor in that I write so tedious a letter.

Praying therefore unto God for your increase of honor in this world and after this life that you may enjoy perpetual blessedness, I most humbly take my leave. The 30th November 1586.

Always at your Honor's commandment,
S.P.

There was procured by Master Secretary twelve of the Council's hands to a letter to the Sheriffs of Middlesex, & other places to inhibit any man from arresting Master Barnby, which was in nature of

a protection for one year and I had
of my cousin Newcom my bond in
of £400 that was forfeited to him
in regard of this favor.

John Chamberlain's Reply to Powle's September 1587 Letter

It is dated from London 25 December "1588" but must have been written in December 1587. It is found in Powle's Letter Book (Tanner MS. 309) in two different places: the complete letter in Chamberlain's hand is inserted on folios 300r–301v, and the end of the letter, as copied by Powle's clerk is on 56r. The following is quoted in full from folios 300r–301v:

Good Master Powle how welcome your letters were to me you may better imagine than I express, for you know things long looked for and much wished are the better accepted at last and yours the rather for that their long tarrying was recompensed with full and long delight. I would I could tell you how much I think myself beholden to you for the extraordinary pains, or that I know readily how to requite it, but though I be not so well stored, yet perhaps *quod defertu non aufertur* [what is deferred is not removed] it may be I shall pay you such interest that you will not think much of the forbearance. But when I bethink me, I see well you have gotten a great start of me and are like enough, if you list, to keep it, for you are there where there is kept a continual mart of news, a place appointed (as it seemeth) for a storehouse of occurrents and advice from all parts; so that to write you news were to send trees to the woods or owls to Athens, and I think there is not much passeth here but you have it sooner than I can send it. But I use not this as an excuse, for you shall have all I remember and new, tag and rag, cut and long tail, that when you have it (though perhaps you will not think it worth having) you may rather blame my indulgence than my diligence.

First, therefore, to begin with that which fell out last: his Excellency [Leicester] returned two days since out of the Low Countries where he hath left the Lord Willoughby lieutenant, and before his coming, upon suspicion of false measure, disarmed the Flushingers so that we have the town in absolute possession. The Earl of Derby, the Lord Cobham, the controller Sir Amias Pawlet, D. Dale, and Master Randall were appointed Commissioners to the Prince of Parma about a treaty and many days and times were prefixed when they should begone but still upon divers causes they have been interrupted, but specially for that the P[rince] maketh great preparation about Dunkirke to what end we know not, some say he had a practice by intelligence upon Flushing, which being discovered Aldegonde Villiers and the Viceadmiral (the P. of Orange's bastard son) are called in question. The Hollanders will in no wise intend to this peace, so that to conform them D. Attabere (master of requests) was sent to the states where he yet remaineth. How it will go forward now his Excellency is come home we shall see hereafter but, for fear of surprise and because we will be *in utrumque parati* [prepared both ways], here is great preparation to sea, for all or most of the Queen's ships are setting forth in all haste and accompanied with the Lord Henry Seymer, the Lord Thomas [   ] the Lord William, the Lord Sheffield and others. Sir Francis Drake with certain of the Queen's ships and others to the number of forty sail is appointed another way. Here hath been a great controversy between him and B Berrows for that he seeks to have justice upon him because in the last voyage he forsook him and carried away the Golden Hind, a ship of the Queen's and best of the company, the want whereof, as he pretends, was cause that he intercepted not the Indian fleet. It hath been long and much debated before the council without any certain determination and now upon my Lord of Leicester's return [torn page] hath renewed it and pursues it hotly. The news [torn corner] of the overthrow of some of his fleet by the Marquess Santa Croce was altogether false, for they are now lately come home and brought with them fourteen sail of portingales[3] laden with sugars and other merchandise from Brazil. Our provisions by land go as fast forward as our sea matters, for we have mustering everywhere and lieutenants and colonels appointed to every shore to be ready upon any sudden invasion. The Earls of Huntington and Cumberland, Sir Henry Lee, Sir Robert Constable and Captain Banborough are appointed like to the North. My Lord Chamberlain is already at Barwicke. Sir Walter Rawley is gone westward; he is sole lieutenant for Cornwall and joined in commission with the Earl of Bath for Devonshire. Sir John Smith is colonel of Essex, Suffolk and Norfolk. Others are likewise named for other places. The chief recusants in England are sent for up and committed to Bishops and others in custody. Now if you ask me upon what ground we have taken this hot alarm, I can answer you no certainty but upon speech of preparation in Spain and upon the Parma's doings at Dunkirke, and some suspicion of Scotland for the Scots are become very lusty and have entered and spoiled within our borders. Besides the King gathereth strength about him under pretence of mistrust of the Hamiltons and Stuarts who are lately linked together by a marriage. The Queen was determined to do him good and to have made him Duke of Richmond with the gift of certain lands (whereby he should have become English) and a pension of six thousand pounds a year. This was once in great forwardness but it is now at a pause or peradventure at a full point.

   On the Queen's Day in November the Earl of Essex made a gallant triumph and performed it well. Her Majesty hath been ever since at my Lord Chauncellor's in Holborn till within these four days that she came to Somerset House.

   Sir William Pelham died a fortnight ago at Flushing. Palavicine is made knight and likewise D. Dale whose son-in-law Master North hath lately played such a prank as would rather become a Turk, Jew or Scythian than any Christian or civil man, for a quarrel growing twixt one Web (whom perhaps you know) and him about six years past at a supper in the Low Countries, he offered at that time to stab him, whereupon Web gave him the bastinado,[4] which he digested till now within this month when, watching a time, he got him trained out between Flushing and Middleborough, and there while his servants held him, cut him overthwart the face with his knife, slit his nose, and then with his thumbs bolted out both of his eyes, that they hung upon his cheeks, and so left him. But by good hap a surgeon passing by put his eyes in their place again, and hath restored him to some sight. This revenge was thought totally inhumane and unfitting our time and country.

The Earl of Northumberland and John Wotton were committed on Sunday last from the council table, the one to the Fleet and the other to the Marshalsea for striking a gentleman in the Countess of Northumberland's house. The matter grew through some lightness in my Lord who is so far in love with Wotton that he would bestow his sister, the Lady Lucy, upon him, which is not thought fit. John Packinton is newly knighted and it is thought he shall be Captain of the Guard. But now that my powder is almost spent let us parle of other matters.

It was strangest for me to hear that you made such a progre[ss] [in] Italy. I thought you durst not have adventured it but I see [some] men have more courage than they make account of and know not [their] own stomach till they be put to it. It was hardily done and I am content it is past but I assure you I would not have been your half in it.

You are marvellously beset with Signoras if you be so round besieged, I see not how you can escape without passing the Pikes. If you live still among such saints you are very obstinate if you be not edified. Ywis your brother [Thomas] would not make it so dainty, for of all things he loves plenty. It was told me that this last summer at Bergen op Zoom [in Brabant in the Netherlands] he kept almost a whole regiment of wenches. He carried two from hence of mine acquaintance, for the rest he furnished himself there and kept four or five in one house. Oh he would have made a goodly Basha![5] But I must seal up your mouth that this come out no more. You write nothing how your diet there contents you, nor what taste you find in those sugared melons and other delicate fruits. Belike you were loath to set my teeth on water, or else you thought me not so licorous of that part as of the other thing.

Now touching the Gentleman your near friend whose welfare you tender so much [Edward Egerton] and of whom you charge me to write what I think unfeignedly, so it is that for myne own part I will not use many words, for you know what good estimation I have always had of the man, but I assure you on my faith that in what company soever (where I come) there fall out any occasion to make mention of him, this continual title or appendix is given him to be a very honest proper sufficient gentleman. This is the general voice of all that are about his uncle and of all others that I meet with, so that I doubt not but the place which you wish him, and I would be most glad he had it for your sake may easily fall to him if his uncle or his cousin[6] will stick to him. But will you have me tell you what I think: these naked praises and applauses are not enough to set him forward, for *virtus laudatur et alget* [virtue is praised and yet neglected] he must work himself into the world and not tarry till he be called, for modesty is grown out of fashion, and therefore he must become more bold and audacious, yea and somewhat importunate; perhaps you will say this is against his nature but this is the way, for so is Daniel Rogers crept in who by report is as fit for that place as I to be Pope, and I guess that Constable aspires to it for I see him much at Court and in great formality. A man of worth would disdain to be out shouldered by such companions. Wherefore you may do well to advise him to spur his uncle and his cousin to the uttermost and to take their time while it last, for I doubt we shall not have them long but that they will drop out of the way one of these days; for his uncle was at last cast not long since (though it were not much spoken of) and his Cousin came little abroad since Shrovetide, so it were good catching hold of occasion while he may.

Thus have I set you down my mind after my plain and Dunstable[7] manner; if you like it you may have more at leisure, for I will not fail to answer you by exchange. Marry I love not to take too much pains nor to wear my wit, and therefore I have sent you this for assay, that you look for no better hereafter. One thing I had almost forgot: that I would not have any spark of unkindness twixt you and Master Gent[8] for lack of a letter. Rather than so I would write for you both myself though I do it ill favoredly. Methinks you should know him too well to judge him either unthankful or unmindful.

I thank you for your gentle token and for the offer of your new relation,[9] which I will not refuse when it shall please God we may meet, that I may enjoy you and them both at once. I did your commendations to the persons you willed me, who all return them twentyfold with hearty prayers for your health and safety. I pray you do the like for me to Master Luther and Master Sioll and lastly to your good self as one that is my second care of all the world out of England, whither I pray God send you an happy and short return.

London this 25 Decembris. 1588 [1587]
Yours assuredly
John Chamberlain

Newsletter from Venice to Principal Secretary Sir Francis Walsingham at the Court dated 13 February 1588 N.S. [3 February 1587/8 in England] (State Papers 101/81, fols. 78r–81v)

Right Honorable, my duty in most humble manner remembered. May it please your Honor to be advertised that my last letter bare date the 30th of January.

Di Roma 30. di Gennaio*

Il Cardinal Gran Maestro di Malta parti di qua dominica con 500. persone et titolo d'Inquisitore Generale nell'Isola di Malta oltra li altri titoli serieta la settimana passata.

Scrivano di Genoa esser arrivati nello porto di vai due Galere di Spagna di quella Signoria con 200 m. scudi de particolari, et con 4. della fuste prese in Corsica et 130. Turchi prigioni, havendo lasciate l'altere 3. a quelle Isolane.

Nel Consistorio di hier mattina s'intende che fosse spedita la Chiesa di Cassano nel regno per Monsignor Ludovici Inglese ad nominatione del Ré di Spagna.

Questo negotiare tanto longamente et cosi alle strette che fa l'Ambasciator Cattolico con li principali Cardinali della Corte fa lambicare il cervello alli curiosi che non possono sottrahere quello que vada sul tavogliero.

Di Polonia s'intende che Monsignor l'Arcivescono di Napoli s'era retirato in Isla castello sicuro, et in virtù d'un breve mandatoli di qua da Sua Santità che desiderando S. B^{pe} come padre universale, la quiete della Rep. Christiana, et di quel Regno et abbracciando l'un et l'altro Principe eletto a quella corona dovesse S. S. Illma a nome di sua S^{te} interporsi con quei Sig^{ri} et doviar li incendii et guerra che da cio potessero nascere, et pero S. S. Sa^{ma} haveva spedito suoi segretarij all'Arciduca Massimiliano, al Principe di Suetia et al Gran Cancelliere, che da loro li sia assicurato il passo per trattar con essi il servitio di S. Sta.

Di Venetia .5. Febraio

Di Spagna avisano con lettere dell'ultimo di Decembre che li 40 vascelli Inglesi che si trattenevano verso il Capo di S. Vincenzo nella Costa di Portugallo facevano di continuo gran da ni, non potendovi passare vascello alcuno che non fosse preso, et gia havevano fatto bottino per piu di 250m. scudi, et che l'armata Cattolica era ancora nel porto di Lysbona; et si bene sollecitana con ogni possibil diliganza per metterla in ordine si teneva pero, che non potrebbe partire piu presto che al principio Maggio, confirmandosi esser. Armata potentissima et e issima provista de soldati et altre cose necessarie, et che del tutto sia destinata per l'impresa d'Inghilterra.

How meanly they be furnished both for men, powder, bullet, sails, victuals, and other necessaries I advertised your Honor in my last letters so that this report is given forth to uphold Spain's greatness in the eye of the world.

Although your Honor have more particular intelligence from Constantinople than possibly may be had from Venice, nevertheless I have

---

*For translation of Italian passages, see pp. 210–11.

thought it my duty to acquaint your Honor of such supposals as be bruited here.

Si è stato detto che il Bailo d'Inghilterra habbia presentata una supplica al Gran Turco, rimemorano che per suo negotio gia fossero stabiliti Capitoli tra S. Alterra, et la sua Regina, nelle quali lei sera obligata muover le armi contra il Ré Cattolico per mare et per terra, si come ha fatto, penetrando non solo li riviere di Spagna et Portogallo, ma anco si puo dire a mezzo il camino della Indie, et per terra nella Frisia, Geldria, et Fiandra in maniera che il Ré irritato hora mantiene due grosse armate: l'uno sotto il Marchese S. Croce et l'altra in mano del Duca di Parma, minacciando di andare ai danni del Regno d'Inghilterra; et che havendo il Gran Sign[ore] promesso di voltar le armi contra Spagna. Hora é venuto il tempo che per lo meno con cento Galere si vadi nelle riviere Spagnuole a fin che matino proposito di disturbare le Regina d'Inghilterra dalla quali esso Bailo aspetta d'esser rivocato.

They serve themselves by this report in .2. purposes: the one is to lessen in the opinion of the world her Majesty's forces as unable of herself to stand against Spain without diverting his power by the mean of the Turk, the other, to make her Majesty odious to the world by bringing into Europe the arms of Infidels to work a private revenge upon Spain.

Di Praga 19. di Gennaio

S'intende che l'Arciduca Massimiliano che si trovava ancora a Crepizzo [Krepitz] con solo 5000. soldati tra Cavalli et farti veniva consigliato andarsene a Velluno [Wielun] et farcusi coronar dalli suoi adherenti, confirmandosi la Corronatione del Principe di Suetia fatta li 27. del passato, dal Cardinale Battori in assentia del vescono di Vilna, al quale per ancora non s'era dato il scettro ni la spada regale, a favore del qua principe si dice che la Polonia maggiore haveva messo una tanza che tutti li huomini di .30. anni pagassero chiascuno di essi un tallero et li giovenetti di .20. anni mezzo tallero, dicendosi anco che il Gran Cancelliere haveva dato libertá alle sue genti di [ ] a suo beneplacito darmegiare con ferro et fuoco la Silesia; le forze della quale et di quella di Moravia (che del continuo si radunavano per favorire le cose di s'Altezza) si dubitava non fossero bastanti, non essendosi per anco li Bohemi risolati di favorir quella Impresa. Excusandosi li capi principali non potervi andare alcuni per indispositione et altre per altre cause.

Da Venetia

Scrivano qua da Milano che Santa Majesta Cattolica haveva poi rimessi et accettati i Capitoli che furono gia discussi per la lega con Suvireri et dato ordine al Signor Duca di Terranova Governatore di quella Citta che si stabilischi. Havendoli S. M^{ta} fatto donar loro 28 mille scudi in questa attione et anco di pagare li le provisioni contenuti ne' Capitoli sudetti. S'intende di Firenza che essendo l'altro giorno Il Cardinal Granduca andato a diporto verso una Isoletta del fiume Arno, et stando in una barchetta a far pescare, nel mettersi la rete da un pescatore, si rivolta la barca et casco in acqua esso Granduca et alcuni Signori che erano seco con grandissimo periculo d'annegarsi, si bene ogni uno si salvo et particularmente il Granduca fu cavato dell-acqua senza offesa alcuna da un suo moro notatore molto prattico.

      Da Roma li .6. di Febraio

S'intende che il Cardinal Giocosa [Joyeuse] faccia instanza verso il Ré Christianissimo di ritornare in Franza per qualche mese per accomodare con la sua presenza le cose della Casa sua, che dopo la morte del fratello sono in confusione at contendosense S. M^{ta} mandi ordine al Cardinal Lenoncourt che si fermi qui alla protettione di quel Regno.

Lunedi sera il Cardinal Farnese fá ad una longa audiensa di S. Sta nolendo dire alcuni giuditarij che fosse per trattare il matrimonio del Principe Ranuttio con la pronipote di S. Sta che tuttavia se ne ragiona.

Powle continues with a few further pages in Italian summarizing news reports from Rome and Venice. After itemizing the various occurrences in Italian, he concludes with his more guarded comments in English.

After I had written this far, I received letters from Padua and Mantua. In the one I understood that Sboroschi was arrived there to be here on this day but in secret to procure men of the Signory for Maximilian. But it is thought his labor will not be with any effectual success because this Signory will not offend the Turk who is all that he may for the Swede. The most that he may hope for is to have some *fuorusciti* [outlaws] and that underhand from hence. From Mantua I am advertized and that for certainty that Don Ippolito Gonzaga is to have charge of 2000. foot forthwith to depart to the aid of Maximilian. Florence will contribute money and Ferrara, as above is written, hath sent 300,000 crowns to the Emperor for the investiture of Modena and Reggio. Besides he will aid his brother with more money so that all the credit the Emperor hath in Italy shall be employed for the recovery of the almost lost kingdom of Polonia, of which occurrence there is most speech at this time in Venice. Charles of Styria sendeth 600. lances, Ferdinand of Tyrol 400. besides certain companies of foot. And the Duke of Bavaria will furnish him with as many as, his own brother's necessity being satisfied, he may conveniently spare.

The reason why the Emperor hath invested the Duke of Ferrara, having so long denied him the same, is partly to procure money to furnish his brother and himself in this action of Polonia and withal to use him for men upon the satisfying of this his request, partly also to have the discontentment with the Pope who hath denied his brother's Ambassadors the loan of money this last summer with this answer: that it was not his office to give wood to nourish the fires in any of his children's countries, for he knew hereby he should greatly offend the Pope that had denied Ferrara this last summer, likewise the Investiture of Ferrara in the person of Don Cesare d'Este.

This morning I had conference with one of especial account that advised me that the 19th of the last month there were seen 40. English sail within the Straits of Gibraltar, as some imagine to meet with an appointed Turk from the Great Signor and by joining their forces together to give him a port in Spain. And (because no man in our nation is better known) they suppose it is Sir Francis Drake. We here know nothing thereof because it is 8 weeks since any letters were received by the way of Cologne by any Englishman.

I thought it my duty to acquaint your Honor with the reports written hither from Antwerp of the Prince of Parma's intents.

D'Annersa li .23. di Gennaio

Il Duca di Parma ha levato da tutti questi presidij li soldati veterani, rimettendone de nuovi gionti ultimamente per unirsi come piu esperti in bello, col suo essercito benissimo al ordine di 30,000 fanti et 7000 cavalli, col quale doneva (come el voce) ritrovarsi ai quindeci del seguente nel Regno di Scotia, da una banda aspettato da quel Ré con altre genti per unirsi seco, et il Marchese Santa Croce con l'Armata dall'altra banda per dare in un medesimo tempo a dorso alla Regina d'Inghilterra da due parti, laqual gagliardamente attende a far delle preparatione per la diffesa del suo Regno.

Di Preslavia li .21. di Gennaio

La Nobiltà della Polonia maggiore resta malissimo sodisfatto di Massimiliano per non volersi partire di quel Regno havendo per cio risoluto di cacciarnele per forza.

Avisi piu freschi da Venetia

Si ragiona che il Persiano haveva maritato una sorella al Ré de Tartari, il quale con 20,000 Cavalli andava verso Babilonia per ricuperare quella Citta per il Cognato, et anch'ergo con potente essercito dall'altra parte marchiana a quella volta, con discegno poi d'andare uniti insieme ad scacciare de Tauris li Turchi.

Scrivono da Praga che havendo il Gran Cancelliere mandato una grossa Banda de soldati per scacciare del Regno Massimigliano, egli haveva rotto li Pollachi con morte di 300. di loro, il capo delli quali s'era retivato in certa terra murata con gli avanzati molto mal trattati. Che in molto luoghi di Germania et d'Ungheria si facevano genti con gran sollecitudine per S. Altezza, nolendo pro sequire la vittoria, et con l'aiuto de Littuani assediare il nuovo Ré in Cracovia.

Di Augusta li .6. di Febraio

Li Francesi che si scrisse essersene ritornati in Francia, hora s'intende che si trovino par nel Contado di Mumbelgardo dameggiando et twanneggiando qui che Turchi poi che violavono virgini, et ogni altra sorte di donne, conducendo via huomini et molti bestianni, ma si crede all'arrivo in detto Contado de 15,000. Suizzeri et 3000. Cavalli mandati presto dalli Landgravij con 5000. fanti del Duca di Wirtenberg debbino scombrare da quel contorno. Hor hora vien detto che i Francesi siano stati circondati in modo dalli 15,000. Suizzeri che non possino retinarsi verso i lor confini.

Thus with the humble remembrance of my duty I beseech Almighty God to bless you in this world with increase of Honor and after this life to bestow on you perpetual happiness.

From Venice the 13. of February, stilo novo 1588. [3 February 1587/8 in England].

Your Honor's
Ever most bounden,
Stephen Powle

Translation of Italian passages in Powle's newsletter of 13 February 1588 to Walsingham.

From Rome $\frac{30}{20}$ January

The Cardinal Grand Master of Malta left here on Sunday with 500 persons and with the title of Inquisitor General of the Island of Malta in addition to other titles received the week before. They write from Genoa that two galleys have arrived at the port from Spain with 200,000 scudi [crowns] belonging to private persons and with four of the galleys taken in Corsica and 130 Turkish prisoners, having left another three with the Corsicans. In yesterday morning's consistory, it was learned, the Church of Cassano in the Kingdom [of Naples] was, on the nomination of the Spanish King, conferred on Dr. Lewis, an Englishman. The very lengthy and secret negotiation of the Spanish Ambassador with the chief Cardinals of the Court makes the curious wrack their brains because they cannot discover what is transpiring.

From Poland it is learned that the Archbishop of Naples retired to Isla, a strong castle, and by virtue of a brief letter sent him from here by his Holiness that he, as the universal father (desiring the peace of the Christian Commonwealth and of that Kingdom and embracing both princes elected to the crown) would have him, in the name of his Holiness, intercede with those Signori and avoid the fires and war which might ensue. He has therefore sent his secretaries to the Archduke Maximilian, the Prince of Sweden, and the Grand Chancellor, in order to be assured of safe passage to negotiate with them as his Holiness wishes.

APPENDIX E 211

Venice $\frac{\text{5 February}}{\text{26 January}}$

Letters of the last day of December from Spain advise us that the 40 English ships which were headed toward Cape St. Vincent on the Portuguese coast continued to do great damage, no ship being able to pass without capture, and they had already taken over 250,000 crowns in booty; and that the Catholic Armada was still in the port of Lisbon and, although they were pushing with all possible diligence to get ready, it was thought that it couldn't depart earlier than the beginning of May. It is confirmed to be very powerful and filled with soldiers and all necessary things and everyone is convinced that it is intended for the enterprise of England.
[See English lines on p. 206].
It has been said that the English ambassador had presented a request to the Grand Turk, reminding him of the already established agreements between His Highness and the Queen by which she will be obliged to take up arms against the Catholic King by sea or land, as she has done, penetrating not only the coasts of Spain and Portugal but also, one might say, the route to the Indies, and on land in Friesland, Gueldria, and Flanders; so that the King, now irritated, maintains two huge armies: one under the Marquis Santa Croce and the other in the hands of the Duke of Parma, threatening the destruction of the kingdom of England, and that the Grand Signor having promised to take arms against Spain, the time has now come when at the least with 100 galleys he should go into the Spanish coasts in order to deter the wicked purpose of disturbing the English Queen by whom this ambassador expects to be recalled.
[See English lines on p. 207].

From Prague $\frac{19}{9}$ January

It is reported that the Archduke Maximilian who was still in Krepitz with only 5,000 soldiers (horse and foot) was advised to go to Wielun and to have himself crowned by his adherents, the coronation of the Prince of Sweden on December 27th by Cardinal Bathory being confirmed in the absence of the Bishop of Vilna, even though he has not yet been given the sceptre and the royal sword. In favor of this prince it is said that greater Poland had placed a tax of a thaler on all men of thirty years of age and half a thaler on the young men of twenty. It was also said that the Grand Chancellor had given his men permission to go at their pleasure with fire and sword to ravage Silesia, where it was feared that their forces and those of the Moravians (who were meeting to assist the affairs of his Highness) would be insufficient, the inhabitants of Bohemia not having made up their minds to support that course.

Seventy-two leaders say in excuse that some cannot go because of illness, and others for other reasons.

From Venice

They write from Milan that his Catholic Majesty had sent back with his acceptance the articles for a league with the Swiss and has given the order to the Duke of Terranova, governor of that city, that it should be concluded, his Majesty having given them 28,000 crowns in the present action and agreed to pay them the provision contained in the said articles. We learn from Florence that the other day the Cardinal Grand Duke had gone for pleasure toward an island in the River Arno and while fishing from the boat, the fisherman in setting the net upset the boat which threw the Grand Duke and some of his gentlemen into the water. Despite a great risk of drowning, they were all saved. The Grand Duke was rescued unharmed from the water by one of his Moors who was an expert swimmer.

From Rome $\frac{6 \text{ February}}{27 \text{ January}}$

It is learned that Cardinal Joyeuse has requested the most Christian King to allow him to return to France for a few months to arrange personally the affairs of his house, now in confusion and dispute since the death of his brother; and his Majesty agreeing to this has ordered Cardinal Lenoncourt to remain here for the protection of that kingdom.

On Monday evening Cardinal Farnese had a long audience with the Pope concerning the marriage of Prince Ranutio to the grandniece of the Pope (which is still being discussed).

[Powle continues with more guarded comments in English—see p. 271—then returns to Italian, which translates as follows:]

From Antwerp the $\frac{23}{13}$ January

The Duke of Parma has removed the veteran soldiers from all these garrisons, replacing them with those recently arrived, in order to add these experienced troops to his army of 30,000 foot and 7,000 horse with which, it is said, on the 15th of next month he is to go into Scotland where he is awaited by that King and other people to join them and on the other side the Marquis Santa Croce with his armada to attack simultaneouusly in two places the English Queen who is bravely making preparations for the defense of her kingdom.

From Breslau January $\frac{21}{11}$

The nobility of Greater Poland remain very dissatisfied with Maximilian for not leaving the kingdom and have decided to turn him out by force.

More recent news from Venice.

It is said that the Persian has married a sister of the King of Tartary who was going with 20,000 horse towards Babylon to recover that city for his brother-in-law who was also marching there from the other side with a powerful army intending to join ranks to chase the Turks from Tauris.

They write from Prague that the Great Chancellor, having sent a large band of soldiers to drive Maximilian from the kingdom, had routed the Poles, killing 300 of them, their leader had then withdrawn with the remainder to a defended position.

That in many parts of Germany and Hungary they were hastily gathering forces for his Highness, for they wished to follow up the victory and, with the help of the Lithuanians, to besiege the new King in Cracow.

From Augsburg $\frac{\text{February 6}}{\text{January 27}}$

The French who were said to have returned to France are now reported to be in the country of Monbeliard, damaging and oppressing it more than any Turks, for they violate virgins and any other women and carry away men and animals. But it is believed that at the arrival in that country of 15,000 Swiss and 3,000 cavalry sent quickly by the Landgrave, with 6,000 foot soldiers from the Duke of Wirtemberg, the French will be chased out of that neighborhood. Now news has come that they have been surrounded by the Swiss in such a way that they cannot withdraw toward their borders.[10]
[See conclusion in English on p. 210]

My Lord Treasurer's Letter which he sent to me to Venice. 15th Febr. 1587 [1587/8] (Tanner MS. 309:46v)
[Powle states in Tanner MS. 78: 101r that Burghley's letter was written in his own hand.]

Master Powle, I should condemn myself deeply if I thought that you did look for my letters, either of thanks or commendations either so often or in so large a measure as you have deserved the same by your continual writing to Master Secretary [Walsingham] whereof being made a participant, I have received towards myself a consolation to see the various proceedings of the world and conceived in you a great liking to see your capacity and judgment in your advertisements and reports, whereto for your commendation I must needs add, a great labor and industry, in writing at such length (as I have observed) in your monthly letters. But setting that apart which concerneth your public letters to Master Secretary, for the which I am sure he giveth you great thanks, I cannot but particularly acknowledge myself very heartily gladdened with a long letter written by you to me in the latter end of November; wherein you did at great length and in a good method anatomize the whole body of Italy, describing the conditions, the sympathies, and jointures of all the states and potentates in such plain and probable manner as any discourser or inward counsellor of their countries were able to do. And truly for my satisfaction therein, I could not find anything lacking to be required. And though I do frequently read the advices which commonly come from Italy and do take pleasure to see the motion of the world that cannot rest; yet the substance of your letter: containing the aspects (as the astronomers say) of every particular state one to the other either by conjunction or opposition, I do the easier judge of the probability of all other common advices which do many times so vary as without a common rule (for which your long discourse doth serve me) it were hard to determine amongst the advertisements what is true and not true. Thus you see what profit I have taken of your writing. And at this time perceiving your servant's purpose to come to you, I could not without some note of unkindness but write to you hereof as I do. And though you may pretend that I may challenge thus much of you because you have knowledged me as your Master, yet surely I esteem your labor bestowed in your large discourse to be of more value than any service at any time since I have had servants hath been. And now to end, I wish you health to continue as you do, and therewith I wish you to be circumspect in the place where you are, to avoid the craftiness of false brethren and the malice of such as may be your enemies for your country's sake.

Of such occurrents here, I doubt not but you have divers of your familiars that have leisure and pleasure also to write thereof whereby you may sometime see that Almighty God doth not forsake the tuition of our Queen and country against the boastings and proud menaces of the sworn enemies of the Gospel of our Saviour Christ. And yet we do not impute our successes to our own powers, which though they are to be balanced with our enemy's, yet they are not to be contemned but of more force by God's favor than any enemy yet hath vanquished. And so it hath pleased God to bless this realm and this age as I dare say no king Christian hath his people (without respect of a number of cowardly recusants and malcontents) so ready, so earnest, yea and well able with bodies, hearts, purses, armour, and weapon to withstand a common enemy that our Lady and Sovereign hath. And this I write of judgment, though I be not ignorant how otherwise in many other proud countries the contrary is commonly reported, partly of envy, part of malice, and in a great part of ignorance of our state.

And so I end with my most hearty thanks, and thereto I must add a

confession of my debt for the delicate and costly token that you sent me which was certain fair spoons of mother of pearl.
From the Court of Greenwich.   15, Febr. 1587
Your assured loving friend,
W. Burghley

To the Lord Keeper Sir John Puckering with a rich cabinet of mother of pearl with sundry pillars of porphyry stone lined with cloth of gold and a great rich glass cut all diamonds covered all over with black velvet edged with broad gold lace which cost me one hundred marks. 2 January 1595/6 (Tanner MS. 309:51r).

My most Honorable Lord,
I have no better present to send than the show of my dutiful service, no other jewel than my wholly devoted heart to your command, either any other gift of price than this Italian trifle. I have kept it long by me, these nine years. I have brought it with me far overland, even out of Bologna. It beareth therefore the characters of time and carriage by some few blemishes. Nevertheless, I offer it to your good Lordship because it hath been heretofore to me highly fortunate: for it hath graced me with the successive favor of two wives: the first honorably descended, being daughter to the cousin germane[11] of Queen Anne Boleyn; the other being an heir to her father of five hundred marks of land and having five hundred pounds the year in possession by her own purchase in Essex. If it may likewise carry with it that fatal power in gaining the continuance of your Lordship's good liking and gracious acceptance thereof, I shall then repute myself richly blessed by this threefold happiness, the which as I hope to obtain so I most humbly crave at your honorable hands. Ending with all submissive reverence, wishing you to live many years in honor with the perfect enjoying of all your contentments.
Chancery Lane this second of January, Anno R.R. Elizabethæ 38.
Your Honor's ever most bounden,
S.P.

Letter written by S.P. for his stepson John Smyth to Mistress Wells, a young sixteen-year-old widow, "fair and rich in state, left by her husband worth £2000 but she had been misinformed of him [Smyth] and therefore made choice of some other." (Tanner MS. 309:4r)

My most dear Mistress Wells,
The most ancient oblation in the infancy of the world was the firstlings and fatlings of their flocks. The best contenting perfume and incense in the time of our forefathers was reputed to be a pure and unspotted soul, and the best accounted sacrifice at this day is esteemed of all men the

unfeigned offering up of a zealous heart. By this is mystically signified that our substance, minds, and bodies must be wholly employed in any worthy to be received oblation. Whereon I make this inference: my kind friends have delivered to your consideration mine estate, myself have presented to you with the view of my person, and this my letter offereth to your gracious acceptance my first and most affectionate love. Now you dear Lady in whose breast the sacred vestal virgins' fire doth as yet burn (and to whom I wholly devote that little all which I am endowed with) if by any kind answer as by an holy heat you further inflame me and that all my mentioned sacrifice ascends smoothly in your sight, you shall cause my often pilgrimage to the Temple of that place you remain in and I will make your sweet self the only saint of my soul. Or if you (resembling the good ground) return me a rejoicing yield of the precious grains of affection I bestow on you, then only and forever hereafter I will employ my whole endeavors for a more plentiful increase. But if either you consume me with any scorching refusal as with the Fire or else deny me a grateful return with the barren Earth, or Cool and quench the burning affection of my heart as with Water, you shall both cause me hereafter to be irreligious in this kind and to live always civilly and solely to myself forsaking utterly the country life forever. Thus resting wholly to be fashioned and formed in the mold it shall please you to work me in by your beautiful hands, I kiss the same with most affectionate Devotion.
The 14 Decembris. 1598.
           Yours, yours, yours,
           Jo: Smyth

To the Mistress of himself
give these.

To Lady Jane Mansell, 1599 (Tanner MS. 309:52r)

My most dear, and worthy to be most dear, Niece,

Although the same way was ever in common conceit from Thebes to Athens as was Athens to Thebes, yet sometimes we find that the steepy descent from the one or the mountainy ascent to the other, or the going in winter or in summer, may alter that grounded opinion. I might make an inference hereof diversely, but indeed between you and me always (be they never so hilly) shall be forever plains and all conveyances (be they never so difficult) shall be equal. For I challenge not at all any prerogative of an uncle. But thus much I might (if I should speak answer for myself) that the last exchange of kindness proceeded from me, for I never received till now by Master Brock any letter or answer to mine date in May was twelve months, and yet plenty of messengers have been afforded every term either to my father, my sister, or other your friends, and I, poor I, as one out of the way had no part at your dole nor was so much as besprinkled with any drop of water of kind remembrance. I will not say I grieved thereat, for then you might think I used complaining expostulations. But this I will say, I might have taken it to the heart if my heart had not been these seven years past heretofore steeled with many crossing discontentments. My man's writing in secretary hand was not for mine ease as you object but for your relief in reading my scribbled lines. Thus much I write as a descant on the ground of your letter. Now (my most sweet Niece) for I will never cease to write kindly to you, because holy waters of love must flow always from the holy fountain of nature, to set down voluntary, I long to see you and have good Sir Thomas and your company here in London. I can now bid you welcome to mine own house. And (before mine own soul I speak it) I will repute myself happy to be able to bid you welcome. Now mine estate is settled so that I can wholly and not dividedly attend my dearest friends. All my storms be overgone (I praise God) so that now I can rest in a calm haven. In one word to say, now I am wholly myself, that is as much to say as all that I am, I am yours. *Tutto quanto che io sono, son vostro.* A great Prince said to me so once for form[12] but I speak it to you materially and effectually.

Look for no news especially of matters of state in these queasy times, for common occurrents would be frivolous and weighty would be dangerous to commit to an uncertain delivery. Thus wishing to you and good Sir Thomas a kind remembrance of your best friends with a desire to have your company, I leave you both to the Lord's mighty protection and end with mine and my wife's most affectionate commendations.

Crown Office this last of November 1599.

Your loving uncle to be commanded,

S.P.

The Earl of Essex his behavior, speech, and prayer at the time of his death. 27 February 1600/1 (Tanner MS. 169:143r–44r).

On Thursday the xxvii of February Anno Domini 1600: about eight of the clock in the morning, was the sentence of death executed upon Robert Devereux, Earl of Essex within the Tower of London where a scaffold being set up in the court and a form [   ] ebre unto the place, whereon sat the Earls of Cumberland and Hertford, the Lord Viscount Bindon, the Lord Thomas Howard, the Lord Darcie of Chiche and the Lord Compton, Sir John Paton [Peyton], Lieutenant of the Tower with some sixteen Swiss lances of the guard. Wa[   ] sent for the prisoner who came in a gown of wrought velvet, a black satin suit, a felt hat black, a little ruff about his neck, and accompanied from his chamber with three deputies, Doctor Manford [Mountford], Doctor [William] Barlow, and Master [Abdy] Ashton his chaplain: them he had requested not to part from him but to observe him and recall him if either his eye, or countenance, or speech should bewray anything which might not become him for that time. All the way he desired the spectators to pray for him and so arriving on the scaffold he waved his hat and with obeisance unto the lords to this effect so spoke:

> My Lords and you my Christian Brethren who are to be witnesses of this my just punishment, I confess to the glory of God that I am a most wretched sinner and that my sins are more in number than the hairs of my head. I confess that I have bestowed my youth in wantonness, lust, and uncleanness; that I have been puffed up with pride, vanity, and love of this world's pleasures but that notwithstanding divers good motions inspired unto me from the spirit of God, the deed which I would I have not done, but the evil which I would not, that have I done. For all which I humbly beseech my saviour Christ to be a mediator to the eternal Majesty for pardon, especially for this my last sin, this great, this bloody, this crying, this infectious sin whereby so many have (for love of me) been drawn to offend God, to offend their Sovereign and to offend the world. I beseech God to forgive that act and to forgive that one most wretched of all. I beseech her Majesty and the state, and ministers thereof to forgive that act and I beseech God to send her Majesty a prosperous Reign and a long if it be his will. O Lord, grant her a wise and understanding heart; O lord, bless Her and her Nobles and her ministers of the church and state; and I beseech you and the world to hold a charitable opinion of me for my intention towards her Majesty whose death I protest I never wanted nor violence to her person. I never was, I thank God, Atheist not believing the word and scriptures, neither Papist trusting my own merits, but hope for salvation from God only by the mercy and merits of my savior Christ Jesus. This faith was I brought up in and herein am now ready to die, beseeching you all to join your selves with me in prayer that my soul may be lifted up by faith above all worldly things in my prayer. Yeah, for that I beseech you to join with me I will speak that you may hear me.

And here as he turned himself aside to put off his gown, Doctor Mountford requested him to remember to pray to God for his sins if he had any. To whom he answered:
I thank you for it.
And so turning himself again to the Lords and the rest, he said:

> I desire all the world to forgive me as I freely forgive and from my heart freely forgive all the world.

Then putting off his gown and ruff and presenting himself before the Block kneeling down he was by Doctor Barlow encouraged against the fear of death. To whom he answered that having been divers times in places of danger where death was never so present nor yet so certain, he had felt the weakness of the flesh and therefore now in this great conflict desired God to assist and strengthen him and so with eyes fixed on heaven after some passionate pants and breathings he began prayer in effect following:

O God, creator of all things and judge of all men, thou hast let me know thy warrant [   ] the world, that Satan is then most busy when our end is nearest, and that Satan being resisted will flee. I humbly beseech thee to assist me in this my last combat, and so nigh. Thou acceptest even of our desires as our hopes. Accept I beseech thee of my desire to resist him as of true resistance and perfect by thy grace that thou seest in my flesh to be feeble and weak. Give me patience to bear as becometh me this just punishment inflicted upon me by so honorable trial; grant me the inward comfort of thy spirit let thy spirit seal unto my soul an assurance of thy mercies. Lift my soul above all early cogitations and when my Life and body shall part, send thy blessed Angels which may receive my soul and convey it to thy joys in heaven.

Then concluding his prayer for all estates of the Realm, he shut up all with the Lord's prayer, reiterating this petition, "Lord Jesus, forgive us our trespasses, Lord Jesus, receive my soul."
Then desiring to be informed what was fit for him to do for disposing himself fit for the block, the executioner on his knees presented himself asking him forgiveness. To whom the Earl said, "I forgive thee, thou art welcome unto me, thou art the minister of Justice."
At which time Doctor Mountford requested him to rehearse the Creed which he did, repeating every article after the reprives.
So opening and putting off his doublet he was in a scarlet waistcoat and then, ready to lie down, he said he would only stretch forth his arms and prove them abroad, for then he was ready. So bowing toward the block, the Doctor requested him to say the first two verses of the fifth psalm which he did, and then declining his body he said:

In humility and obedience to thy commandment, in obedience to thy ordinance, to thy good pleasure, O God, I prostrate myself to my deserved punishment. Lord be merciful to thy prostrate servant.

So lying down flat along the boards and laying down his head and fitting it upon the block stretching out his arms with these last words, "Lord, into thy hands I commend my spirit."
His head was severed from his body by the aid of three strokes but the first deadly and absolutely and depriving all sense and motion.

Love letter written by S.P. for his servant Dick Hoskyn to Mr Dr Franke's daughter Kesie. (Tanner MS. 169:142r).

Dear heart,
For so I will style thee, because my first and dearest love hath been bestowed upon thee; and my dearest and daily thoughts be continually of thee. Dear heart, I say, be not like the barren ground to yield me small increase of my labour and all of my grains of passionate affection cast

upon thee. It began and was sowed in the spring and youth of the year at St. Valentine's day; it doth continue in this season of summer and shall remain and be of force with me to the winter of mine age and end of my life. I challenge the same at thy hands by the law of nature because our years be not unequal, and by the law of requital because the reward of love is and must be only love. Let to me make trial of my truth as thou didst write unto me and let my unfained passions be made known and rewarded as they deserve. Then I doubt not that I shall be rewarded with that which to enjoy I shall esteem my sole and only happiness. In hope thereof I live and without that path I shall perpetually languish. Thus I end resting ever

        Thyne, thyne, only thyne
          R. Hoskyn

(probably written ca. 1610)

To the right worshipful my much respected friend Sir Robert Bassett knight   8 June 1616 (Tanner MS. 169:147v)

Against a representation by Fictions

Forma homine fragile; Una mutabilis hora:
Luce nova nulla est; vel nova luce nova.

Sir
There is nothing more befitting a worthy gentleman than the keeping of his naked and bare word but when the same is clothed by protestations in written letters and sealed up with all the assurances that your directions to your own scrivener could by your own appointment devise, it is in my simple judgment from any honest man an infallible security. And therefore, sir, because I hold you by birth honorable and by condition and carriage justly to be skilled and upright, therefore I will never be persuaded that you mean to swerve from any of such true endowments which God and nature hath bestowed upon you. It was your pleasure to desire my house, you being to me before unknown nor never heard of. Having as you pretended a purpose to match your son in these parts, you made means by your often letters and messages for the same. The price after long conference was agreed on, the party by your direction named who should have the possession thereof delivered and that with all expedition (for these were your words in your last letter) which was accordingly performed by me. The house cost me in ready money £2250 to the hinges, readers in Gray's Inn, besides the charges in present reparations which come to £56. I have been offered sundry times £1300 for it. I at the first stood (to some men) to have £1500 and to some others £2000 and yet of late after six years' forbearance of rent and income, then £100 spent in reparations in building again the overgrown brick walls, I was contented to take £1400, being a lesser sum. This

circle and course held by me I set down to show you first my proceedings therein and then to acquaint you what is the center and period of my resolution which is to take it unkindly if you fail the payment at the time appointed and made by your own mature consideration thereof. Yet I will never misconceive so of you (that before you and Master Lassells[13] entered to the statute as of £2000 to me) that you had conveyed away your Land to any other. Thus in hope of your sincere dealing with me in this my important business, I commit you to God and rest,

                    Your loving friend,
                    S.P.

Mile end this 8 of June 1616

(Apparently the sale of Mylende to Sir Robert Bassett was never consummated. Powle was still living there in 1620 when he wrote to his niece Lady Jane Mansell [see page 171]. However, by the time of Sir Stephen's marriage to Lady Wigmore in 1623 Mylende had evidently been disposed of, as there is no further mention of it.)

Notes

Preface

1. See appendix B for a listing of the few references to him in print.
2. Evidence for this is found in a poem of his (see p. 99) in which his name is rhymed with "soul." Furthermore, he was registered at Cambridge as "Pole."
3. C. R. Cheney, ed., *Handbook of Dates for Students of English History* (London, 1978), pp. 4–5, 10–11.
4. In Powle's time, according to a statement of his on what is now Tanner MS. 314, fol. 89r, the original letter was placed by him following this folio. This is one of the examples of how much the original material had become jumbled by Tanner's time.

Chapter 1. Education in the Liberal Arts and the Law

1. On 5 April 1556, when Stephen's father was granted a coat of arms (ADD MS. 37687G, fol. 41v), he was described as Thomas Powle of Cranbrook, Essex, esq., and on 31 July 1565, when Stephen's oldest brother Thomas entered Middle Temple, he was registered as Thomas Poule, son and heir of Thomas P. of Cranbroke, Essex. esq. (H. A. C. Sturgess, *Middle Temple Admissions*, London, 1949). However, by 1566 the family was living and paying taxes in Barking, Essex (E115 299/63). Le Nève's statement that Thomas the elder was the son of Sir Richard Powle of Shotesbroke, Berkshire, is apparently incorrect.
2. According to E. S. Leedham-Green (assistant keeper of Cambridge University Archives), there are no further records of "Pole at Cambridge beyond that of incorporation in July 1571." Miss Leedham-Green asserts that Venn (in *Alumni Cantabrigienses*) was wrong, having confused Stephen with Richard Poley, whose Grace and Supplicat are listed as 1572.
3. Probably the Thomas Fanshawe of the well-known Exchequer family.
4. Sturgess, *Middle Temple Admissions*.
5. Edited by Charles Henry Hopwood (London, 1904), p. 202 as extracted from MS. Book D (1551–1610).
6. W. Herbert, *Antiquities of the Inns of Court and Chancery* (London, 1804), chap. 3.
7. Arthur Robert Ingpen, ed., *Master Worsley's Book on the History and Constitution of the Honourable Society of the Middle Temple* (London, 1910), pp. 35, 38, 138.
8. Sir John Fortescue, *De laudis legum Angliae*, ed. and reprinted by Cambridge University Press: 1942, chap. 49, p. 3.
9. Thomas Powle's escutcheon is on the north side in window X, shield 7

(Az. a fess pean between three lions passant or). He was admitted to the Middle Temple 31 July 1565 (according to Alexander Pulling, *Order of the Coif* [London, 1884], pp. 430–31).

10. Confirmed by an entry in the Middle Temple's Book D, fol. 126v.

11. *Middle Temple Records*, edited by C. H. Hopwood (London, 1904), pp. 214, 215, 219.

12. A mark was equivalent to 13s 4d (about two-thirds of a pound sterling).

13. In George Gascoigne's *Steele Glasse*, 1576, appears a commendatory poem whose author is described as "Walter Rawely of the middle Temple."

14. The moots and most of the readings were in "Law French," a conglomeration of English, French, and Latin.

15. In Stephen's advice to John Chamberlain about choosing a spouse (169:206v) he recommended that the husband be taller than the wife. His other recommendations to Chamberlain seem to tally with the facts of his experience, so one may expect that this does also.

In a 24 October discourse sent to Master John Clapham (169:4r) Powle expressed his view that, since the man is exemplar, he should exceed his wife in power, place, providence, circumspection, and in stature also.

Judging by the tomb effigy at Blackmore of Powle's second wife, Margaret, whom he married in 1593, she was of more than average height. I have found no indication of the height of his other two wives.

Chapter 2. Travel: A Modified "Grand Tour"

1. This may have been Thomas Bodley, who was later to become the great benefactor of the Bodleian Library. He had left England in 1576 and was in France at about this time.

2. Powle included in his memoranda drafts of a series of letters to Audrey "Buttes" and copies of the letters James received from her in 1578–79 (Rawlinson MS. D 913:72v–73r, 75v; Tanner MS. 169:47v, 53r, 54r, 58v). These are apparently the first of a number of love letters that Powle wrote for various people. There is no indication whether or not any funds were finally collected from James.

3. "Ottoman" was apparently Grynaeus's first name. It is recorded that he had originally held an important professorship at Heidelberg but had left when the Palatine Elector Ludwig imposed conformity to Lutheranism. After Ludwig's death, Grynaeus had been invited to return to Heidelberg but by that time he was happily settled at Basel.

4. *Petri Rami Basilea ad Senatum Populumque Basilensem*, 1571.

5. A batt was equivalent to a shilling, according to Powle's notes (309:205v).

6. "Unamini" should undoubtedly read "unanimi."

7. (Strasbourg, 1855), p. 322.

8. (Strasbourg, Neustadt in 4o).

9. Sturm was humanist, pedagogue, theologian and writer.

10. For further details on Sturm's difficulties with the Lutheran Church of Strasbourg, see Walter Sohm's *Die Schule Johann Sturms und die Kirche Strassburgs* (Munchen and Berlin, 1912). For a discussion of Jacob Andreae and the *Formalis Concordia*, see *Encyclopedia of the Lutheran Church*, ed. Julius Bodensieck for the Lutheran World Federation (Minneapolis, Minn., 1965).

11. Some years before a fine portrait of Johann Sturm was painted by Tobie Stimmer depicting a handsome clear-eyed scholar with flowing beard. In 1617 an engraving was made from it by Jacques von der Leyden. It appears as frontispiece in Charles Schmidt's *La Vie et les Travaux de Jean Sturm,* Strasbourg, 1855.

12. A full description of the clock is given in a 20 June 1581 letter to William West, one of the clerks of chancery (309:22r), and a copy of this was enclosed in Powle's letter to his father.

13. See, for example, Sir John Davies's long poem "Orchestra."

14. The Palatinate (a territory in Germany under jurisdiction of the counts palatine, who were electors of the Holy Roman Empire) was divided into two parts. The lower, referred to above, that of the Rhine, extended on both sides of the river south of the Main.

15. A "German mile" was equivalent to about five English miles.

16. See Edward Mallet, *History of Oxford* (London, 1924), 2:170; James M. Osborn, *Young Philip Sidney* 1972); and Millicent V. Hay, *Life of Robert Sidney* (Washington, London, and Toronto (New Haven, 1984), p. 2.

17. Among Sturm's works were his *Book on the Right Method of Founding Schools for Literary Education,* 1537, and *Nobilitas Literata,* translated into English by T. B(rowne) in 1570.

18. Eagles were used for hunting in the same way as falcons. "Thayned" (perhaps derived from "thane") is apparently a term relating to the training of eagles for such service. See the *Oxford English Dictionary.*

19. Rich, open country unenclosed by hedges or fences but apportioned in strips to various owners.

20. Henry III, son of Henry II, upon the death of his brother Charles IX became king of France in 1574 and reigned until he was murdered in 1589.

21. "The Joyeuse Magnificences," in *Astraea: The Imperial Theme in the Sixteenth Century* (London, 1975) pp. 149–72. However, it does not include the final portion of the "Magnificences" that Powle saw.

22. Louise de Vaudemont of the House of Lorraine.

23. *Art and Power: Renaissance Festivals, 1450–1650* (Berkeley and Los Angeles, 1984), p. 122.

24. After the death of King Henrico of Portugal, the illegitimate Don Antonio made a claim to the throne, but Philip II of Spain, by means of military force under the duke of Alba, asserted his stronger genealogical claim and overcame Don Antonio's resistance (R. B. Wernham, *The Making of Elizabethan Foreign Policy* [Berkeley, 1980], p. 56).

25. See Wallace T. MacCaffrey, *Queen Elizabeth and the Making of Policy, 1572–1588* (Princeton, 1981), chap. 11.

26. R. B. Wernham, *Before the Armada* (London, 1966), p. 362.

27. See *Poems of Robert Sidney edited from the poet's autograph notebook with commentary by P. J. Croft* (Oxford, 1984).

28. Apparently the famous "Shroud of Turin" fabricated in the twelfth or thirteenth century and put forth as a relic of Jesus' crucifixion. (See *New York Times,* 14 October 1988, p. 1.)

29. Shrovetide was the hilarious period of the Mardi Gras carnival preceding the solemn session of Lenten fasting. The "zany" was a kind of clown who tried to entice youngsters with sweetmeats dangling on strings.

30. Powle undoubtedly meant *dextra.*

Chapter 3. England and Scotland

1. *Victoria County History* 5:196 (Becontree Hundred).
2. George Carew (1555-1629), first baron Carew of Clopton and first earl of Totnes, became a prominent statesman.
3. A heavy weight that could be lowered to measure depths at sea.
4. Cooke was a nephew of Lord Burghley's wife Mildred Cooke Cecil. Her father was Sir Anthony Cooke. See transcript of this letter in appendix E, p. 191.
5. *The first booke of the Christian Exercise appertayning to resolution* was published at Rouen in 1582. Other editions with slightly different titles were published in the ensuing years. There is no indication to which edition Powle refers.

Chapter 4. Agent for Queen Elizabeth at Casimir's Court

1. Elizabeth Godfrey, *Heidelberg: Its Princes and Its Palaces* (London, 1906), p. 221.
2. According to Dr. Häusser's *Geschichte der Rheinische Pfalz*, as quoted by Elizabeth Godfrey in *Heidelberg*, pp. 216-17:

> Archbishop Gebhardt Truchsess had been for some time inclined to favour the Reformed Doctrine, but was driven to take it up in earnest by a scandalously unworthy motive. The beautiful Countess Agnes von Mansfeld had lived with him as his mistress, and her brother, discovering the connection, forced upon him the necessity of marrying her; finding himself compelled to choose between his bishopric and his love, it occurred to him that if he could not only turn Protestant himself, but bring the Reformation into his diocese, he might secure both.

Casimir attempted to bolster the archbishop's position by marching with an armed force to Bonn; Henri of Navarre took up the cause, but there was lack of union between the two Protestant groups, and the emperor insisted on deposing Gebhardt, who eventually was obliged to relinquish his bishopric.

3. D. C. Peck, ed., *Leicester's Commonwealth* (Athens, Ohio, and London, 1985), p. 5.
4. Parker to Burghley, 11 September 1573, as referred to by Peck, *Leicester's Commonwealth*, p. 259.
5. In Powle's Commonplace Book (169:92r-131r) is a manuscript copy of an early version of *Leicester's Commonwealth* written in what is evidently the hand of Powle's current secretary-clerk (as are entries on a number of other pages). See pages 185-86 for discussion of the possible authorship of the tract and of Leslie Hotson's incomplete reading of Powle's comment on it.
6. Tanner MS. 78:104r (May 1586, after his return to London).
7. After returning to England, Powle informed Burghley of this and, as a result, received thirty pounds from Her Majesty's purse. (78:105r).
8. Calendar State Papers, Foreign, 1586-88, p. 263. See also Lawrence Stone, *An Elizabethan: Sir Horatio Palavicino* (Oxford, 1956), p. 20.

Chapter 5. Agent for Queen Elizabeth in Italy

1. William Thomas, *The History of Italy*, ed. George B. Parks, (1549; reprint, Ithaca, N.Y., 1963), pp. 155, 65–67, 83.

2. A galleass, or galliass, was a heavy, low-built vessel, larger than a galley, propelled both by sail and oars, chiefly employed in war.

3. At this time the Franche Comté was a Spanish territory.

4. When the election finally took place, none of the above was chosen. Instead, the non-native Polonian Sigismund, son of King John III of Sweden, was elected, largely because the nobility hoped (although vainly) that he would bring them Swedish aid against Muscovy.

5. In the margin Powle noted that this was the young earl of Orange, with whom he became acquainted at Strasbourg in 1580.

6. Parts of two different letters have been incorrectly placed in sequence in MS. 309.

7. Walsingham, having lived and studied in Padua before Elizabeth's accession, was, of course, fluent in Italian.

8. Butera is in Sicily, between Agrigentum and Syracuse.

9. The Fuchers (or Fuggers) were a family of German merchant princes, among the richest in Europe. They had extensive holdings of real estate throughout the Continent and were important international bankers.

10. François, duke of Montpensier.

11. After becoming king, Navarre was at first unable to unify France because of the bitter division between Huguenots and Catholics. Realizing that the problem was aggravated by his own Protestantism, he relinquished his religion for the sake of his kingdom and converted to Catholicism while retaining broadminded sympathy for his Huguenot subjects.

12. In a rough duplicate of this letter (314:85ff) is noted in Powle's hand, "I sent with this letter a token of mother of pearl."

13. Probably Powle's servant Daniel Simpson, who had been sent back to England with various messages.

14. "After we were warmed by the wine."

15. Messenger, a carrier of the post.

16. Chamberlain apparently knew of the despotism of Stephen's father.

17. This probably refers to his father's homestead in Aldersbrook.

18. Powle noted in 309:55ᵛ that the latter part of this letter "was but the substance of what I wrote to Master Chamberlain, for I could not have leisure to copy it out verbatim by reason of my number of letters sent to England by Master Egerton at one time."

19. I am grateful to Professor Paul Oskar Kristeller for calling to my attention the source of this quotation: Virgil's *Aeneid*, bk. 1, line 135.

20. Tom Powle eventually died in the wars shortly before November 1597 (see C2 D10/34, and Calendar State Papers, Domestic, Elizabeth, vol. 273, #65). Chamberlain's view of Stephen Powle's brother as a bit of a "playboy" is confirmed by his father's testimony in a Chancery suit brought by Tom's widow, Elizabeth (C2 D10/34 at P.R.O.).

21. Obviously a reference to the wanderer Odysseus.

22. This presages Claudio's remark to Lucio in *Measure for Measure* (1.2.129). It was perhaps a characteristically English feeling.

23. "N.N." stood for *Nomen nescio* (I do not know the name).

24. The rest of the letter is apparently not extant.

25. "Melior est certa pax qam sperata victoria" (Livy, bk. 8).
26. The actual letter is missing from the State Papers, but Powle's draft or copy can be found in Tanner MS. 169, fols. 40v–41v.

Chapter 6. Home

1. The arms were later hung in the hall of the six clerks' office in Chancery Lane. The book jacket shows Powle's coat of arms, although not in full color as in escutcheon at Folger Library [Z.c.22(1)].
2. The circumstances of his stepmother's involvement are unclear, as no further mention of her is made by Powle from this time on.
3. Eventually Clay-hall Manor was retained temporarily through a complicated series of transactions by which it was left in trust to the London Guild of Fishmongers (C2 Eliz D10/54 at P.R.O.). Stephen was staying at Clay-hall in March 1590/1, as evidenced by a long "Meditation" written from there (309:79v).
4. This probably refers to Thomas Powle's sale of the clerkship of the Crown (see p. 106).
5. Powle also referred to Burghley's fatherliness in a letter now in the State Papers (Elizabeth, Domestic, 1589, 24 Feb.) in which Powle, then in a penurious state with no lucrative work in sight, wrote that he had received much comfort from Burghley's fatherly speeches, which had settled his uncertain thoughts and quieted him. He solicited "either a pension" by which he might be able to live in his own country "or else get a passport to go to Hamborough [Hamburg?] and Switzerland there to spend the remainder of my wretched days."
6. See Garrett Mattingly, *The Defeat of the Spanish Armada* (Oxford, 1959), chap. 23–28.
7. Bowes was persuaded to return as ambassador in 1590 because of the good rapport he had had with King James (Hardwicke MSS. 96 & 97 at the New York Public Library). There seems to have been no official ambassador during the preceding interim.
8. Elizabeth, who came from the same parish as Powle's mother, was the widow of Miles Hobart (or Hubburt) of London, Norfolk.
9. There was a Barnaby Gooch who was master of Magdalene College, Cambridge. It is uncertain whether or not this is the Dr. Gooche referred to above.
10. Where I do live.

Chapter 7. Interlude: Recovery from Tragedy

1. Son of Thomas Joye of Wiltshire, who died in 1593. Inquest Post Mortem (35 Elizabeth) is C142 237/136.
2. For procedures in wardships, see Joel Hurstfield's *The Queen's Wards* (London, 1958), pp. 33–107.
3. A 20 November 1593 Letter of Powle's is dated from Smyths-hall and makes evident that he was then married (Lansdowne MS. 75:132).
4. Her promise probably was that she would make their eldest son, John, her heir and that she would erect a tomb for her husband in which at her death she would be buried beside him, for in 1592 an altar tomb with the recumbent figure of Thomas Smyth in full armor was placed in the chancel of the Priory

Church of Saint Laurence at Blackmore. In 1621, when Margaret Smyth Powle died, she was buried there and her recumbent effigy was placed beside that of her first husband. The base of the tomb shows that many, if not all, of their children were also buried there. Thomas Smyth's will is D/AEW 10/192 at E.R.O.

5. C2 Eliz PS/58 K/457 at P.R.O. According to Philip Morant, *History and Antiquities of the County of Essex*, I, 1:17, 2:57 17, II, 57, Blanche was the daughter of Nicolas Colshill of Middlesex.

6. Will of Christian Turner is D/AEW 7/163 at E.R.O.

7. Philip Morant, *History and Antiquities of the Borough of Colchester in the County of Essex* (Colchester, 1810), p. 233, states that Christian Turner, daughter of William Fisher, married John Turner, son of Thomas Turner, and that she purchased these properties after her husband's death.

8. Powle had apparently returned to France for a brief visit at that time.

9. This was a little over half a year after his own marriage.

10. A painting believed to be of her with her third husband, Sir Thomas Mansell, and their little daughter, Mary, now hangs at Penrice in Glamorganshire.

Chapter 8. Early Years in Chancery

1. W. H. Jones, *The Elizabethan Court of Chancery* (Oxford, 1967), p. 132. The hanaper, or "hamper," was so called because of the miscellaneous nature of its duties.

2. Ibid., p. 134.

3. The story contained in Powle's notes is partly recounted by Conyers Read in *Lord Burghley and Queen Elizabeth* (1960; reprint, London, 1965), p. 522. Egerton lived until 1617, but Burghley died in 1598.

4. C216 1/17 at P.R.O.

5. As reported in an 11 March 1620 letter of John Chamberlain's to Sir Dudley Carleton (see McClure, *Letters of John Chamberlain*, 2:293). In Calendar of State Papers, Domestic, 1595–97, p. 353, the grant of the office of clerk of the Crown to George Coppin is dated 28 January 1597.

6. About this time Thomas Powle was appointed master extraordinary in Chancery, purely as an honorary title, for he was then virtually in retirement. He had served the queen since 1549 (Jones, *Elizabethan Court of Chancery*, p. 134).

7. Ibid., p. 135

8. M. S. Giuseppi, *Guide to the Contents of the Public Record Office* (London, 1928), 1:7.

9. Thomas Duffy Hardy, *A Catalogue of Lord Chancellors . . . and Principal Officers of the Court of Chancery* (London, 1845), p. 107.

Chapter 9. Family Life

1. The "yoll" is a loud cry or howl. "Qwitbendy tatrayammatry" are apparently nonsense words.

2. There are a number of examples of very persuasive love letters written by Powle for others, that is, those of James Buttes to Audrey, whom he eventually

married (Rawlinson MS. D 913:72v–73r & 75r&v, and to Kesie Franke for Powle's servant Dick Hoskyn (169:142r). See appendix E, pp. 215 and 219.

3. In a letter to his niece (169:177v) he referred to her "saintlike mother."

4. See tomb inscriptions at Margam Abbey, and also Walter de Gray Birch, *Penrice and Margam Manuscripts in the Possession of Miss Talbot of Margam* (London, 1894), pt. 2, p. 112.

5. In January 1596/7 Thomas Powle, being in much financial duress, had sold the office of clerk of the Crown to George Coppin, to take effect after Thomas Powle's death. Although it was officially retained by him during his lifetime, by the time of the sale he had become old and infirm. Therefore Stephen Powle as deputy clerk exercised the full duties of clerkship of the Crown (see p. 105).

6. Among these would have been deputy clerk of the Crown, justice of the peace for Essex, to which he was first appointed in 1597 (see p. 127), and commissioner of Oyer and terminer for Kent, Sussex, Suffolk, Herts., and Essex. These are listed on the Patent Rolls of Grantees.

7. By this is meant Powle's activities in the court of Chancery.

8. He was created one of the first baronets in 1611, was M.P. for Glamorgan in 1614, and died 20 December 1631 (Alexander Brown, *Genesis* [1899], 2:942).

9. In 1780 the old mansion was pulled down and its contents removed to Penrice Castle on the Gower peninsula.

10. Powle was touched by this phrase when Don Antonio greeted him with an Italian version of it 1582 (cf. p. 48).

11. Jane's husband, Sir Thomas Mansell, had been at court during this period.

Chapter 10. Recording the Essex Rebellion

1. George Long, *The Decline of the Roman Republic* (London, 1866), 2:308.

2. Henry Cuffe, a rather Machiavellian character who was constantly scheming and planning, was a staunch adherent of Essex and carried his letters from Ireland to the queen (Robert Lacey, *Robert, Earl of Essex* [New York, 1971], pp. 109, 265).

3. Essex had awarded 170 knighthoods in the course of his campaigns—more than one-quarter of the total in the whole of England (ibid., p. 238).

4. Rumor has it that when Elizabeth's Portuguese physician, Dr. Roderigo Lopez, ministered to Essex in early years he suspected that Essex had venereal disease, as was then quite common in court circles. Lopez's release of this information so angered Essex that he relentlessly pursued the doctor's condemnation for treason. Although the evidence was inconclusive and Elizabeth questioned the validity of the verdict, she seems to have been unable to prevent Lopez's execution in 1594 (ibid., p. 201).

5. There is also a copy of this account in Rawlinson MS. C 744, fol. 100r.

6. A commission "to hear and decide."

7. The "Teste" is the final clause in a royal writ, naming the person who authorizes affixing the royal seal.

8. The "privy signet office" is that closest to the sovereign and of a more private nature than even the privy seal (J. Harvey Bloom, *English Seals* [London, 1906], p. 101).

9. See illustration in E. M. Tenison, *Elizabethan England* (Royal Leamington Spa, Warwick, 1956), pl. 11, opp. 488.

10. The large initial "E" is written in a shaky hand, but the rest of the signature is firm and elaborate.

Chapter 11. Suits, Paradoxes, and Slanders

1. R. E. Bennett has transcribed the four paradoxes and published them together with a brief introduction in *Harvard Studies and Notes in Philology and Literature* (Cambridge, Mass., 1931), 13:219–39.
2. *Leicester's Commonwealth: The Copy of a Letter Written by a Master of Art of Cambridge (1584) and Related Documents* (Athens, Ohio & London, 1985).
3. According to insinuations of the tract, Walter, earl of Essex, was poisoned because the earl of Leicester was enamored of Lettice, then countess of Essex, whom he later married.
4. She married Sir Thomas Mansell circa 1599.
5. Salisbury, Cecil papers 63/24. See p. 85, concerning the Giraldo plot.

Chapter 12. Lord of the Manor of Smyths-hall

1. *The History and Antiquities of the County of Essex* (London, 1768), 2:57.
2. He was a descendant of King Richard II's standard bearer, John Carington, who changed his name to Smyth (Frederick Chancellor, *Ancient Sepulchral Monuments of Essex* [London, 1870], p. 358).
3. E115,309/136 at P.R.O. This seems to be standard phraseology. *Commorant* is the anglicization of the Latin *commorans*, meaning "sojourning." Smyths-hall was his principal residence at that time.
4. However, those serving in a large town were usually selected from that urban area.
5. The material on justices of the peace derives from the excellent chapter on this subject in Wallace Notestein's *The English People on the Eve of Colonization 1603–1630* (New York, 1954), pp. 211–28; also D. H. Allen, *Essex Quarter Sessions Order Book* (Chelmsford, n.d.), pp. ix–xiii; and J. S. Cockburn, *History of English Assizes 1558–1713* (Cambridge, 1972).
6. Q/SR 137/2 at the Essex Record Office.
7. Q/SR 139/25 at E.R.O.
8. Q/SR 139/88–94 at E.R.O.
9. Q/SR 144/29 at E.R.O.
10. Q/SR 151/34 at E.R.O.
11. Q/SR 208/123 at E.R.O.
12. Perhaps a comic piece.
13. Q/SR 129/75, 105 at E.R.O.
14. Principal Secretary Sir Francis Walsingham had died in 1590. In 1596 Sir Robert Cecil was appointed to the office. In May 1607 Cecil yielded to the urging of King James and relinquished to him the handsome estate of Theobalds in exchange for the king's gratitude and what was then a far more modest estate at Hatfield.
15. W. C. Metcalf, *A Book of Knights* (London, 1885), p. 154.
16. "Stopes" were devices with holes through which flames could be introduced, probably for the purpose of heating foods.
17. I have been unable to ascertain what these were.

Chapter 13. Country Squire at Mylend

1. G. W. Hill and W. H. Frere, eds., *Memorials of Stepney Parish; Vestry Minutes 1579–1662* (Guildford, 1890–91), pp. 46, 61, 70, 73, 81, 83.
2. Tanner MS. 169, fol. 199r.
3. A. H. French, etc., "Population of Stepney in the early seventeenth century . . . an analysis of the Parish Registers 1606–1610" (1729 folio pamphlet at London Guild Hall).
4. *History of East London* (London, 1939), p. 169.
5. In 169:138v he referred to Mylend as "a petty place of contentment."
6. One wonders whether "Sir Peputy" was little Durk's version of "Sir Stephen Powle."
7. Thomas Duffy Hardy, p. 105.
8. Tax records (E115 306/13 at P.R.O.) show that he was living there on 15 July 1606.
9. Powle occasionally mentions the name of a current servant. Among others referred to are: Robert Newcomen ca. 1576 (309:10r); Daniel Simpson in April 1587 (309:67r) through 1592 (246:3r); and Francis Saunders in 1617 (169:117v).
10. In Breton's hand are the lines:

> Una cortisana: perdo tempo
> Merranamente honesta: passa tempo
> Via donna da bene: guadagna tempo.

11. Today he is usually referred to as Andrew Melville.
12. Melvyn's outspoken speeches in behalf of freedom of assembly in 1606 and a bitter epigram in 1607 on the subject of Anglican ritual had caused him to be imprisoned in the Tower. In 1611 he was released by the intercession of Henri, duc de Bouillon, who had him appointed professor of biblical theology at the University of Sedan.

Chapter 14. Sir Stephen Powle as "Adventurer" in the Virginia Company of London

1. He was born about 1558 and was educated at Oxford. Despite the identity of names, there is no reason to believe that he was related to Margaret Powle's first husband.
2. Sir Stanley Spurling, *Sir Thomas Smythe, knt.* (New York, 1955), pp. 15–16.
3. In a joint-stock company, members pooled their resources in a common fund for investment under direction of the company's officers.
4. Edward Thompson, *Sir Walter Ralegh* (London, 1935), p. 250.
5. See Louis B. Wright, ed., *A Voyage to Virginia in 1609* (Charlottesville, 1965), containing William Strachey's "A True Repertory of the Wreck and Redemption of Sir Thomas Gates, Knight" and Silvester Jourdain's "Discovery of the Bermudas."
6. According to Alexander Brown's *Genesis of the United States* (1890; reprint, New York, 1964) 1:231–2, the ship was the "De La Warr."
7. The two spaces left blank for the date should read "first" of "April" (ibid.).
8. Powle contributed £50 on 9 March 1608/9 (168:iv r), £37 10s in 1610/11,

7. The two spaces left blank for the date should read "first" of "April" (ibid.).
8. Powle contributed £50 on 9 March 1608/9 (168:iv^r), £37 10s in 1610/11, and £100 in 1618 or 1619 (Susan Myra Kingsbury, *The Records of the Virginia Company of London* [Washington, D.C., 1933], 3:86, 331).
9. (Cambridge, 1912) 2:185. An assessment of £12 10s was levied on those Adventurers who wished to participate in the division of land. Some large areas were granted to groups of men for private self-governing plantations.
10. Edmund S. Morgan, "The First American Boom: Virginia 1618–1630," *William and Mary Quarterly*, 3d ser., 28: 75.
11. (Richmond, 1930), pp. 33–34.
12. *Quo warranto* was a high prerogative writ by the Crown questioning by what authority a claim was supported and was normally used against an institution holding by royal charter or patent. It was to prevent a continued exercise of authority misused or unlawfully asserted.
13. *English Politics in Early Virginia History* (1901; reprint 1968), p. 54. Although this volume has been criticized as overly polemical, it nevertheless has some valid insights.
14. *Dissolution of the Virginia Company* (New York, 1932), chap. 9.
15. *The Government of Virginia in the Seventeenth Century* (Williamsburg, Va., 1957), p. 9.
16. *The Records of the Virginia Company of London* (Washington, D.C., 1906), 1:115.
17. According to Brown, *English Politics*, p. 60, this was after the arrest of Sandys in June 1621 because of his leadership against monopolies and opposition to the Crown.
18. Kingsbury, *Records of the Virginia Company*, 1:111, states that this was accomplished during the brief period when the Crown returned records to the colonists for them to answer the quo warranto.
19. For example, that when in the custody of the Indian chieftain Powhatan, Smith's life was saved by the pleading of the Indian princess Pocahontas, and he subsequently married her.
20. Kingsbury, *Records of the Virginia Company*, 4:523.
21. This was the statement of the earl of Middlesex to the board of the company.
22. This was during the governorships of Sir George Yeardley and of Sir Francis Wyatt.
23. For further references to the Virginia Company of London, see: Thomas J. Wertenbaker, *Virginia under the Stuarts, 1607–1688* (Princeton, 1914), chaps. 1 and 2.

Chapter 15. Later Years at Smyths-hall and Mylend

1. D/DAC 236 at E.R.O.
2. Powle does not mention her first name.
3. Civil lawyers.
4. Inherited from her second husband, John Fuller, who mentioned them in his will.
5. Plaice is a flat fish that has a thick, black, unattractive skin on the upper side and is white and delectable looking on the underside.
6. Exon MS. 88, folios 55r–56r.

7. Charles K. Sisson, *Thomas Lodge and Other Elizabethans* (New York, 1966), p. 85, refers to a 1594 lawsuit (C 24/243/56) in which it is mentioned that Lodge frequented this tavern at the corner of Chancery Lane and Fleet Street.

8. He was so listed in Thomas Heywood's *Troia Britannica*, 1609.

9. Three contemporary methods of internal cleansing: bleeding by cutting open a vein, emptying the bowels, and sneezing.

10. This lease may have been consummated, for vestry records show that Powle temporarily moved away from Mylend in 1618.

11. Both letters are originals in Lodge's hand.

12. It is in the same hand as many of Powle's notes of this period. The handwriting is easily identifiable, as is the continual spelling of the word "of" as "oft".

13. Ralegh began his great *History of the World* while imprisoned. He completed only the first volume, which deals with the history of the Jews, early Egypt, Greece, and Rome to 130 B.C. It was published in 1614.

14. Tanner MSS. 168:v^v., 169:43r, 147r, 173v.

15. PROB 11/135 4 Soame (31 December 1619).

16. Vexing.

17. On 19 July 1608 Francis Mansell of Muddlescombe, Camarthen County, brother of Sir Thomas Mansell of Margam, had made a grant to the latter's wife, Lady Jane, "of the enclosed grounds called the New Park, Castle Park, or Great Park for her life" (Birch, *Penrice and Margam Manuscripts in the possession of Miss Talbot of Margam* (London, 1894), 2:24.

Perhaps Francis Mansell's grant was in return for his brother's financial assistance in December 1605, when Sir Thomas joined with him in a four hundred pound bond to Henry Smith of London (p. 23).

Now, in 1620, Lady Jane may have wished to transfer the park property to one of her two children.

18. Mary eventually married Sir Edward Stradling of Saint Donat's Castle (Edward Phillips Stratham, *History of the Family of Mansell* [London, 1917–20], II, ii, p. 681). Presumably he was a son who had already inherited.

19. Now at the Essex Record Office.

20. According to D/DB in T5/31 at the Essex Record Office, on 9 December 1597 her oldest son, John Smyth, was twenty-seven. If Margaret was seventeen when he was born, she would have been about sixty-eight when she died.

21. T 5/32, 31 December 1597, E.R.O.

22. D/ACW 6/261 at the Essex Record Office. He left his estate to be divided equally between his sister Cole, his sister Lenton, and his nephew John Smith. The testator's older brothers, Charles and Thomas, had died earlier.

23. Tax records show that he was there at least as late as 26 April 1620 (E115 308/12).

Chapter 16. "Indian Summer"—A Third Marriage

1. I am grateful to Miss Jane C. Apple for calling this entry to my attention.

2. Perhaps Powle's servant by referring to him as M^r rather than Sir was emphasizing the fact of Powle's rise in the world from young *Master* Powle to the present husband of *My Lady* Wigmore.

3. Devereux Papers, box V, 76, 77, at Longleat.

4. Salisbury (Cecil) Papers XIV, XVI.

5. John Chamberlain to Dudley Carleton from London, 23 January 1609, as printed in McClure, *Letters*, 1:282.
6. He was buried on 27 May 1621 at the Church of Saint Margaret, Westminster.
7. PROB 11/137 (60 (Dale).
8. E 151 (1617–24), Westminster Library Archives. This rate book shows that Powle paid four pence weekly (sixteen shillings in toto) in taxes.
9. E 179 143/330 (membrane 1 dorse) at P.R.O.
10. E 152 at Westminster Library Archives.
11. The Saint Margaret's Parish Register is kept at the Westminster Library.
12. PROB 6 14B 160 at P.R.O.

Appendix A: Catalogue of Manuscripts and Their Provenance

1. Corrections and changes of wording indicate that these were drafts rather than final letters. Usually they were signed in an abbreviated manner,"SP."
2. It is worth noting that Powle's papers do not contain copies of letters received from his father. Perhaps his father did not take the time to write to him. Or, perhaps if Thomas Powle did write to Stephen, the letters were belittling ones that the son did not care to preserve.
3. They are chiefly among the Landsdowne manuscripts or in the Elizabethan State Papers.
4. Fourth son of John Monke of Herston, Sussex.
5. Henry Powle was a grandson of Richard Powle (d. 1628), lord of the manor of Shottesbrooke, Berkshire, who was deputy register of the court of Chancery in early Elizabethan times. He seems to have been a first cousin of Thomas Powle, Sir Stephen's father. The arms and crest of Richard and Thomas were quite similar.

Appendix C: Funerary Monument of Powle's Parents

1. "The Hamper" was a term for "The Hanaper" not only because of its miscellaneous functions but also because of a basket in which papers relating to the post were kept. Thomas Powle received license for the controller's post in 1549.
2. Two sons apparently died in childhood. Stephen in his letters mentions only two brothers (Thomas and William) and a sister, whose married name was Dutton.
3. The body is a fetid prison;
   Death a liberation;
   Life is a stormy sea.
     The tomb a harbor;
   The world is an unsteady wandering;
     Heaven one's homeland.
   Therefore learn to die;
     Forget living.

Appendix E: Transcripts of Typical Letters from and to Powle and Other Representative Pages from His Notebooks

1. "Brother" is being used in a general sense. Anthony Cooke was a nephew of Lord Burghley's wife and seems to have been a close friend of Powle's at this time.

2. Jacques Ségur-Pardailhan was agent of Henry of Navarre and envoy to England in 1585.

3. Portuguese ships.

4. A beating with a cudgel.

5. Tom Powle eventually died in the wars shortly before November 1597 (see C2 D10/34 at P.R.O. and Calendar of State Papers Reign of Elizabeth Vol. 273 #65). Chamberlain's view of Stephen Powle's brother as a bit of a "playboy" is confirmed by his father's testimony in this Chancery suit brought by Thomas's widow, Elizabeth.

6. Edward was related to Thomas Egerton, who in 1594 became keeper of the rolls, and in 1603, lord chancellor.

7. A proverbial phrase for anything plain and direct.

8. William Gent of Gloucester Hall, Oxford, with whom Powle had been friendly in Paris (see p. 49).

9. Powle had probably offered to introduce his niece Jane and her new husband, Sir John Bussy, to Chamberlain.

10. I am grateful to Miss Irene Cassidy for her translation of the above Italian passages.

11. First cousin.

12. In the margin Powle noted that these words had been addressed to him and Master Robert Sidney by Don Antonio, king of Portugal, in Paris at the Hostel della Regina Madre. See p. 48.

13. According to 169:146v, Lassells was Powle's cousin.

Index

Note: In this index, SP is used for Stephen Powle.

Abbey Saint Germain (Paris), 45
Alençon, Francis, duc d' (also duc d'Anjou ["Monsieur"]), 32, 48, 49, 80
Aldersbrooke, Essex, 21
Altanni brothers, 77
Amy, Master Doctor, 135
Andreae, Jacob, 37–38
Angelo, Signor (religious counselor at Middle Temple), 27, 33
Anjou, Francis, duc d'. *See* Alençon
Anne of Denmark (later Queen of England and Scotland), 98
Antonio, Don (pretender to throne of Portugal), 48, 49, 88, 229 n.10, 235 n.12
Antwerp, 49, 63
Arcadia (Sidney), 102
Aristotle, 39, 163
Armada. *See* Spanish Armada
Arundel, Charles, 123
Ashton, Abdy, 120
Astrology, 41
Augsburg, 65–66, 67, 68

Bacon, Anthony, 117
Bacon, Sir Francis, 139
Bagford, John, 181
Bailey, Doctor (Earl of Leicester's surgeon), 123
Baker, Doctor (Queen Elizabeth's surgeon), 98
Balzac, Jean Louis Guez de, 154–56; *Le Prince*, 155
Bargrave, Isaac, 178
Barlow, Dr. William, 112, 120
Basel, 35–36, 57; university of, 15, 36
Bassett, Sir Robert, 220–21
Battori, Stephen, 72
Battori family, 73, 74

Bede, the Venerable, 39
Bergen Abbey, 37
Bergen op Zoom, 85
Bermudas, the, 143, 145
Beuter, Doctor, of Nuremburg (genealogist), 42
Beza, Theodor, 27, 34
Blackmore (village), 126, 128, 131, 132, 161
Blanton, Wyndham: *Medicine in Virginia in the Seventeenth Century*, 150
Blount, Sir Christopher, 106, 120
Bodleian Library, 11, 12, 26, 182
Bodley (Bodleigh, Bodligh) (father and son), 33, 223 n.1
Bohemia, 57, 58, 85
Bois de Vincennes, 44
Boleyn, Anne, 98
Bonna, Jieronimo di, 73–74, 78
Book of Resolutions (Parson), 57
Borgo Santo Sepolchro, 71–72, 83
Bourbon, Cardinal de, 45
Bowes, Lady, 55
Bowes, Ambassador Robert, 55, 98
Brentwood, 128, 129, 131
Breton, Elizabeth, 135
Breton, Nicholas, 16, 135–36, 164–65; *The Court and Country*, 11, 133, 164–67, 168–69
Breton, Richard, 135
Breton, William, 135
Brill (Netherlands), 63
Bristowe, Richard, 20
British Museum (Lansdowne Collection), 181
Broadgates Hall (Pembroke College), Oxford, 20, 44
Bromley, Sir Thomas (Lord Chancellor), 27, 56, 57; SP's letter to, 190

237

Brooke, Sir George, 141
Brown, Alexander, 151
Buckhurst, Lord (Thomas Sackville), 63, 119
Burghley, Lord (William Cecil, First Baron Burghley), 11, 15, 16, 131; attitude toward/relationship with SP, 60, 66, 79, 80–81, 100, 104; death of, 122; SP in service of, 54, 55, 58, 59–66, 61–62, 79, 80–81; SP's letters to/from, 95, 181, 182, 192–93, 213–15; SP named secretary to, 97, 98
Burghley, Lady (Mildred Cooke Cecil), 225 n.4
Bussy, Cecily Mansell, 111, 157, 172
Bussy, Sir John, 110, 235 n.9
Bussy, Sir Rawleigh, 111, 157, 158, 160, 172; death of, 179
"Buttes," Audrey, 33, 228 n.2
"Buttes," James, 33, 158, 228 n.2
Buttes, Lady Will, 33

Calendar: New Style/Old Style, 12
Calvinism ("Reformed Religion"), 20–21, 27, 34–35, 36–37, 38, 58–59
Cambridge (University), 20–21
Camden, William, 20
Capezucchi, Captain Biaggio, 79
Cardanus, Hieronymus, 41
Carew, George (1st Baron of Clopton and 1st Earl of Totnes), 20, 36, 55–57, 113
Carew, Richard, 20
Carington, John, 230 n.2
Carleton, Sir Dudley, 228 n.5
Caron, Antoine, 45
Casimir, Duke John (count palatine of the Rhine), 16, 42–43; Elizabeth's support for, 80; letter to Lord Burghley, 63–65; SP at court of, 58–67. *See also* Rhenish Palatinate
Cassells, 67
Catch, The (ship), 143
Catherine de Medici, 49
Catholic League (Holy League), 45, 59, 72, 80
Catholics and Catholicism, 20, 72, 76, 226 n.11
Cecil, Robert (Principal Secretary), 125, 131, 141
Chamberlain, John, 13, 16, 24, 124, 223 n.15, 228 n.5; SP's correspondence with, 81–85, 86, 102–3, 202–5
Chancery: SP official in, 11, 13, 104–7; SP's records of, 15; T. Powle official of, 19
Chancery Lane: SP's home in, 103, 106, 111, 127, 135
Charles I (king of England), 152, 154
Charles V (Holy Roman Emperor), 42
Charles IX (king of France), 224 n.20
Chelmsford, 128, 129, 130, 131
Cheyney, Sir Francis, 167–70
Cheyney, Frauncis, 170
Cheyney, John, 27
Cheyney, Lady Mary, 109, 167–70
Christ Church, Oxford, 44
Church of St. Dunstan the West (London), 187
Church of Saint Dunstan (Stepney), 132
Church of Saint Laurence (Blackmore), 228 n.4
Church of Saint Margaret (Barking, Essex), 98–99
Church of Saint Margaret (Westminster), 164, 175, 178
Church of the Holy Ghost (Heiligen Geist) (Heidelberg), 43
Clapham, John, 106, 133, 223 n.15
Clay-hall Manor, Essex, 54
Clerkship of the Crown, 104–6
Cobham, Henry, 32
Cobham, Lady, 32
Coke, Sir Edward, 119, 141
Cologne, archbishop of, 59
Columbus, Christopher, 41
Condé, prince of, 93
Constitution and Finance of English, Scottish, & Irish Joint-Stock Companies to 1720, The (Scott), 147
Controller of the Hanaper, 107; T. Powle, 19
Cooke, Sir Anthony, 57, 191–92, 225 n.4
Cope, Walter, 65, 84
Coppin, George, 100, 106, 229 n.5
Cornwallis, Sir William, 122
Cornwallis family, 122, 123
Corpus Christi, Oxford, 20, 44
Correspondence (SP), 11, 12, 13–14, 157, 158, 181–82; G. Carew, 55–57;

J. Chamberlain, 81–85, 86, 102–3, 202–5; E. Egerton, 86–87; Jane (niece), 110–12, 159–61; T. Powle (father), 39–42, 181; transcripts of, 190–99, 200–221. See also Intelligence letters (SP)
Council of the Virginia Company of London, 11, 137
Counterblaste to Tobacco, A (James I), 147
Court and Country, The (Breton), 11, 133, 165–67, 168–69
Court Party, 150–51, 152
Cranbrook, Great Ilford, 19
Craven, Wesley Frank, 151
Crompton family, 134–35
Cuffe, Henry, 116, 120, 229 n.2

Dale, Sir Thomas, 144–45
Danneus (theologian), 34, 36
Danvers, Sir Charles, 106, 120
Danvers, Sir John, 152
Dare, Ananias, 138
Davison, William (Master Secretary), 200–202
Dee, Dr. John: *De virtutibus et magnalibus Dei* . . . , 67, 82; *Liber de secretis et magnalibus Dei* . . . , 67
Dethick, Sir William, 95, 101, 133
Devereux, Robert. See Essex, 2d Earl of (Robert Devereux)
"Discourse of the Old Company, A" (Sandys and Ferrar), 153–54
Discovery (ship), 138
Discovery of the Bermudas, A (Jourdain), 143
Drake, Sir Francis, 76, 77, 90, 93, 94; and defeat of Spanish Armada, 97–98
Du Moulin, Pierre, 154–56
Dutton (sister of SP), 75, 103, 134, 157, 158, 170; death of, 158–59; SP relationship with, 109–10
Dutton, Jane (later Lady Mansell; niece of SP), 75, 103, 124, 125, 157, 158, 233 n.7; Death of, 179; Marriages of, 110–11, 235 n.9; SP's correspondence with, 158, 159–61, 171–72, 216–17; SP Relationship with, 109–12

East London, 132

Eastward Hoe! (play), 143–44
Edinburgh: SP visit to, 55
Egerton, Edward, 82, 86
Egerton, Thomas, 105, 106, 122, 235 n.6; Essex and, 113, 116, 117, 119
"Elegy for Himself" (Tichborne), 199–200
Elizabeth I (queen of England), 11, 48, 62, 89, 97, 105, 120–21, 138, 156; candidates for hand of, 48–49; court of, 42; death of, 131; and earl of Essex, 113, 116–17, 119–20; and foreign relations, 63, 80; plot to poison, 85–86, 125; SP in service of, 58–94; relationship with Casimir, 59; relationship with Ralegh, 164
England, 15, 40; international relations, 80; SP in, 53–57, 95–179; proposed peace with Spain, 88–89, 91–93, 138
"Enterprise of England." See Spanish Armada
Epistola apologetica contra Jacobum Andreae . . . (Sturm), 37
Erasmus, Desiderius, 35–36
Essex (county): SP justice of peace for, 11, 127–31; T. Powle justice of peace for, 19
Essex, 1st earl of (Walter Devereux), 123
Essex, 2d earl of (Robert Devereux), 112, 113–21, 114, 175, 178; execution of, 106, 119–20; SP on death of, 217–19
Essex Rebellion, 15, 105–6, 111–12, 113–21

Fage, Master, 128–29
Fanshawe, Thomas, 21
Ferdinand, Archduke, 71
Ferrar, Nicholas, Jr., 150, 152, 153
Ferrara, 83, 90, 91
Ferrara, duke of, 71, 74
Filliasi, Giacomo, 98
Fimbria, Gaius Flavius, 115–16
Flaccus, L. Valerius, 115–16
Florio, John, 136
Flushing (Netherlands), 63
Formalis Concordia (Andreae), 37–38
France, 15, 35, 40, 78, 88–89; heir to throne of, 80; influence in Low

Countries, 63; Protestants in, 75; Turkey and, 49
Franche Comté, 72
Franke, Master Doctor, (SP's Mylend tenant), 158
Franke, Kesie, 158, 219–20, 229 n.2
Franke, Master, 136
Frankfurt Mart, 65, 75
Frankfurt on Main, 43, 62, 66, 67
Fuchers (or Fuggers), 79, 93
Fuller, John, Esq., 110, 232 n.4

Gascoigne, George, 135–36
Gates, Sir Thomas, 142–43, 144
Genealogy, 42; Casimir, 60, 62, 65; Powle, 180
Generall Historie of Virginia, New England and the Summer Isles (Smith), 153
Geneva, 26, 27, 33–34, 40; SP in, 34–35; university of, 15
Genoa, 75, 76, 78
Genoa, duke of, 47, 48
Gent, Master William, 49, 84, 124
Geratt, Master, 86
Germany, 15, 35, 40, 42; safe passage through, 71
Gilpyn, Lucas, 20
Giraldo, Giuseppe, 85
Giraldo, Michael, 85–86, 88, 125
Godspeed (ship), 138
Golden Hind, The (anthology), 200
Gondomar, conde de, 151
Gooch, Doctor (Barnaby Gooch?), 98
Goraisky, Adam de, 35, 57
Goraisky, Peter de, 35, 57
Gozzi, Niccolo di, 74, 77, 78
Gray's Inn (Inns of Court), 21
Great seal, 104, 105
Gretham, 101
Grynaeus, Ottoman Jacobus, 36
Guiana, 141, 142
Guicciardini, Francesco, 39, 83
Guise, Henri, duc de, 46–47, 48, 80
Guise party (France), 45

Hakluyt, Richard, 137, 138; "Particular Discourse Concerning . . . the Western Discoveries," 138
Hamburg, 66, 67, 94
Hastings, Henry, 36, 38–39
Heidelberg, 42, 43, 58–68; university of, 15, 60
Henrico (settlement in Virginia), 144–45
Henry, king of Navarre (later King Henry IV of France) 79–80, 86, 93, 225 n.2
Henry II (king of France), 224 n.20
Henry III of Valois (king of France), 49, 80; program of entertainments (Paris), 45–48
Henry V (king of England), 44
Henry VIII (king of England), 111, 126
Hesse, William: landgrave of, 63, 67, 82
Hickes, Michael, 97, 100, 104, 123–24, 125; knighted, 131
Hobart (Hubburt), Miles, 122, 227 n.8
Holland, Lady Mary, 176
Holland, Sir Thomas, 176
Holliband (French schoolmaster), 66
Hopkins, Master (SP's childhood schoolmaster), 20, 24–26
Hoskyn, Dick, 158, 219–20, 229 n.2
Howard, Lord Admiral Charles, 97
Howard, Thomas, 118–19
Hubert, Francis, 106, 167
Huguenots, 58, 80, 86, 93, 226 n.11
Hutton, Dr. Matthew (Bishop of Durham), 101

Indies, 88, 90, 93, 94
Inns of Court, 21, 24, 27, 128; "Grand Christmas," 22; SP at, 21–25
Innsbruck, 71
Inquisition, Papal, 69, 73
Intelligence letters (SP): from Casimir's court, 62; from Frankfurt, 66; from Holland (Leicester's headquarters), 63–65; from Italy, 65–66, 69–94, 205–13
Intelligence work (SP): danger in, 68, 95; precautions in, 75–76, 78, 87–88, 94, 95
"Invective Against Women as the Champions of Luxury" (St. Jerome), 108
Ireland, 116–17
Italy, 40, 66, 74–75; SP agent in, 11, 15, 69–94; soldiers levied in, 78–79

INDEX 241

James I (king of England), 11, 121, 131, 141; death of, 152; and Virginia Company, 138, 147, 148, 150–51, 152, 154, 156
James VI (king of Scotland): relationship to England, 89; declared king of England as James I, 131
Jamestown (settlement), 138–39, 142, 144
Jefferson, Thomas, 153
Jerome, St.: "Invective Against Women as the Champions of Luxury," 108
Jerrari (Spanish ambassador), 72
Jews, 43
John (servant to Signor Richard Shelley), 77–78
Johnson, Alderman, 139, 150
Jourdain, Silvester: *Discovery of the Bermudas, A*, 143
Joye, Master, 97, 100
Joyeuse, Anne, duc de, 45, 47, 48, 80
Justices of the peace, 128–30

Kearns, Sir John, 172
Kiddemister (Kederminster), Master, 124
Kingsbury, Susan Myra, 152
Knights of Malta, 77–78
Kristeller, Paul Oskar, 37–38
Kyrton, Master, 90–91, 93–94

la Valetta, Monsieur, 47, 48, 49
Lacey, Robert, 117
Languet, Hubert, 44
Lassells, Master, 157
Law: a state of, 155–56; SP on the study of, 24–26, 41
le Groate, Master, 163
le Jeune, Claude, 45
Leedham-Green, E. S., 222 n.2
Leicester, earl of (Robert Dudley), 60, 62–63, 79, 123
Leicester's Commonwealth, 62–63, 123, 225 n.5
Letters of John Chamberlain, The (McClure), 81
Lidcote (godfather of SP), 57
Lodge, Thomas, 13, 16, 109, 162–63
Lopez, Dr. Roderigo, 229 n.4
Lorraine, 44, 72, 78

Lorraine, duc de, 46–47
Lorraine, Marie de, 45
Louis, Saint (Louis IX of France), 51
Louis XIII (king of France), 155
Louise (queen of France and wife of Henry III), 46
Low Countries, 63, 78, 88, 93, 95
Ludwig VI of the Palatinate, 58–59
Lutheranism, 36–37, 58–59
Lyons, 33, 34

McClure, Norman Egbert: *The Letters of John Chamberlain*, 81
Machiavelli, Niccoló, 39
Maiden Lane, 75
Malta, 35, 93
Mansell, Anthony, 157
Mansell, Francis, 158, 159, 233 n.17
Mansell, Lady Jane. *See* Dutton, Jane
Mansell, Sir Thomas III, 111, 112, 157, 159, 160, 161, 171–72, 228 n.10, 230 n.4, 233 n.17
Mantua, duke of, 71, 75
Margam (Wales), 111, 171
Margam Abbey Church, 111
Mary queen of Scots, 62; death of, 67, 73, 90
Maximilian (duke of Bavaria), 71, 72–74, 90
Maye, Cordell, 101–2
Maynard, Henry, 65
Medicine in Virginia in the Seventeenth Century (Blanton), 150
Medina Sidonia, duke of, 93–94
Melvyn (Melville), Andrew, 16, 54, 55, 136
Middle Temple, 15, 21–26
Milan, 35, 72, 75, 79; intelligence reports from, 76
Milan, duchy of, 74
Monke, John, 179
Monke, Philippa Sleight, 179
Monke, William, 178–79, 181
"Monsieur." *See* Alençon
Morant, Philip, 126
Mordaunt, Mary, 111
Mundy, John: *Songs and Psalmes*, 199
Murcot, Job, 135
Mylend (SP's retreat), 103, 132–36, 157–74, 175

Naples, 72, 74, 75, 78, 93
Netherlands, 49, 63, 89
Neustadt, 38
Newcom, Cousin, 124
Newcomen, Robert, 231 n.9
Newport, Sir Christopher, 132, 138, 143
"Nova Britannia" (Virginia Company broadside), 139, 140
Nuremberg, 60

O'Neill, Hugh, 116
Opechancanough (Indian chief), 149
Orange, prince of, 48–49, 63
Oxford (university), 15, 20, 44

Padua, 65, 83
Palavicino, Horatio, 66, 79, 82, 83
Paris, 32–34, 44–51; university of, 33
Parker, Archbishop Matthew, 63
Parma, duke of, 75, 88, 94, 97
Parson, Robert: *Book of Resolutions*, 57
"Particular Discourse Concerning . . . the Western Discoveries" (Hakluyt), 138
Patriots' Party, 150, 152
Peck, Dwight C., 123
Penrice Castle (Wales), 229 n.9
Perron, Cardinal, 154
Persia, 35, 78, 84
Persia, king of: son Emirdas, 74
Philip II (king of Spain), 51, 72, 73, 74, 76, 77, 88, 90, 91–93, 94, 97, 224 n.24
Piacenza, duke of, 75
Pickerd, Elias, 131
Plato, 41
Pocahontas (Indian princess), 149
Poland (Polonia), 40, 57, 72–73, 76, 84
Poland (Polonia), king of, 74, 78
Poole, George, 135
Popham, Sir John, 118, 119
Portugal, 35, 88, 91
Portugueses Indies, 76
Powhatan (Indian chief), 149, 232 n.19
Powle, Lady Anne Wigmore (Wygmore) (3d wife of SP), 175–79
Powle, Elizabeth (wife of T. Powle [younger]), 235 n.5
Powle, Elizabeth Woodhouse Hobart (Hubburt) (1st wife of SP), 98–99, 122; death of, 98–99, 100
Powle, Henry, 181
Powle, Jane Tate (mother of SP), 19–20; death of, 27; funerary monument, 187
Powle, Margaret (or Margareta) Turner Smyth (2d wife of SP), 102–3, 106, 108–9, 126, 131, 132, 133, 223 n.15; death of, 172–73, 175, 228 n.4; illness of, 157
Powle, Richard, 234 n.5
Powle, Stephen: album of musings and memoranda, 26; appointed ambassador to Scotland, 98; catalogue of manuscripts of, 181–84; childhood and early life, 19–20; coat of arms, 95, 96; death of, 178–79; and death of first wife, 99, 100–101; education, 15, 19–31, 33, 53, 60; family life, 108–12; feelings about the law, 24–26; financial situation/problems, 23–24, 27, 32–33, 39, 57, 62, 63, 89–90, 95–97, 98, 100, 103, 104, 124; friends and friendship, 24, 35, 57, 133, 136, 141; government service, 54, 141; government service at Casimir's Court, 58–68; government service in Chancery, 11, 104–7; government service as clerk of the Crown, 11, 104–7, 110, 112, 118, 127, 129, 141, 173, 229 n.5; government service as justice of the peace, 11, 127–31, 161, 174; government service as six clerk, 107, 135, 141; health/illness, 53, 55, 109, 158, 162–63; homesickness for England, 86–87; importance of, 13–14; knighted, 11, 131; land transactions, 157–58; love for the countryside, 167; marriage to E. Hobart, 98–99; marriage to M. Smyth, 102–3; marriage to A. Wigmore, 175–79; personal characteristics, 22, 24, 53, 156; physical appearance, 27–31; printed references to, 185–86; "A Problematical discourse of the Judges' Robes and Habits . . . ," 161; relationship with father, 19, 26–27, 39, 53, 55–57, 65, 106; relationship with stepmother, 27; reli-

gious belief of, 26–27, 34, 41, 53, 100, 122, 142–43; significance of manuscripts of, 15–16; skill in languages, 26, 33, 53, 60, 76, 156; study and meditation, 133, 134, 161, 173, 174; views on marriage, 102–3
Powle, Stephen (infant son of SP), 98, 99
Powle, Thomas (brother of SP), 19, 33, 74–75, 84–85, 234 n.2; death of, 226 n.20, 235 n.5
Powle, Thomas (father of SP), 19, 75, 228 n.6; books dedicated to, 188–89; Clerk of the Crown, 21, 23, 104–5; financial reverses, 65, 89–90, 95–97; funerary monument, 187; leased Clay-hall Manor, 54; SP's letter to regarding value of his travels, 39–42; SP's letters to, 23, 26, 181; relationship with SP, 19, 26–27, 53, 55–57, 65, 106; sale of office of Clerk of the Crown, 106, 227 n.4, 229 n.5; service as justice of the peace, 130; widowed, remarried, 27
Powle, Thomas (infant son of SP), 98, 99
Powle, William (brother of SP), 53–54, 234 n.2
Powle, Winifred Mordaunt Cheyney (stepmother of SP), 27, 75, 106
Prince, Le (Balzac), 155
Privy Council, 63, 94, 148, 153
"Problematical discourse of the Judges' Robes and Habits . . . , A" (SP), 161
Protestant League (proposed), 59, 63, 72
Protestants, 72, 75
Public Record Office, 11, 13, 182
Puckering, Sir John, 105, 215

Ralegh, Lady, 157
Ralegh, Sir Walter, 16, 24, 25, 32, 36, 109, 157, 158; execution of, 164; letter to in preparation for death, 163–64; Roanoke Colony, 137; and Virginia Company, 138, 141
Ramée, Pierre de la (Ramus), 36, 223 n.4
Rammekens (fort in Netherlands), 63

Regis Declaratio pro Jure Regio (James I), 154
Religion, 20–21, 58, 69
Religious persecution: in Italy, 73. See also Inquisition, Papal
Regiomontanus, 39, 41
Rhenish Palatinate, 11, 15, 38, 42–43, 58–68, 141. See also Casimir, Duke John
Rich, Nathaniel, 150
Rich, Robert (earl of Warwick), 150
Richard II (king of England), 178, 230 n.2
Riding clerk, 107
Roanoke Colony (Virginia), 137, 138
Robsart, Amy, 62
Rodwey, Stephen, 82, 85, 94, 103, 123–25
Roe, Sir Thomas, 141, 142
Rolfe, John, 148, 149
Rome: English College at, 76
Rudolph II (Holy Roman Emperor), 42
Russell, Lady (Essex's aunt), 117
Rutters, 67, 72
Ryder, William (lord mayor of London), 118, 119

Saint Andrews University (Scotland), 15, 54, 55, 136
Saint Bartholomew's Day massacre (Paris), 58
Saint Denis (France), 32
Samoisky (strongman in Polonia), 72–73
Sandys, Sir Edwin, 139, 148–49, 150–52, 153, 154
Sandys, George, 149
Santo Clemente, Guglielmo, 76
Saunders, Francis, 163, 231 n.9
Savage, John, 159, 160
Savage, Lady, 158–60
Savoy, duke of, 74–75
Scheinam Abbey, 43
Schmidt, Charles: La Vie et les Travaux de Jean Sturm, 37
Scotland, 15, 40, 76, 88–89; SP appointed ambassador to, 98; SP in, 53–57
Scott, William Robert: Constitution and Finance of English, Scottish, &

Irish Joint-Stock Companies to 1720, 147, 154
Sea Adventure (ship), 143, 144
Secret writing: methods of, 52, 94
Ségur, Master (ambassador to the king of Navarre), 60, 62
Shakespeare, William: *The Tempest*, 143
Sharplisse, Thomas, 147
Shelley, Richard, Lord Prior, 76, 77–78
"Shroud of Turin," 224 n.28
Sicily, 72, 74, 76, 78, 93; Spain's kingdom in, 93
Sidney, Sir Philip, 44, 63; *Arcadia*, 102
Sidney, Robert, 16, 44–45, 48, 49–51, 50, 235 n.12
Simier, Jean de, 24, 32
Simpson, Daniel, 66, 81, 88, 101, 231 n.9
Six Clerks, 11, 19, 106–7
Sixtus Quintus, Pope, 71–72
Smith, Arthur, 173
Smith, Catherine, 167–70
Smith, Captain John: *Generall Historie of Virginia, New England and the Summer Isles*, 153
Smith, Sir Thomas, 137, 138, 139, 144, 148, 150, 153
Smyth, Blanche, 102
Smyth, Hubert Llewelyn, 132
Smyth, John, 102, 103, 109, 126, 160–61, 215–16, 233 nn. 20 and 22; death of, 173
Smyth, Kate, 109, 170–71
Smyth, Thomas, 102, 172–73
Smyths-hall (Blackmore, Essex), 102, 132, 133, 173; SP at, 126–31, 157–74; theft by servants at, 131
Somers, Sir George, 143
Songs and Psalmes (Mundy), 199
Southampton, earl of (Henry Wriothesley), 120–21, 139, 150, 151, 152–53
Spain, 40, 48–49, 59, 63; interests in Italy, 74; proposed peace with England, 88–89, 91–93, 138; soldiers levied, 78–79
Spanish Armada, 15, 77, 78, 88, 89, 91, 93, 94, 97–98
Spencer, Richard, 65

Stafford, Sir Edward, 24, 32
States General of the United Provinces, 48–49
Stella Evidale, La (ship), 85–86, 88
Stepney (parish), 132
Strachey, William, 143
Stradling, Sir Edward, 233 n.18
Strasbourg, 36–39, 42, 43–46; university of, 38
Strong, Roy, 48
Sturm, Johann, 36, 37, 38, 44; *Epistola apologetica contra Jacobum Andreae . . .* , 37
Sturmianum (home of J. Sturm), 44
Susan Constant (ship), 138
Suthcours, Master (counsel), 124
Swabian *Concordia*, 37
Swiss (people), 40

Tanner, Thomas, 12–13, 182
Tanner manuscripts, the, 11–13, 26, 122–23, 137, 154, 166
Tempest, The (Shakespeare), 143
Thames River, 135
Thomas, William, 69
Tichborne, Chidiock: "Elegy for Himself," 199–200
Tobacco, 142, 147–48, 149, 153; customs duties on, 150
Tothyll, William, 106, 170
Tower of London, 105, 118, 119, 120, 141
Travel (SP), 15, 27, 32–52; effect on SP, 53; map of, 70; SP's letter to father on value of, 39–42
Turks, 40, 72, 74, 76, 78, 91–93
Turner, Christian, 102, 173
Turner, John, 228 n.7
Turner, Thomas, 228 n.7

Urbino, 78, 83
Urbino, duke of, 75

Vambolt, Master, 193, 194
Vasques de Ayllon, Lucas, 137
Venice and Venetians, 35, 65, 67–68, 69, 82–83; danger for foreigners in, 87–88; description of, 69; SP's intelligence work in, 66, 69–94
Venice, signoria of, 71, 74
Vere, Edward de (earl of Oxford), 102
Verona, 91

Virginia: beginnings of democracy in, 145, 148, 152, 153–54; code of laws, 144–45; colonization of, 137–56; disease in, 149–50; exports, 142, 147–48
Virginia Company of London, 11, 15–16, 24, 121, 136, 137–56, 157, 161, 175; charters, 138–41, 142, 145, 148, 151; dissolved, 151–52, 156; lotteries, 145–47, 146, 148

Wakes Colne, Essex, 161–62
Walsingham, Sir Francis, 11, 15, 55, 58, 62–63, 66, 92; death of, 230 n.14; SP as agent of in Venice, 71–94, 95; SP's reports/letters to, 66–68, 181, 182, 205–13
Watson, Roland, 104, 105
Wells, Mistress, 215–16
Wertenbaker, Thomas, 151
West, Thomas, lord DeLaWare, 144, 145

West, William, 178, 224 n.12
Westminster, 178
Westminster Hall, 22
Whitaker, Reverend Alexander, 145
White (master doctor, of St. Dunstan's, London), 90
White, John, 138
Wigmore, Lady Anne. *See* Powle, Lady Anne Wigmore
Wigmore, Michael, 175
Wigmore, Sir Richard, 175–76
Wilkinson, Richard, 106
Wilson, Master, of Wakes Colne, 171
Worsley, Charles, 21
Worme, John, 130
Wyatt, Sir Francis, 233 n.22

Yates, Frances, 45
Yeardley, Sir George, 233 n.22

Zouche, Edward Lord, 66, 67, 82
Zwingli, Huldreich, 38

DATE DUE

			MAR 2 1 1998
AUG 2 4 1998			
SEP 0 1 2000		MAR 1 9 2003	
		JAN 1 2 1999	MAY 2 8 1999
		NOV 0 3 1999	JUL 1 5 2002
MAR 1 0 2000			
JAN 2 7 2001			
SEP 2 0 2001			
JAN 1 1 2002			
			Printed in USA